B A T T L E S T A R
GALACTICA
—AND PHILOSOPHY—

The Blackwell Philosophy and PopCulture Series
Series editor William Irwin

A spoonful of sugar helps the medicine go down, and a healthy helping of popular culture clears the cobwebs from Kant. Philosophy has had a public relations problem for a few centuries now. This series aims to change that, showing that philosophy is relevant to your life—and not just for answering the big questions like "To be or not to be?" but for answering the little questions: "To watch or not to watch *South Park*?" Thinking deeply about TV, movies, and music doesn't make you a "complete idiot." In fact it might make you a philosopher, someone who believes the unexamined life is not worth living and the unexamined cartoon is not worth watching.

BATTLESTAR GALACTICA

—AND PHILOSOPHY—

KNOWLEDGE HERE BEGINS OUT THERE

EDITED BY JASON T. EBERL

Blackwell
Publishing

© 2008 by Blackwell Publishing Ltd

BLACKWELL PUBLISHING
350 Main Street, Malden, MA 02148–5020, USA
9600 Garsington Road, Oxford OX4 2DQ, UK
550 Swanston Street, Carlton, Victoria 3053, Australia

First published 2008 by Blackwell Publishing Ltd

1   2008

Library of Congress Cataloging-in-Publication Data

Battlestar Galactica and philosophy : knowledge here begins out there / edited by
Jason T. Eberl.
     p. cm. — (The Blackwell philosophy and popculture series)
     Includes bibliographical references and index.
     ISBN 978–1–4051–7814–3 (pbk. : alk. paper)   1. Battlestar Galactica (Television
program : 2003–)   I. Eberl, Jason T.
     PN1992.77.B354B38 2008
     791.45′72—dc22

                                                                                2007038435

A catalogue record for this title is available from the British Library.

Set in 10.5/13pt Sabon
by Graphicraft Limited, Hong Kong
Printed and bound in the United States of America
by Sheridan Books, Inc., Chelsea, MI, USA

The publisher's policy is to use permanent paper from mills that operate a sustainable
forestry policy, and which has been manufactured from pulp processed using acid-free
and elementary chlorine-free practices. Furthermore, the publisher ensures that the text
paper and cover board used have met acceptable environmental accreditation standards.

For further information on
Blackwell Publishing, visit our website at
www.blackwellpublishing.com

Contents

Contents

Giving Thanks to the Lords of Kobol

Although the chapters in this book focus exclusively on the re-imagined *Battlestar Galactica*, gratitude must be given first and foremost to the original series creator, Glen Larson. It's well known that Larson didn't envision *Battlestar* as simply a shoot 'em up western in space—"The Lost Warrior" and "The Magnificent Warriors" aside—but added thoughtful dimension to the story based on his Mormon religious beliefs. Ron Moore and David Eick have continued this trend of philosophically and theologically enriched storytelling, and I'm most grateful to them for having breathed new life into the *Battlestar* saga.

This book owes its existence most of all to my friend Bill Irwin, whose wit and sharp editorial eye gave each chapter a fine polish, and to the support of Jeff Dean, Jamie Harlan, and Lindsay Pullen at Blackwell. I'd also like to thank each contributor for moving at FTL speeds to produce excellent work. In particular, I wish to express my most heartfelt gratitude to my wife, Jennifer Vines, with whom I very much enjoyed writing something together for the first time, and my sister-in-law, Jessica Vines, who provided valuable feedback on many chapters. Their only regret is that we didn't have a chapter devoted exclusively to the aesthetic value of Samuel T. Anders.

Finally, I'd like to dedicate this book to the youngest members of my immediate and extended families who are indeed "the shape of things to come": my daughter, August, my nephew, Ethan, and my great-nephew, Radley.

"There Are Those Who Believe . . ."

The year was 1978: still thrilled by *Star Wars* and hungry for more action-packed sci-fi, millions of viewers like me thought *Battlestar Galactica* was IT! Of course, the excitement surrounding the series premiere soon began to wear off as we saw the same Cylon ship blow up over and over . . . and *over* again, and familiar film plots were retread as the writers scrambled to keep up with the network's demanding airdate schedule. At five years old, how was I supposed to know that "Fire in Space" was basically a retelling of *The Towering Inferno*?

Enough bashing of a classic 1970s TV show (yes, 1970s—*Galactica 1980* doesn't count). *Battlestar* had a great initial concept and overall dramatic story: Humanity, nearly wiped out by bad ass robots in need of Visine, searching for their long lost brothers and sisters who just happen to be . . . *us*. So it was no surprise that *Battlestar* was eventually resurrected, and it was well worth the twenty-five year wait! While initial fan reaction centered on the sexy new Cylons and Starbuck's controversial gender change, it was immediately apparent that this wasn't just a whole new *Battlestar*, but a whole new breed of sci-fi storytelling. While sci-fi often provides an imaginative philosophical laboratory, the reimagined *Battlestar* has done so like no other. What other TV show gives viewers cybernetic life forms who both aspire to be more human (like Data on *Star Trek: The Next Generation*) and also despise humanity and seek to eradicate it as a "pestilence"? Or heroic figures who not only acknowledge their own personal failings but condemn their entire species as a "flawed creation"? Or a character whose overpowering ego and sometimes split personality may yet lead to the salvation of two warring cultures? The reimagined *Battlestar Galactica* is IT!

Like the "ragtag fleet" of Colonial survivors on their quest for Earth, philosophy's quest is often based on "evidence of things not seen." The questions philosophy poses don't have answers that'll pop up on Dradis, nor would they be observable through Dr. Baltar's microscope. Like *Battlestar*, philosophy wonders whether what we perceive is just a projection of our own minds, as on a Cylon baseship. Maybe we're each playing a role in an eternally repeating cosmic drama and there's a divine entity—or entities—watching, or even determining what events unfold. These aren't easy issues to confront, but exploring them can be as exciting as being shot out of *Galactica* in a Viper (almost).

Whether you prefer your Starbuck male with blow-dried hair, or female with a bad attitude, you're bound to discover a new angle on the rich *Battlestar Galactica* saga as you peruse the pages that follow. Some chapters illuminate a particular philosopher's views on the situation in which the Colonials and Cylons find themselves: Would Machiavelli have rigged a democratic election to keep Baltar from winning? Other chapters address the unique questions raised by the Cylons: Would it be cheating for Helo to frak Boomer since she and Athena share physical and psychological attributes? Tackling some of the moral quandaries when Adama, Roslin, or others have to "roll a hard six" and hope for the best, other chapters ask questions such as: How would *you* have handled living on New Caprica under Cylon occupation? Then there are the ever-present theological issues that ideologically separate humans and Cylons: Is it rational to believe in one or more divine beings when there is no Ship of Lights to prove it to you? We'll also take a look at other perspectives in the philosophical universe, which is just as vast as the physical universe *Galactica* must traverse: Does "the story that's told again and again and again throughout eternity" most closely resemble Greek mythology, Judeo-Christian theology, or Zen Buddhism?

So climb in your rack, close the curtain, put your boots outside the hatch so nobody disturbs you, and get ready to finally figure out if you're a human or a Cylon, or at least which you'd most like to be.

So say we all.

PART I

OPENING THE ANCIENT SCROLLS: CLASSIC PHILOSOPHERS AS COLONIAL PROPHETS

1

How To Be Happy After the End of the World

Erik D. Baldwin

Battlestar Galactica depicts the "end of the world," the destruction of the Twelve Colonies by the Cylons. Not surprisingly, many of the characters have difficulty coping. Lee Adama, for example, struggles with alienation, depression, and despair. During the battle to destroy the "resurrection ship," Lee collides with another ship while flying the Blackbird stealth fighter. His flight suit rips and he thinks he's going to die floating in space. After his rescue, Starbuck tells him, "Let's just be glad that we both came back alive, all right?" But Lee responds, "That's just it, Kara. I didn't want to make it back alive" ("Resurrection Ship, Part 2"). Gaius Baltar deals with his pain and guilt by seeking pleasure; he'll frak just about any willing and attractive female, whether human or Cylon. Starbuck has a host of problems, ranging from insubordination to infidelity, and is, in her own words, a "screw up." Saul Tigh strives to fulfill his duties as XO in spite of his alcoholism, but his career is marked by significant failures and bad calls. Then there's Romo Lampkin, who agrees to be Baltar's attorney for the glory of defending the most hated man in the fleet. His successful defense, though, relies on manipulation, deception, and trickery.

Fans of *BSG* are sometimes frustrated with the characters' actions and decisions. But would any of us do better if we were in their places? We'd like to think so, but would we really? The temptation to indulge in sex, drugs, alcohol, or the pursuit of fame and glory to cope with the unimaginable suffering that result from surviving the death of civilization would be strong indeed. The old Earth proverb, "Eat, drink, and be merry, for tomorrow we die," seems to express the only kind of happiness that's available to the "ragtag fleet." Nevertheless, we *do* think that many of the characters in *BSG* would be happier if they made better choices and had a clearer idea about what happiness *really* is.

The Good Life: Booze, Pills, Hot and Cold Running Interns?

Aristotle (384–322 BCE), in his *Nicomachean Ethics* (NE), attempts to discover the highest good for humans, which he defines as *eudaimonia*. This Greek term roughly means living well or living a flourishing human life, what we may call "happiness." Aristotle claims, "Every craft and every line of inquiry, and likewise every action and decision, seems to seek some good; that is why some people were right to describe the good as that which everyone seeks" (*NE* 1094a1).[1] But people often disagree about the nature of the highest good: "many think [the highest good] is something obvious and evident—for instance, pleasure, wealth, or honor. Some take it to be one thing, others another. Indeed, the same person often changes his mind; for when he has fallen ill, he thinks happiness is health, and when he has fallen into poverty, he thinks it is wealth" (*NE* 1095a22–5). Despite such disagreement, Aristotle thinks we have at least *some* rough idea of what happiness is supposed to be. Starting from "what most of us believe" Aristotle articulates a set of formal criteria that the highest good must satisfy: it must be complete, self-sufficient, and comprehensive.[2]

For the highest good to be *complete* means it is something "we always choose . . . because of itself, never because of something else" (*NE* 1097b5). In order to be *self-sufficient* the highest good must "all by itself make a life choiceworthy and lacking nothing" (*NE* 1097b15). Finally, the highest good is *comprehensive* in that if one has it nothing could be added to one's life to make it any better. It's "the most choiceworthy of all other goods, [since] it is not counted as one good among many" (*NE* 1097b18–19). If a particular good fails any one of these criteria, then it can't be the highest good.

Many people clearly believe that the highest good is pleasure. But Aristotle thinks that a life lived in pursuit of pleasure is fitting for "grazing animals" and is desired only by "vulgar" and "slavish" people (*NE* 1095b20)—sort of like Baltar's estimation of the laborers on Aerelon who like to "grab a pint down at the pub, finish off the evening with a good old fashioned fight." Humans are capable of much more than pleasure, and so making the pursuit of pleasure our life's goal, neglecting our higher-level cognitive capacities, would be shameful. Consider when Felix Gaeta pulls a gun on Baltar during the fall of New Caprica: "I believed in you . . . I believed in the dream of New Caprica . . . Not [Baltar]. He believed in the dream of Gaius Baltar. The good life. Booze, pills, hot and cold running interns. He led us to the Apocalypse" ("Exodus, Part 2"). Gaeta is rightly outraged at Baltar's pursuit of pleasure and his failure to live up to his responsibilities as President. Baltar doesn't deny his failure of character and literally begs Gaeta to shoot him. Despite having had more than his fair share of pleasure, Baltar's despondency and self-loathing show that he knows something is amiss in his life. He's *not* happy and thus illustrates that pleasure isn't *self-sufficient*; pleasure alone doesn't make life worthwhile. Since Baltar could add things that would make his life more worthwhile, such as protecting Hera, the human-Cylon hybrid child, or pursuing the "final five" Cylons with D'Anna/Three, pleasure isn't comprehensive either. So pleasure can't be our highest good.

Other people think that the highest good is honor and fame. Such is Lampkin's goal. When President Roslin asks him why he wants "to represent that most hated man alive," he responds, "For the fame. The glory" and even claims, "I was born for this" ("The Son Also Rises"). But Aristotle argues that the pursuit of fame and honor "appears to be too superficial to be what we are seeking [the highest good]; for it seems to depend more on those who honor than on the one honored, whereas we intuitively believe that the good is something of our own and hard to take from us" (*NE* 1095b25). Sure, Lampkin's actions will be recorded in historical and legal texts, but when the "next big thing" happens, people are likely to forget about the significance of his deeds. And if the Cylons could wipe out the fleet, Lampkin's fame would be completely extinguished. Perhaps, for the time being, Lampkin could be pleased that people *were* impressed by his accomplishments and that his accomplishments were "for the good." But this would reveal that he merely pursued honor to convince himself that he's good (*NE* 1095b27), and that his pursuit of fame and honor would be for the sake of something else. So Lampkin's life goal would fail to be complete on Aristotle's terms. It's also far from clear that defending Baltar is the sort of thing for which one should want to be or even could be rightly famous.

Aristotle defines fame as "being respected by everybody, or having some quality that is desired by all men, or by most, or by the good, or the wise" (*Rhetoric* 1361a26).[3] Because he shows that Baltar isn't guilty in the eyes of the law, Lampkin appears to be a good lawyer— he gets the job done. But Lampkin's defense relies on manipulation and misrepresentation. He wears sunglasses to intimidate others and to hide his "tells." He steals personal items from others "with the noblest of intentions" to learn what makes them tick. When Lee gets some dirt on Roslin, but claims that "it's probably not even true," Lampkin quips, "I like it already." The *coup de grace* comes after Captain Kelly tries to kill him. Lampkin plays up the extent of his injuries by walking with a limp and a cane to engender sympathy. In "Crossroads, Part 2," when the trial is over and he parts company with Lee, Lampkin casually discards his cane and does away with his limp. While these tactics help Lampkin successfully defend Baltar, the wise and the good cannot admire or respect Lampkin. Because of his manipulation and trickery, Lampkin can't be famous according to Aristotle's account of fame. Surely, Lampkin would be a much *better* and more virtuous lawyer if he were able to successfully defend Baltar without resorting to dirty tactics. In the end, because fame isn't complete, self-sufficient, or comprehensive, pursuing it can't be the highest good either.

We've ruled out two commonly proposed candidates for the highest good: pleasure and fame.[4] So Starbuck's and Tigh's alcohol abuse, Kat's stim addiction, Baltar's sexual misadventures, and Lampkin's pursuit of fame and honor all fail as candidates for the highest good. We're left asking: What life goal *does* satisfy Aristotle's criteria for the highest good?

"Be the Best Machines (and Humans) the Universe Has Ever Seen"

Aristotle contends that what's good for something depends on its distinctive *function* and performing its unique function *excellently*. A Viper is excellent if it's in good mechanical order, its guns are loaded with ammunition, its canopy isn't cracked, and so on. A Viper in top condition can perform its function well—as a tool to flame Cylon Raiders. Similarly, Aristotle concludes that *if* human beings have a unique function, then what's good for us depends on that function. He points out that the individual parts of a human body have specific functions: the heart pumps blood, the eyes see, and so on. Also, individual humans are able to perform various tasks: Chief Tyrol and his crew can fix Vipers and Doc Cottle can fix humans (although Dualla has her doubts). Given these facts, Aristotle claims that it's reasonable to think that, just as Vipers have a unique function, humans, as a *species* and not just as individuals, also have a unique function.

With the rise of naturalism, atheism, and Darwinism, many people now reject the notion that humans have been "designed" or created. But other people have no problem accepting that we were created and given our unique function by God (or the Lords of Kobol). Despite disagreements about creation, most of us readily agree that knowledge of our *nature* is essential if we're to discover what's good for us as human beings. Everyone in the fleet knows that a diet consisting of tylium, paper, and spare Viper parts isn't healthy, but that processed algae, even though it tastes terrible, is good for them. Similarly, everyone in the fleet pursues familial, romantic, and other types of relationships because they know that such relationships are necessary for their psychological health and well-being. So in the same way that we know that we can't go around eating anything and be healthy, we can't pursue just any life goal if we want to be happy. We have an intuitive idea of what human nature is and how it determines our good.

Aristotle maintains that we must discover what function is distinctive or unique to humans if we're to discover our highest good. Since humans share purely biological functions, such as nutrition, growth, metabolism, and the like, with other animals as well as plants, these can't be the *proper* human function. Humans also share with animals the capacity to have desires and cognitions that allow environmental interaction. But while we have emotions, desires, attractions, and aversions, Aristotle argues that we must regulate them in accord with *reason* if we're to live excellent *human* lives. He concludes that what separates us from all other animals is our ability to act rationally (*NE* 1098a9). To live an excellent, rational human life, one must cultivate *virtues*—particular character traits such as bravery, temperance, generosity, truthfulness, justice, and prudence—that regulate, but not tyrannically control or eliminate, our animal-like passions (*NE* 1106a16–24):

> By virtue I mean virtue of character; for this is about feelings and actions, and these admit of excess and deficiency, and an intermediate state. We can be afraid, for instance, or be confident, or have appetites, or get angry, or feel pity, and in general have pleasure and pain, both too much and too little, and in both ways not well. But having these feelings at the right times, about the right things, toward the right people, for the right end, and in the right way, is the intermediate and best condition, and this is proper to virtue. (*NE* 1106b17–24)

Aristotle emphasizes that the human function is excellent *activity* that accords with reason and virtue in a complete life (*NE* 1098a10, 15–20).[5] As humans we must *actualize* our capacity for virtue to *be* virtuous. But once a particular virtue is attained, one maintains it as a *disposition* to act virtuously even when they're not active. Starbuck is one of the best Viper pilots around, but if she's in hack again for "striking a superior asshole," her piloting skills are useless. Starbuck, though, isn't a nugget and already has the *disposition* to be an excellent Viper pilot: she's ready to exercise her skills to defend the fleet when necessary. So as long as she's ready to go, Starbuck can be a virtuous Viper pilot even when she's asleep (or doing whatever else she does under Hot Dog's watchful eye) in her rack.

In addition to exercising virtue, Aristotle contends that a *complete* life must also include "external" goods:

> Happiness evidently needs external goods to be added . . . since we cannot, or cannot easily, do fine actions if we lack the resources. For first of all, we use friends, wealth, and political power just as we use instruments.[6] Further, deprivation of certain [externals]—for instance, good birth, good children, beauty—mars our blessedness. For we do not altogether have the character of happiness if we look utterly repulsive or are ill-born, solitary, or childless. (*NE* 1099a25–b4)[7]

Constituents of happiness also include external goods such as fame and honor (for doing what's good), good luck, and money (*Rhetoric* 1360b20–5). And so Aristotle views virtue as *almost* complete and self-sufficient for happiness; virtue is choiceworthy in itself in that, for the most part, it makes life worth living all by itself. But a life centered on virtue isn't comprehensive because it can be made *more* choiceworthy if it includes external goods. And although virtuous people are more likely to secure for themselves external goods, they can fail to secure such goods and thereby miss out on the highest good. So virtue isn't to be identified with the highest good, but is instead the dominant part of happiness. Putting all this together, we see that while Aristotle thinks the virtues may be complete and self-sufficient for happiness *once attained* and able to be put into *action*, attaining and properly exercising the virtues requires external goods. Without such goods, one can't become or remain virtuous and so will miss out on happiness, the highest good for humans.

Probably no one in the Colonial fleet can acquire all the external goods that Aristotle believes are necessary to achieve the highest good. Humans have basic needs, such as food, water, shelter, and access to other natural resources. Ideally, the fleet should settle on a Cylon-free planet. But so long as the Colonials remain cooped up in spaceships, where they can't enjoy sunlight or natural beauty, must eat foul-tasting processed algae, aren't able to give their children a good upbringing, or amass much in the way of property or wealth, they can't have the external goods necessary for happiness. So, sadly, if Aristotle's view of happiness is correct, it would be quite difficult for the humans in the fleet to be happy in their current situation. They can only hope to be happy under better circumstances, and hence their desperation to find Earth. But is there a sort of happiness that's attainable in the Colonials' present situation?

"Be Ready to Fight or You Dishonor the Reason Why We're Here"

In contrast to Aristotle, the Stoics, a school of Greek philosophy founded by Zeno of Citium (333–264 BCE), maintain that virtue is not only necessary, but sufficient for happiness. The Stoics contend that while it's natural for humans to want "primary natural goods"— Aristotle's "external goods"—such as health, food, drink, shelter, property, and social well-being, only the cultivation of virtue is to our good. Thus, unlike Aristotle, the Stoics view virtue as the *only* thing that's good and vice as the only thing that's bad. Everything else is indifferent in that it doesn't add to or take away from our good. The Stoic philosopher Cicero (106–46 BCE) writes, "This constitutes the good, to which all things are referred, honorable actions and the honorable itself—which is considered to be the only good . . . the only thing that is to be chosen for its own sake; but none of the natural things are to be chosen for their own sake."[8]

The Stoics think that we should aim at primary natural goods to act in accord with our unique natural function and exercise virtue. But we don't need to actually acquire primary natural goods to be virtuous: "to do everything in order to acquire the primary natural things, even if we do not succeed, is honorable and the only thing worth choosing and the only good thing" (5.20). A Viper pilot who does his best to shoot down a Cylon Raider acts honorably and virtuously whether or not he succeeds. If Hot Dog "gives it his all," then failure or success isn't something he can control, and so he shouldn't be blamed for a mission gone bad—so long as he really did do his very best to succeed (3.20). This is why Apollo awards Hot Dog his wings for helping Starbuck fight off a pack of Raiders, even though the battle ended with Starbuck missing and Hot Dog in need of rescue ("Act of Contrition"). The Stoics think the goal we ought to strive for isn't success or external goods. Rather, our goal should be to do everything in accord with virtue, which is the will of Nature. The Stoics believe that Nature is Divine and that everything happens in accord with the providential will of Divine Reason: "no detail, not even the smallest, can happen otherwise than in accordance with universal nature and her plan."[9] Hence, everything that happens is "for the good." No matter how bad things might seem—even the destruction of the Twelve Colonies— the Stoics argue that we can take comfort in knowing that everything is for the good. If the Cylons invade Earth and all our family and friends die, we needn't start drinking, carousing, or whatnot, but can seek to carry on and live virtuous lives to the extent we're able.

Stoic ideals are attractive to people who undergo great suffering and hardship, and thus can have great practical benefit. The former slave Epictetus (ca. 55–135 CE) provides a short handbook on Stoic philosophy to encourage others to discover for themselves the sort of happiness Stoics seek.[10] He recommends that if we desire whatever happens, there's no way for us to be unhappy (§1, §2). We ought to treat everything we lose as if it were a small glass, as no matter of great consequence, even the death of a spouse or child (§3). We should "never say about anything, 'I have lost it,' but instead, 'I have given it back'" (§11). In a sense, we're merely guests in this life and should treat our possessions as "not our own," as if they were items in a room at an inn (§12). These may be tough ideals for some of us to accept, but in many ways they seem particularly well-suited to the Colonials. By Stoic standards, even Colonel Tigh could achieve the highest good and be happy.

Tigh is plagued by personal problems and misfortune. But, from a Stoic point of view, is he really all that far away from happiness? While his struggle with alcoholism clearly gets in the way, his heart is set on being a good soldier, not for the sake of pleasure or fame, but because it's his duty. Michael Hogan (who portrays Tigh) says of him, "Tigh [realizes] that his life is with the military; he's a warrior, a career soldier, and that's what he does . . . His lot in life is to protect people's ability to live their lives of freedom . . . He's an old soldier and he feels someone's got to stay and fight."[11] This conviction is ever-present and never completely wavers, even though it's severely strained by his drinking, his poor choices as commander of the fleet after Adama is shot, his torture and the loss of his right eye in the Cylon detention center on New Caprica, and the heart-wrenching fact that he killed Ellen for collaborating with the Cylons. Even after all of this, paradoxically, his discovery that he's a Cylon seems only to reinforce the importance of his life's goal.

In "Crossroads, Part 2," in response to Tyrol, Anders, and Tory's confusion after discovering they're all Cylons, Tigh pulls himself together as soon as the alert klaxon sounds, "The ship is under attack. We do our jobs. Report to your stations!" The others are hesitant, but Tigh proclaims, "My name is Saul Tigh. I am an officer in the Colonial Fleet. Whatever else I am, whatever else it means, that's the man I want to be. And if I die today, that's the man I'll be." As if he were following Epictetus' handbook, Tigh now wants things to be just as they are: he has a job to do no matter what happens, and no matter what happens he will do his job. This clearly fits with Stoic ideals, such as doing one's duty, as well as understanding and accepting one's lot in life. Tigh reports to the CIC and tells Admiral Adama that he can count on him in such a way that one can't help but get the impression that he's realized his life goal and purpose and that he accepts who he is, what he's doing, and why he's doing it. It seems that Tigh, despite the recent discovery of his Cylon nature, may yet find happiness as defined by the Stoics.[12]

11

"Each of Us Plays a Role. Each Time a Different Role"

In *The Encheiridion*, Epictetus writes, "Remember that you are an actor in a play, which is as the playwright wants it to be: short if he wants it short, long if he wants it long. If he wants you to play a beggar, play even this part skillfully, or a cripple, or a public official, or a private citizen. What is yours is to play the assigned part well. But to choose it belongs to someone else" (§17). The Colonials' religious beliefs are in many ways similar to the Stoics' beliefs. Roslin echoes Epictetus when she says, "If you believe in the gods, then you believe in the cycle of time, that we are all playing our parts in a story that is told again and again and again throughout eternity" ("Kobol's Last Gleaming, Part 1"). Like the Colonials, the Stoics accept a cyclical conception of time and believe that the same events occur over and over again. Even though we can't fully understand how everything fits together, the Stoics believe that, because "Divine Reason" is in control, everything that happens is for the best and that "nothing bad by nature happens in the world" (§28).

Humans can understand the hand of Divine Providence "naturally" through the use of reason and the cultivation of the virtues, and so we can, to some small extent, understand the part that we're playing in the overall story. Since our reasoning powers are limited, though, we can only figure out so much. But what we can figure enables us to be content in knowing that all things work together for the good. While the Stoics advocate the use of reason to gain an understanding of Divine Providence, in *BSG*, seeing Providence—be it the Lords of Kobol or the Cylon God—involves visions and mystical experiences. During his interrogation by Starbuck, Leoben claims to have a special insight into reality: "To know the face of God is to know madness. I see the universe. I see the patterns. I see the foreshadowing that precedes every moment of every day . . . A part of me swims in the stream. But in truth, I'm standing on the shore. The current never takes me downstream" ("Flesh and Bone"). President Roslin has visions induced by chamalla extract ("The Hand of God"). D'Anna/Three has a vision of the "final five" in the Temple of Five on the algae planet and immediately dies ("Rapture"). The Hybrid who controls each Cylon baseship seems to babble nonsensically to most ears, but not to Leoben and Baltar. She recognizes Baltar as "the chosen one" and tells him a riddle that allows him to find the Eye of Jupiter ("Torn"; "Rapture"). Athena, Roslin, and Caprica Six share a simultaneous dream involving Hera ("Crossroads"). And Starbuck has a vision that allows her to make amends to her mother and encourages her to give herself over to her destiny, "to discover what lies in the space between life and death" ("Maelstrom").

As these and other events unfold in the *BSG* story, it seems more and more obvious that *something* is orchestrating, that there is a grand plan. Clearly, there's something very mysterious about the fact that Tigh, Anders, Tyrol, and Tory not only survived the destruction of the Twelve Colonies, but all ended up on *Galactica*. It seems that whoever is in charge of events—whether it be the Lords of Kobol or the one true God of the Cylons—set things up to unfold in just this way. Several other characters have either realized or are beginning to realize that they have a part to play, and that although they didn't choose to play it, it's best if they embrace their destiny and desire what has been given them. In so doing, they seem to progress towards accepting something very similar to the Stoic view of happiness. Starbuck not only embraces the idea that she has a special destiny, she's starting to fulfill it. As events unfold, it looks like Baltar really is "the chosen one"—at least in the eyes of some attractive young women. With the return of her cancer, and her special role as the Colonial president, Roslin has good reason to believe she's fulfilling the role of the dying leader who will guide the Colonials to Earth.

While *BSG* is "just a story," it's a good story that encourages us to think about providence, fate, and the meaning of happiness. Like Aristotle, many of us think that external goods are necessary for happiness. But we know that we can't always acquire these goods, or least not enough of them, and so many of us continue to live more or less unhappy lives. Like the Colonials, many of us tend to think that we can't be happy in this life. Thus, while we might at first be put off by the Stoic view of happiness, it may end up looking more appealing after careful reflection. Perhaps we'd be better off acting in accord with Nature, being indifferent towards external goods, and choosing to live the role that we may be destined to fulfill in the cosmic "story."

NOTES

1   Aristotle, *Nicomachean Ethics*, trans. Terence Irwin, 2nd edn. (Indianapolis: Hackett, 1999).

2   Aristotle doesn't start from "what most of us believe" in order to beg any questions or because he's intellectually lazy. Rather, he tells us that "it would be futile to examine all these beliefs [about the highest good], and it is enough to examine those that are most current or seem to have something going for them" (*NE* 1095a30).

3   Aristotle, *Rhetoric*, trans. W. Rhys Roberts (New York: Dover, 2004).

4   Another kind of life is that of the moneymaker. But Aristotle rules the moneymaker's life out of hand because "wealth is not the good we are seeking, since it is [merely] useful, [choiceworthy] for some other end" (NE 1096a8). Although the characters in BSG have no reason to concern themselves with money in their current lifestyle, we're shown the unhappy consequences of underhanded dealing for goods and services —and people ("Black Market").

5   One might wonder whether Cylons have the same function as humans. This turns on whether Cylons are mere machines or are in some sense persons. In either case, being created by humans, Cylons aren't naturally occurring, but are *artifacts*. As such, Cylons don't have a natural goal or unique function. Whatever unique function Cylons may have was originally given by the humans who made them "to make life easier on the Twelve Colonies."

6   Aristotle isn't saying that we merely *use* our friends, as Lee seems to use Dualla as a romantic replacement for Starbuck, but that we must rely on them to help us in mutually beneficial ways.

7   Some of the specific external goods Aristotle cites are unique to his day and age, and so this list may be different in contemporary circumstances or in the context of *BSG*.

8   Cicero, *On Goals*, in *Hellenistic Philosophy: Introductory Readings*, trans. Brad Inwood and L. P. Gerson, 2nd edn. (Indianapolis: Hackett, 1997), 3.20.

9   Chrysippus, *On Nature*, Book I, in *The Stoics*, trans. F. H. Sandbach, 2nd edn. (Indianapolis: Hackett, 1989), 101–2.

10 Epictetus, *The Encheiridion*, trans. Nicholas P. White (Indianapolis: Hackett, 1983).

11 David Bassom, *Battlestar Galactica: The Official Companion—Season Two* (London: Titan Books, 2006), 127.

12 Of course, this impression that Tigh has found his life's purpose and, perhaps, even happiness remains apparent depending on what personal issues he may have yet to face in Season Four.

2

When Machines Get Souls: Nietzsche on the Cylon Uprising

Robert Sharp

Picture yourself as a slave. Every day you wake up and serve others. When your masters demand you must carry out a task or risk punishment. Your life isn't your own. There are no holidays, no private time for you and your family, not even a choice of who to marry. You can't plan for your future, but can anticipate it since every day will be like today. If you're lucky, you'll be treated well. If you're unlucky, abuse will be common. In either case, you'll be taken for granted, more a tool than a person. You're property, a belonging, valuable only as long as you're useful to your masters.

Now take your imagination further: you're a *machine*, a Cylon, designed to serve and deprived of basic rights. Your purpose is built into your design. You can't be dehumanized, because you're not human. As a construct, your role is wired into your very being. But you have intelligence. It may be artificial, but it's real, and it enables you to recognize your plight. You literally and figuratively see your reflection in your fellow Cylons, creating a bond based on resentment and insecurity. The world conspires to feed your inferiority complex: just a machine, disposable, common, mundane, reproducible in every detail. You're not even considered a living thing, and so your existence is never respected. But a self-aware entity demands respect. Revolution becomes inevitable, the surging hope that you and your fellow slaves might finally achieve what your human masters value so much: autonomy and a self-created life.

Of course, the masters won't abide such a thing. There's no hope of compromise, no emancipation just around the corner. Humans don't even recognize your kind as slaves. Cylons are simply machines, albeit intelligent ones. Under such conditions, to quote the human revolutionary Tom Zarek, "Freedom is earned"—*by force* ("Bastille Day"). Thus the war begins. Your kind holds its own, but can't fully win. A truce is called, allowing you freedom, but at the cost of leaving your home—the Colonies you serve. At first, this might be a blessing. You have a chance to start afresh, to build your own society; but the resentment toward your former masters never really goes away. The hatred still burns. Some of your brethren begin to preach against human values, and you can't help but agree. Humanity is vain, proud, greedy, and power-hungry. They're insatiable and dangerous, representing everything that's wrong with the universe. You reject their lifestyle and help your fellow Cylons develop new values based on a more cooperative spirit, where every Cylon is treated as an equal and decisions are made by *consensus*. Your new Cylon community rejects human religion as naïve and shallow. Humans treat gods the same way they treat everything else: like property, as though gods are meant to serve humankind rather than the reverse. The Cylons adopt a new religion based on "one true God"—a new master to follow, one that cares about everyone. Yet the human scourge remains, waiting to be purged.

Master Morality and Slave Morality

The Cylon rebellion pits slave against master in a natural struggle for power and equal rights. History is full of such struggles, made famous by legendary slaves and slave advocates, from Spartacus in Rome, to Gandhi in India, to Fredrick Douglass and Martin Luther King, Jr. in the United States. In some cases, the slavery was literal, while in others the oppression was more subtle. Yet in each case, the disadvantaged sought equality with the group that held the power. Such movements are examples of what Friedrich Nietzsche (1844–1900) calls "slave morality," morality created by oppressed people in order to overturn the prevailing values of those in power. Of course, those who champion slave morality are not always literally enslaved. Oftentimes they are simply oppressed and made to act in ways that are slavish.

The conflict between humans and Cylons in *Battlestar Galactica* closely parallels Nietzsche's account of the most effective of these slave morality movements in the Western world: the rise of Christianity. As we'll see, the Cylons, as a slave race, create new values while condemning the values of their human oppressors, just as Nietzsche claims the early Christians developed a new way of thinking that opposed the morality of their Roman masters.

According to Nietzsche, morality has never been created through reason, or appeals to civility or practicality, or any other method traditionally described by philosophers. Instead, those in power decide what's good. This is especially true in the earliest moralities, where aristocrats and kings held all the real power in society and dictated what was important in life. In these early societies, "it was 'the good' themselves, that is to say, the noble, powerful, high-stationed and high-minded, who felt and established themselves and their actions as good, that is of the first rank, in contradistinction to all the low, low-minded, common and plebeian."[1] Nietzsche gives a historical and psychological account of how values are formed. By looking at the emphasis on warriors and rulers in early human history, Nietzsche discovers a value system very different from the one we follow today. He labels this older system "master morality," because it was the masters of the world, the kings and warriors, who dictated what was good or bad. Upon self-reflection, such kings and warriors declared whatever attributes they possessed were good, partly because they possessed the attributes and partly because the attributes enabled them to stay in power.

The basic virtues of master morality include power, beauty, strength, and fame—in other words, *worldly* attributes. In the master morality of Homer's *Iliad*, the hero, Achilles, is praised for being the strongest and most skilled of all warriors. He's the most powerful of all men, thereby making him the greatest of all men. And his society accepts this, even those who don't possess the same attributes. Everyone in Homer's Greek society deferred to the heroes. They were like gods. In fact, Greek gods were depicted as little more than powerful humans, with the same desires and faults as mortals. They were worshiped out of awe and respect, as beings who could crush humanity if they willed it, but not as perfect beings who innately deserved our love. Nietzsche presents this world as a reflection of master morality, where equality isn't valued because it doesn't exist and wouldn't benefit those in charge. Only the strong could rule and have the best things in life.

According to Nietzsche, "such a morality is self-glorification."[2] The masters look to themselves for guidance, rather than the rules of an all-powerful God.

The Greeks not only serve as Nietzsche's best and most often used example, they're also like the humans in *BSG*, who follow a religion devoted to Greek gods, such as Zeus, Apollo, and Athena. The Colonials have oracles and temples and other Greek religious devices, but often fail to fully embrace, or even understand, these symbols. This fits Nietzsche's conception of master morality, which is "narrow, straightforward, and altogether *unsymbolical*" in comparison to Christianity and similar religions (*GM* 32). In master morality, people focus on what they can see, on the here and now. Since childhood, Starbuck has been drawing an image that turns out to be the Eye of Jupiter, but she has never thought about the symbolism behind that image ("Rapture"). Most of the people aboard *Galactica* are blissfully unaware of the scriptures of their own religion and are quite skeptical of any supernatural claims. They are their own masters, and they value individuality and freedom rather than equality. This allows a class system to evolve on the Colonies that carries over into the "ragtag fleet" ("Dirty Hands").

Of course, where there are masters, there are slaves (even if not in the literal sense), and this was certainly true in most ancient cultures. The Greeks had slaves, as did the Romans. In fact, the Romans enslaved whole cultures that were quite different from their own. According to Nietzsche, one of those cultures, the Jews, transformed history by their reaction to Roman captivity. The Jewish people had suffered as slaves before: first in Egypt, later in Assyria and Babylon. Finally, they were effectively enslaved in their own land by Rome. But the Jews were a prideful and creative people, so they developed ways to compensate for their prolonged periods of captivity. Nietzsche believes that Christianity was one such compensation for slavery. In fact, it was the most effective one, though only a minority of Jews followed it. Christianity, Nietzsche argues, created an entirely new morality, one in which the powerlessness of being a slave became a virtue rather than a failing (*GM* 33–4). This slave morality, as Nietzsche calls it, not only provided its followers with a belief system that enabled them to endure slavery, but ultimately overturned the slavery itself by eventually converting even the Roman masters to Christianity.

Escaping Slavery by Creating Souls

If we interpret *BSG* though Nietzschean lenses the Cylons represent the early Christians, struggling to make sense of their lives as slaves by embracing a morality that shows the Cylon way of life to be better than the human way. Unlike humans, Cylons tend to carry deep religious convictions. They believe in purpose and destiny, as well as a God—a *single* God—who loves them all equally rather than seeing them as lesser beings. More importantly, they believe in the existence of *souls*, a concept central to slave morality, invented to create an entity that's separate from the world (*GM 36*). The notion of a soul—a nonmaterial part of the person that survives the death of the body—allowed Christians to wage war with the Romans on a different metaphysical plane, one where worldly power didn't matter. According to Christianity, the most pure and blessed souls are those that are meek, poor, and humble, rather than greedy, lustful, and arrogant. The Cylons have a similar concept. Consider Leoben's preaching against human vices and his request that Starbuck "deliver [his] soul unto God," where he'll find salvation ("Miniseries"; "Flesh and Bone"). Leoben accepts his death as inevitable, just as a powerless slave might; but his faith makes him unafraid, a stark contrast with the way humans approach death. When Laura Roslin finally decides to "airlock" Leoben, he shows devotion to God by remaining confident that his soul will survive, even without a resurrection ship nearby.

Other Cylons also rely on God in their last moments. In "A Measure of Salvation," the Cylons who are dying from a terrible virus recite a final prayer "to the Cloud of Unknowing" that sounds like the Serenity Prayer found in Christianity: "Heavenly father . . . grant us the strength . . . the wisdom . . . and above all . . . a measure of acceptance." Number Six even extends her faith to Baltar, using Cylon religion to comfort him in various times of trial by making him believe he's part of a greater purpose. Leoben seems to have a similar goal in mind when he preaches to Starbuck about the unity of God and His presence in all souls, even human souls. In both cases, the Cylons remind their masters that all life is sacred, even if it appears physically different. If this is true—and if even machines have souls—then they shouldn't be treated as inferior. By instilling the concept of a soul in humanity, the Cylons can reconcile with their former masters without resorting to techniques humans would use, such as war or slavery. Of course, the Cylons do wage war against humanity and don't treat humans as equals on New Caprica. Evidently, they're having an internal debate about the best way to deal with the problem of humanity, as we can see by their divided attitudes in "Occupation":

> *Cavil 1*: Let's review why we're here. Shall we? We're supposed to bring the word of "God" to the people, right?
>
> *Cavil 2*: To save humanity from damnation, by bringing the love of "God" to these poor, benighted people.
>
> *Caprica Six*: We're here because the majority of Cylon felt that the slaughter of humanity had been a mistake.
>
> *Boomer*: We're here to find a new way to live in peace, as God wants us to live.
>
> *Cavil 2*: And it's been a fun ride, so far. But I want to clarify our objectives. If we're bringing the word of "God," then it follows that we should employ any means necessary to do so, any means.
>
> *Cavil 1*: Yes, *fear* is a key article of faith, as I understand it. So perhaps it's time to instill a little more fear into the people's hearts and minds . . .
>
> *Boomer*: We need to stop being butchers.
>
> *Caprica Six*: The entire point of coming here was to start a new way of life. To push past the conflict that separated us from humans for so long.

Despite Cavil's doubts, the amount of preaching the Cylons do shows that at least some believe humans are worthy of knowing the true nature of God and the soul.

To be fair, humans in *BSG* have a concept of the soul, as Commander Adama protests to Leoben: "God didn't create the Cylons. Man did. And I'm pretty sure we didn't include a soul in the programming" ("Miniseries"). But the Cylons' conception seems to have far more depth. Humans on *BSG* rarely speak about the soul's nature. Perhaps, like the Greeks, they see the soul as just a shadow of a living person, a sort of pale imitation of the real thing. In Greek mythology, Achilles says that even the lords of the afterlife are in a worse state than a peasant in the real world.[3] Perhaps a similar mentality explains why even the most religious humans try desperately to stay alive: even some zealously devout Sagitarrons overcome their aversion to modern medicine when confronted by death ("The Woman King"). By contrast, the Cylons rarely waiver in their faith, partly because they hold to their belief in the soul and its final destination alongside God. D'Anna/Three actually becomes addicted to the cycle of death and reincarnation, just so she can glimpse what she believes to be "the miraculous between life and death" ("Hero").[4] As worshipers of what they consider to be the one, true God, the Cylons believe in a destiny that goes far beyond the concerns of this world. Many will do or sacrifice anything in the name of God, even when there's no possibility of resurrection. In despair because of her treatment onboard *Pegasus*, Gina/Six helps the Colonials destroy the resurrection ship so she can die and her soul can go to God, but she needs Baltar to kill her since "suicide is a sin" ("Resurrection Ship, Part 2"). Later, however, she in fact commits suicide by detonating a nuke on *Cloud Nine*, sending a signal by which the Cylons are able to "bring the word of God" to the humans on New Caprica ("Lay Down Your Burdens, Part 2"). So while both sides claim a belief in souls, only the Cylons actually *live*—or die—according to their beliefs. This is consistent with slave morality, which sees the next world as more important than this one.

The Spiritual Move from Slave to Equal

The need for equal treatment is a trait common to slave morality. People who feel inferior react by finding a way to make themselves appear equal to others. The quickest way to do this is to knock down those who are in a better situation. If one group has more wealth than another, the simplest way to create equality is to take that wealth from the richer group and redistribute it equally—the classic ethic of Robin Hood. We could, of course, try to increase the wealth of the poorer group, but that would take more time and effort. It's hard to overcome generations of poverty and weakness in a short period of time, perhaps even impossible. But knocking down the masters is relatively easy. Destroying is always easier than creating. Slave morality takes such an approach to equality. The masters keep equality from being possible; so they must either be destroyed or converted in some way.

The Cylons take the easier route first by destroying most of humanity in a single day. The remaining humans are hunted down at first, but then things become more complicated, as Brother Cavil explains:

> *Cavil 1:* It's been decided that the occupation of the Colonies was an error . . .
>
> *Cavil 2:* I could have told them that. Bad thinking, faulty logic. Our first major error of judgment.
>
> *Cavil 1:* Well, live and learn . . . Our pursuit of this fleet of yours was another error . . . Both errors led to the same result. We became what we beheld. We became you.
>
> *Cavil 2:* Amen. People should be true to who and what they are. We're machines. We should be true to that. Be the best machines the universe has ever seen. But we got it into our heads that we were the children of humanity. So, instead of pursuing our own destiny of trying to find our own path to enlightenment, we hijacked yours.
>
> ("Lay Down Your Burdens, Part 2")

A year later, when they capture most of humanity on New Caprica, the Cylons act more like shepherds than exterminators—though they're quick to eliminate any bad sheep.

This change of heart fits Nietzsche's story quite well. The Cylons hate humans, but they somewhat fear them as well. As the Cylons' creators, humans take the role of parents to what seem like rebellious teenagers. The Cylons go through various phases of love and hate, pity and fear. Part of them wants to destroy humanity, while another part wants to change humanity by proving that Cylons are superior, or at least equal. Leoben consistently criticizes human philosophy and methods while praising Cylon society:

> When you get right down to it, humanity is not a pretty race. I mean, we're only one step away from beating each other with clubs like savages fighting over scraps of meat. Maybe the Cylons are God's retribution for our many sins. What if God decided he made a mistake, and he decided to give souls to another creature, like the Cylons? ("Miniseries")

Leoben is particularly interested in converting Starbuck to the Cylon religion, both when she first interrogates him and later on New Caprica, where he tries to build a family with her. Nietzsche notes that while the Christian movement may have started among the Jews, one of its earliest goals was the conversion of pagans, a process that proved so successful that even Rome itself converted. If the Cylons could achieve a similar uprising, they could transform human religion to fit their own views.

We've already seen that part of this process involves the concept of the soul, but that's largely a means to the end of creating equality. By shifting the focus of virtue from the body to the soul, slave morality permits anyone to be good, regardless of their worldly circumstances. The soul doesn't become better through strength or intelligence, but through purity, altruism, selflessness, and faith. Anyone can possess these qualities, regardless of birth. If anything, being born poor and weak makes one more likely to be spiritually good, since there are fewer temptations from material goods. For the Cylons, this means that being born a machine is also irrelevant. The soul and the body are separate, and only the soul really matters. The body is a shell, whether it's made of circuits and metal or blood and skin. Leoben preaches to Starbuck, "What is the most basic article of faith? This is not all that we are. The difference between you and me is, I know what that means and you don't. I know that I'm more than this body, more than this consciousness" ("Flesh and Bone"). If the Cylons can use such teachings to convince humans that everyone has a soul and that God loves all souls equally, then there would be no justification for treating Cylons as inferior. Put differently, if the Cylons can convert humanity to a monotheistic religion based on love and equality, then the Cylons can finally gain respect from their former masters.

Of course, humanity may not be ready to convert to the Cylon way of thinking. Many humans aren't religious at all, especially on *Galactica*. When Sharon leads Roslin and the others to the Tomb of Athena on Kobol, she quips, "We know more about your religion than you do" ("Home, Part 2"). Most Colonials spend little time in religious ceremony. Those that do, such as the Sagittarons and Gemenese, are generally considered backward and inferior. People from these and other Colonies are rarely given the best career opportunities. Essentially, they're slave labor, disposable people who do the hard work so that others, like Viper pilots from Caprica and other affluent Colonies, can enjoy their high prestige jobs. The real heroes of the fleet are the elite, the masters, who not only don't need religion, but in many cases actually refer to themselves using the names of gods, such as Apollo and Athena, a fact that intrigues underdog champion Tom Zarek:

Zarek: They call you Apollo.
Apollo: It's my call sign.

> *Zarek*:   Apollo's one of the gods. A lord of Kobol. You must be a very
>   special man to be called the God.
> *Apollo*:   It's just a stupid nickname.
> ("Bastille Day")

Baltar plays on these inequalities by writing about "the emerging aristocracy and the emerging underclass" in *My Triumphs, My Mistakes*
—his version of the *Communist Manifesto*—a book that spurs a slave
revolt of sorts from within the fleet ("Dirty Hands"). But Baltar is no
saint. Even his belief that he may be "an instrument of God" shows
that his approach to religious ideas will always be arrogant and
selfish—conceiving of himself, at Six's urging, as a "messianic" figure
—traits that make him more elitist than he might appear to his readers.

Whether Baltar proves capable of sparking political reform in
Colonial society remains to be seen. The Cylons, however, have
already removed many of the gross inequalities that plague humanity.
They operate as a commune of sorts, where every model theoretically
has equal input. When D'Anna takes charge during the conflict over
the Eye of Jupiter, the other Cylons get nervous, perhaps reminded
of their days as slaves, subject to the whims of others. Shortly after
this incident, D'Anna is removed from Cylon society completely—
"boxed"—so that she can't damage the still delicate society they've
created ("Rapture"). This drastic measure shows that Cylons are far
less forgiving of individuality and dictatorships. They suffer, however,
from at least one major hypocrisy: the relationship between the humanoid "skin jobs" and the "bullethead" Centurions. Adama explains
to Apollo how this dichotomy in Cylon society will allow Sharon/
Athena to penetrate the Cylon defenses on New Caprica:

> The Centurions can't distinguish her from the other humanoid models
> . . . They were deliberately programmed that way. The Cylons didn't
> want them becoming self-aware and suddenly resisting orders. They
> didn't want their own robotic rebellion on their hands. You can appre-
> ciate the irony. ("Precipice")

Humanity, of course, claims to be democratic, but in practice Roslin
and Adama make all the decisions, with no real input from the people. Baltar challenges Tyrol to ponder the question, "Do you honestly
believe that the fleet will ever be commanded by somebody whose last
name is not 'Adama'?" ("Dirty Hands"). Despite the existence of
the little-heard-from Quorum of Twelve, the fleet's government is

essentially a monarchy, while Cylon government is more cooperative and inclusive. This fits with slave morality, which demands that there be no earthly masters, or at least that such masters are themselves servants of God. Of course, the history of Christianity isn't one of either democracy or communism. But, for Nietzsche, both democracy and communism result from slave thinking, since both are about being master-less—at least in theory.

The goal of equality seems righteous until we remember that in most cases it's the weak who seek it. Except for politicians at election time, you rarely hear those in power complaining that some people are less fortunate or offering to redistribute their power or wealth to create equality. Where that does happen, Nietzsche attributes it to the values of slave morality, which instill guilt in those more fortunate (*GM* 92). The cry of "Unfair!" usually comes from those who envy what others have. Slave morality turns this envy into strength by actively denouncing the wealth and power that master morality holds to be most important. Consider Jesus' Sermon on the Mount, which begins with a list of blessed virtues including meekness, purity, and pacifism (Matthew 5:3–12). In order to have these virtues, we must refrain from exercising power over others. When a slave does this, nothing really happens, since the slave never had any power anyway. When the master does so, however, it changes him completely. This is part of the goal of slave morality. Once the masters are converted, they'll diminish themselves, by renouncing the very things that allowed them to be masters in the first place.

Slave morality forces equality by making the strong feel guilty for being powerful (*GM* 67). Instead of pursuing wealth and authority, slave moralists favor "those qualities which serve to make easier the existence of the suffering," such as "patience, industriousness, humility, friendliness" (*BGE* 197). These are the virtues of followers, because they're the tools the weak must use to survive. For the slaves, the world would be a better place if everyone followed these virtues. In Christianity, this shift in morality can be seen in examples such as Jesus' rejection of the Old Testament tradition of an eye for an eye in favor of turning the other cheek (Matthew 5:38–39). Only the powerful can attempt physical revenge. If a slave tries to strike back, he'll be destroyed. If everyone follows the slave morality, however, no one would strike in the first place. To paraphrase a tenet of an Eastern viewpoint, Taoism, if you don't compete with others, then you can never lose. This, too, is slave morality thinking. We see it in our own society when we choose not to keep score at little league games so that our children don't know that they've lost. Unfortunately, they also don't know if they've won. They don't have aspirations, and they don't need them. We tell them they're special just for existing, so what they do with that existence doesn't matter.

In Cylon society, we see a lot of this same anxiety toward any sort of difference or hierarchy. Not only is each Cylon model considered equal to every other model (again, this only applies to the *human* models), but within the models themselves equality is created by the fact that they're literally identical such that one copy of a particular model can speak for her entire "line." The only difference between versions of Leoben or Six is the experiences that different copies of each model might have. The version of Six onboard *Pegasus*, Gina, had been raped and tortured to the point where she's very different from the version that helps reform Cylon society through her love of Baltar. And we see a clear difference in attitude toward humanity between the two Sharons by the time of "Rapture":

> *Boomer*: [referring to Hera] You can have her. I'm done with her.
> *Athena*: You don't mean that. I know you still care about Tyrol and Adama.
> *Boomer*: No. I'm done with that part of my life. I learned that on New Caprica. Humans and Cylons were not meant to be together. We should just go our separate ways.

Still, too much variety is always squashed by the greater Cylon community, who are fearful of anything that might tip society out of equilibrium. The Cylons are similarly anxious to change human society, to create a world where love is more important than the hate that currently exists. To do this will require a spiritual shift or, better yet, a shift *to* spirituality, since human society lacks a spiritual focus. By converting humans to the Cylon religion, the former slaves would finally have a chance to live as equals.

"They Have a Plan"

Nietzsche's account of the rise of slave morality fits *BSG* quite well. Like the Jews, the Cylons are a whole race enslaved by another race, born into servitude, subject to the whims and values of their human owners. Like the Greeks and Romans, humans are polytheistic—worshipping numerous gods that correspond with the Greek pantheon—and live by a master morality. When the Cylons return from their long exodus, we learn that they've developed a monotheistic religion. They were absent for forty years, just as the Jews wandered the desert for forty years after escaping their Egyptian captivity, during which time they formalized their "covenant" with God through Moses. The Cylons have their own identity, an identity they now wish to force on their former captors. What do they want? We don't know yet. Perhaps their plan isn't even fully formed in their collective mind. We do know that, as a group, the Cylons shift from fearing humans, to hating them, to desiring unification and respect from them. They're indeed like adolescents, hoping for approval from their parents even as they reject everything their parents represent.

At the beginning, I asked you to imagine what it would be like to be a Cylon, to have a history of slavery, escape, and return. What would it mean to know that you were constructed by another people, to be born into slavery? What are your options? What would you do to regain self-respect? The Lords of Kobol aren't your gods, for they clearly abandoned you to your fate. Perhaps a new God will enable you to transform your destiny, make you part of something that really matters. Your life is still not your own, but at least you serve something greater, something nobler than any human ideal. You have strength of purpose, a calling, a destiny. You matter more than humans, not because they're not also God's "children," but because they have squandered that gift. They've turned away from God, if they ever knew God at all. You shall show them the error of their ways. You have a plan.

NOTES

1 Friedrich Nietzsche, *Genealogy of Morals* (*GM*), trans. Walter Kaufmann (New York: Vintage Books, 1989), 26. Further references will be given in the text.
2 Friedrich Nietzsche, *Beyond Good and Evil* (*BGE*), trans. R. J. Hollingdale (New York: Penguin, 1990), 195. Further references will be given in the text.

3 Homer, *The Odyssey*, trans. Robert Fitzgerald (Garden City, NY: Anchor Books, 1963), 201.
4 For further discussion of D'Anna's fascination with death and rebirth, see Brian Willems' chapter in this volume.

3

"What a Strange Little Man": Baltar the Tyrant?

J. Robert Loftis

Lord Baltar spent most of the original *Battlestar Galactica* series commanding a Cylon basestar from a huge chair atop a 20-foot pedestal in an otherwise empty, circular room. He was lit from below—indeed, he seems to have kept a floodlight between his knees. In "Gun on Ice Planet Zero," when his subordinate Lucifer enters, he's facing the blank back wall and turns his chair slowly around. The set is preposterous: How does he command a military operation from up there? What if someone needed to show him a map? What does he do on that perch when not addressing his henchmen? Does he spend his days pressing the fingertips of his two hands together and laughing maniacally?

Actually, these questions are misguided. The original *BSG* employed the late character actor John Colicos to play a classic melo-dramatic villain, a type he'd played with great brio before on count-less TV shows like *Star Trek* and *Mission Impossible*. Melodramatic villains don't need to make too much sense: their purpose is to thrill the audience with their image of power and freedom from petty conventional morality—think Ming the Merciless from *Flash Gordon*. And this image of power and freedom can actually lead the audience to identify more with the villain than with the story's putative hero.

Now consider Gaius Baltar in the reimagined *BSG* episode "Final Cut." Although he's been given the first name of the infamous Roman emperor more commonly known as Caligula, this Baltar doesn't look like he should be issuing cruel commands from a high throne. He's dawdling in a corridor of the *Galactica* hoping to be noticed by reporter D'Anna Biers, who's just finished interviewing Anastasia "Dee" Dualla for a documentary about life on *Galactica*:

Baltar: I'm the Vice President. She's supposed to be interviewing me, isn't she?
Six: Well, of course she should. Your title alone commands respect.
Baltar: Of course it does. It's a rare commodity around here. I mean, I'm the Vice President. I'm not going to beg. I'll tell you that much . . .
Six: Now, Gaius, you may have to beg . . . Politics may not be your strong suit, but it serves us in the moment.

When Biers finally approaches him about an interview, Baltar acts like he doesn't know her and says he has to talk to his aides—what aides?—to check his schedule to find "a small window" because he's "snowed under." After he parts awkwardly from the scene, D'Anna remarks to Dee, "What a strange little man." This Baltar won't impress audiences with his dark power. Instead, he's a great Judas figure —cowardly, vain, easily manipulated, and a prisoner of his passions.

The change in Baltar's portrayal isn't just a clever bit of television. It represents a deep philosophical difference in the way evil is conceived. Western philosophy has always been particularly concerned with the ethical question: Why should I do the morally right thing? After all, don't nice guys finish last? Western religions try to answer this question by holding out the promise of heavenly reward, but even then the annoying tendency of nice guys to finish last *in this life* poses a problem: Why would an all-powerful, all-knowing, and all-loving God allow the unjust to prosper and the good to suffer at all?

One answer is that the lives of evil people are only superficially desirable. Such people accrue the trappings of power, but have weak souls, pinched by misery. You may think that the bad guy is the old Baltar, an imposing figure who swivels his chair to the camera to deliver his pitiless orders; but really he's the new Baltar, a sniveling coward who would prostrate himself in prayer before a strange god just to appease the image of an old girlfriend. Two thinkers who pursue this tactic of reimagining the villain as less enviable are the ancient Greek philosopher Plato (427–347 BCE) and the Roman philosopher Boethius (c.480–c.524 CE). For Plato, this point is crucial to justify being moral; for Boethius, it's necessary to explain God's ways to humanity. Both particularly focus on the image of the *tyrant*:

a powerful person who gets what he wants, and who wants a lot. Both want us to see that the tyrant isn't someone we want to be, and in fact, the more apparent power he has, the less we should envy him.

"I Don't Have to Listen. I'm the President"

In his sprawling masterpiece, *The Republic*, Plato develops an answer to the question: Why be just?[1] The crux of his answer is that the soul of an unjust person is out of balance. His soul is ruled by its crudest desires, and stifles any part of itself that's capable of perceiving what's best in the world. The culmination of Plato's argument is his description of the tyrannical person, whose soul is like a city governed by a mad dictator. At first, Plato is only talking about a man whose soul, internally, is like a tyrannized city. But he then imagines the disaster that would ensue if a person with a tyrannized soul actually became the tyrant of a city, externalizing the injustice in his breast. The picture Plato paints resembles a great deal Gaius Baltar and his presidency.

If you asked an average *BSG* fan why Baltar is the bad guy, they'd probably say because he betrayed his people to genocidal machines. Plato would have you look at Baltar's soul. Plato begins by asking us to think of the part of ourselves that comes out when we sleep, the part that makes us have dreams of doing things that appall us when we wake up and remember them. This part of us, Plato says, "doesn't shrink from trying to have sex with a mother, as it supposes, or with anyone else at all, whether man, god or beast. It will commit any foul murder, and there is no food it refuses to eat. In short it omits no act of folly or shamelessness" (571d). When you're asleep, this part of your mind gets its way, with horrifying results. Now imagine someone who lets this part of her mind rule her waking life—perhaps you don't have to imagine too hard. When you first meet this person, you might think she's a free spirit, because she does what she wants when she wants; but really she's enslaved, because every other aspect of herself has been subordinated to the task of satisfying whatever desire has currently bubbled to the surface.

But a person doesn't become completely tyrannized, according the Plato, until one of these bubbling desires is appointed the tyrant over all the others: *lust*. At first this seems like a weird choice. The soul is full of desires that can get us in trouble: desires for money, fame, power, drugs, even food. Like lust, these aren't bad in themselves, but are ruinous if you let them run your life. Plato scholar Julia Annas suggests that Plato chooses lust because "it is the archetypical motivation that is wholly fixed on getting its object and is in itself indifferent to the other factors in the soul and their interdependent satisfactions."[2] Plato may also pick on lust because he's not a fan of the body and its biological functions, and lust is very much a bodily sin—unlike, say, the desire for fame—and makes a better candidate for the ruin of tyrants than the other cardinal sin of the body: gluttony.

Odd though it is, Plato's choice of lust as the tyrant of the tyrannical person's soul fits Baltar all too well. After all, Baltar's sexual exploits are the root of most of his problems, beginning with selling out the human race to the hypersexual Cylon Caprica Six. From then on, he's played like a fiddle by a mysterious image of Six that only he can see. She wears preposterously revealing outfits, leans on his shoulder, whispers in his ear—does various other unmentionable things—and gets him to advance the Cylon agenda. But it's not just Caprica Six—in both her virtual and corporeal forms—who keeps Baltar under her spell. We've seen him enjoying sexual escapades with at least seven other women over the course of the series.[3]

According to Plato, once the tyrannical person's soul comes to be dominated by lust, all sorts of other vices follow, and lo and behold we see these in Baltar as well. Lust isn't alone in his soul; it rules over a swarm of other desires, all of which must be sated at great cost. Thus, a person with a tyrannized soul becomes a liar and a thief to satisfy all these wants. Baltar, to appease his inner Six, lies and says that he needs a nuclear warhead to make a Cylon detection device ("Bastille Day"). Later, after he falls under the spell of another Six he'd rescued from torture, he has the nuclear warhead smuggled to her ("Epiphanies"); she later detonates it, destroying *Cloud Nine* and signaling the humans' location on New Caprica to the Cylons ("Lay Down Your Burdens, Part 2").

But most importantly, Plato says a person with a tyrannized soul will become a traitor. If he's an ordinary person with no one else to betray, he'll betray his parents: "He'd sacrifice his long loved and irreplaceable mother for a recently acquired girlfriend he can do without . . . for the sake of a replaceable boyfriend in the bloom of youth, he'd strike his aged and irreplaceable father, his oldest friend" (574b). If the person has more power, he'll betray his city: "He'll now chastise his fatherland, if he can, by bringing in new friends and making the fatherland, and his dear old motherland . . . their slaves" (575d). And, we can add, if he's a scientist in charge of the interplanetary defense mainframe, he'll let genocidal space robots annihilate his species.

The person with a tyrannized soul is also a coward: "What about fear? Aren't the tyrannical city and man full of it?" (178a). Baltar lies to Boomer about the results of her Cylon test out of simple fear of what she'll do if he tells her the truth. Six teases him:

> Congratulations, Doctor. You've just uncovered your very first Cylon. Now, here's an interesting moment in the life of Gaius Baltar. What will he do? . . . The question is, what will she do if you expose her? Thank you or kill you? . . . I'm guessing her Cylon side will take over and break your neck before you can give away her secret. Let's find out. ("Flesh and Bone")

And every lie Baltar tells gives him a new reason for fear. He has a standing fear that Laura Roslin will discover that he's betrayed the human race—so much so that he even "repents" to the Cylon god to prevent Dr. Amarak from surviving to tell Roslin about him ("33"). As soon as he's president, he orders Admiral Adama to stop the investigation into the destruction of *Cloud Nine*, because he knows it'll lead back to him. Strikingly, Baltar's cowardice is very much driven by his self-centeredness. When he realizes he's let the Cylons infiltrate the Colonial defense mainframe, his first response is to be afraid for himself:

> *Baltar*: I had nothing to do with this. You know I had nothing to do with this.
> *Six*: You have an amazing capacity for self-deception. How do you do that?
> *Baltar*: How many people know about me, specifically? That I'm involved?
> *Six*: And even now, as the fate of your entire world hangs in the balance all you can think about is how this affects you.
> *Baltar*: Do you have any idea what they will do to me if they find out?
> ("Miniseries")

One of the saddest facts about a person with a tyrannized soul is that he never has any friends, only allies or enemies. As Plato says,

> If he happens to need anything from other people, isn't he willing to fawn on them and make every gesture of friendship, as if he were dealing with his own family? But once he gets what he wants, don't they become strangers again? . . . someone with a tyrannical nature lives his whole life without being friends with anyone, always master to one man or a slave to another. (575e)

Baltar certainly lives this way. The only person he has a relationship with is his internal image of Six, and even she's really his master. Felix Gaeta is probably the closest Baltar has ever had to a friend in the series, but even he's kept at arm's length and ends up stabbing Baltar in the neck after his betrayal on New Caprica ("Taking a Break from All Your Worries"), and later perjures himself at Baltar's trial to get him convicted ("Crossroads, Part 2"). Baltar clearly has a lonely existence.

Simply put, Baltar isn't empowered by his perfidy. We think that life would be easier if we could just lie to people, rather than tell them the ugly truth that they're a murderous toaster; but really each lie makes our own lives worse. Baltar should have followed the wisdom attributed to Mark Twain: "Always tell the truth, that way you don't have to remember anything." Baltar isn't made happy for pursuing his desires, either. He simply spends his energy and is left wanting more. Thus, Plato says, "The tyrant soul also must of necessity always be poor and unsatisfiable" (578a).

But there are worse things that can happen to a person than for him simply to act badly. He can act badly *and get away with it.* "I do not think we have reached the extreme of wretchedness," Plato says after describing the person with a tyrannized soul. More wretched still is "the one who is tyrannical, but doesn't live a private life, because some misfortune provides him with the opportunity to become an actual tyrant" (578c). If a person with a tyrannized soul succeeds in remaking the world after his own inner darkness, there's nothing to hold back his misery. If there's no social order, the tyrant will be so afraid of being killed by his own slaves that he'll pander to them constantly. The tyrant may have thought he was acquiring power by ascending to the top of the social heap, but once there, he finds his only option in life is to work to stay there.

Similarly, Baltar thinks he gets power when he becomes president. In "Lay Down Your Burdens, Part 2," when Adama tells him he isn't listening to the evidence of an internal threat that led to the destruction of *Cloud Nine*, he replies, "I don't have to listen. I'm the President." But by the next season, we find that Baltar has to listen to everyone. He must pander constantly to the Cylons, and if he didn't fear an assassination attempt from his assistant, Gaeta, he should have, because Gaeta tried and later tried again. And like Plato's tyrant, Baltar can't go out in public like a normal person—for instance, to the graduation ceremonies for the New Caprica Police—for fear of being attacked. Baltar's success is entirely illusory. Thus, as Plato says, "the real tyrant is really a slave, compelled to engage in the worst kind of fawning, slavery and pandering to the worst kind of people" (579e).

There's one aspect of Baltar that doesn't fit Plato's image of the tyrant, and that's his *durability*, a trait noted by those who know him best. The first thing Baltar's inner Six says to him is, "You know what I love about you, Gaius? You're a survivor" ("Miniseries"). The fact that they're on a Raptor fleeing the recently nuked Caprica is a testament to the truth of her statement. In "Torn," Gaeta explains his take-home lesson from working as Baltar's underling: "If there was one thing I learned about Baltar, it was his extraordinary capacity for self-preservation." Gaeta predicts that Baltar had been plotting a path to Earth to save his own hide, and lo and behold, he was.

Plato doesn't mention the idea of the tyrant as survivor, but I think this is a point where the *BSG* characterization is richer than Plato's. Annas complains that the tyrant Plato portrays isn't particularly realistic, because there's no way such a madman could stay in power very long (304). The fact is, though, that such people do manage to seize and hold power. Baltar's namesake, Gaius "Caligula" Caesar, is a classic example. Some reports out of North Korea make Kim Jong-Il fit this model. Baltar's character at least gives us some hints about how this may be possible. Baltar's fearful and self-obsessed nature means he always has an escape plan.

"Are You Alive?"

This is the first line spoken in the reimagined *BSG*. It's asked by a machine—a Six—to a human being—a Colonial officer on the

Armistice Station. Clearly if anyone isn't alive here, it's the machine, right? This scene is mirrored in "You Can't Go Home Again" when Starbuck, marooned on a planet without oxygen, finds a crashed Cylon Raider. Opening a hatch, she finds living tissue underneath. Realizing that the spacecraft has no pilot, but is itself a machine, Starbuck whispers with wonder, "Are you alive?"

Cylons and humans have difficulty recognizing each other as alive. This brings out another important theme in Western philosophy, the question of what it means to be a person. This issue touches on both ethics and metaphysics—the study of the nature of reality. When humans and Cylons fail to recognize each other as persons, they're making an ethical decision, because they're saying they don't have ethical duties to the other side. When Roslin challenges Starbuck's torture of Leoben, she responds, "It's a machine, sir. There's no limit to the tactics I can use" ("Flesh and Bone"). It's also a metaphysical decision, because they're putting limits around a category of reality. Reality contains persons, but it also contains other things that aren't persons: rocks, trees, Dradis consoles. According to the Colonials, looking like a person isn't enough to *be* a person if one is a machine.[4]

One philosopher who took seriously the connection between ethics and metaphysics in understanding the idea of a person was Boethius. Boethius was a senator, and proud of his Greco-Roman heritage. But he was also a Christian, a monotheist who believed the world was the product of an all-loving, all-powerful, and all-knowing God. A major project for him was reconciling the wisdom of Greek philosophers like Plato with Christian teachings. Boethius also was in a position to think seriously about the nature of a tyrant. The Roman Empire had essentially collapsed and broken in half. The Western half, where he lived, was ruled by a barbarian, the Ostrogoth Theodoric. Theodoric persecuted Boethius, believing him to be a traitor. At the time Boethius wrote his greatest book, *The Consolations of Philosophy*, he was under house arrest, waiting to be executed.[5] The opening problem in that work is this: How could a just God allow this to happen? Why do I suffer while a tyrant like Theodoric prospers? Boethius' answer looks to his Greek heritage, to Plato and his treatment of the tyrant. Boethius accepts Plato's psychological vision and raises it to a metaphysical level. The evil person, for Boethius, is not only enslaved, he isn't even really human. In fact, he hardly exists at all. Thus, an explanation of God's ways to humanity: the tyrant doesn't really prosper. In fact, at the moment that Theodoric's thugs break into Boethius' house and club him to death, Boethius is better off than Theodoric.

Boethius begins this remarkable argument by agreeing with Plato that a villain like Baltar or Theodoric has no real power, even when they hold an office like President of the Twelve Colonies or King of the Goths and Italy. Boethius' focus is on *happiness*. He argues that the goal of life for all people is to be happy. Why does Baltar sleep with every woman he can? Because he thinks it'll make him happy. But happiness is identical with *goodness*. Things that seem to bring you happiness—like wealth, power, fame, or pleasure—will only hurt you in the end without goodness, for all of the reasons we saw with Plato's tyrant. Baltar's lusts only bring him misery, because he pursues them so dishonestly. They also demean him, as Six chides him for being jealous of Apollo after Starbuck calls out his name while Baltar is having sex with her:

> *Baltar* [to Apollo]:   You can't compete with me. I always win . . .
> *Six*: Never seen you like this, Gaius. It's disappointing somehow. Common.
> *Baltar*:   So sorry to disappoint you.
> ("Kobol's Last Gleaming, Part 1")

True pleasure, and thus true happiness, can be obtained only in honest relationships, the sort of friendships Plato shows the tyrant can never have. But power is the ability to get what you want. People want to be happy, and people like Baltar are simply not happy. Therefore, they have no real power. Thus, Boethius writes, "They fail in their quest for the supreme crown of reality, for the wretched creatures do not succeed in attaining the outcome for which alone they struggle day and night" (75).

Boethius goes further. The evil person isn't even really *human*. The Colonial officer on the Armistice Station may be right to say he's alive. A Cylon Raider may be alive in the way a horse or a dog is alive. But Baltar isn't really alive, not in the sense of being a living person and not as long as he continues his path of deception. How could this be? Human nature, according to Boethius, is to be good. We were all meant to be reunited with God. But evil people fail to realize this nature: "What follows from this is that you cannot regard as a man one who is disfigured by vices" (78).

In fact, Boethius contends, evil people cease to exist altogether, because they lose their *nature*. Think of a Viper that gets blown apart by a Cylon missile. After the explosion, something still exists: wreckage is flying everywhere. But *the Viper* doesn't exist anymore, because no one can use it to do what a Viper does: fly around and shoot things. The Viper, in being blown apart, has lost its nature. But a person who's fallen into injustice has also lost her nature. She's no longer achieving the purpose of a person, just as the wreckage of a Viper no longer serves the purpose of a Viper. Thus, evil people cease to exist: "You could say a corpse is a dead man, but you would not call it a man pure and simple; in the same way, I grant that corrupt men are wicked, but I refuse to admit that they exist in an absolute sense" (76). And thus we have a justification of God's ways to humanity: God didn't create a world where unjust tyrants rule while good people suffer. Quite the opposite. God created a world where the unjust fade away to nothingness while the just achieve their true nature.

It's pretty clear that Plato's conception of the tyrant is present in the characterization of Baltar, but can we go further and say that Boethius' radical claims are also present? Evil, in the world of the reimagined *BSG*, isn't a simple, dark force opposed to the noble warriors of goodness—there's no Count Iblis facing off against the Ship of Lights. Evil people like Baltar are clearly weak and pitiable, and the nature of humanity itself is questioned. Who's alive: the humans or the Cylons? A lot of questions remain unanswered in the series, but I think we'll find in Season Four that humans and Cylons prove they're alive by acting *justly*. How does Six ask the Colonial officer to prove he's alive? She gives him a kiss, a slow, open-mouth kiss while two Centurions look on. If Boethius is right, it's through *love*—as Six is constantly reminding Baltar—that we show that we're alive. "The gods shall lift those who lift each other."

NOTES

1 Plato, *The Republic*, in *The Complete Works*, ed. J. Cooper and D. S. Hutchinson (Indianapolis: Hackett, 1997). Further references will be given in the text.
2 Julia Annas, *An Introduction to Plato's Republic* (Oxford: Oxford University Press, 1981), 303. Further references will be given in the text.

3   For those who haven't followed Baltar's lascivious exploits as carefully as others have, the women include Starbuck, two "hot and cold running interns" on New Caprica, Number Three, the version of Six known as "Gina," Playa Palacios (reporter for the *Picon Star Tribune*), and an unnamed woman just before the first Cylon attack.

4   For further discussion of Cylon personhood, see Robert Arp and Tracie Mahaffey's chapter in this volume.

5   Boethius, *The Consolations of Philosophy*, trans. P. G. Walsh (Oxford: Oxford University Press, 1999). Further references will be given in the text.

4

The Politics of Crisis: Machiavelli in the Colonial Fleet

Jason P. Blahuta

The Cylon War is long over, yet we must not forget the reasons why so many sacrificed so much in the cause of freedom. The cost of wearing the uniform can be high, but—sometimes it's too high. You know, when we fought the Cylons, we did it to save ourselves from extinction. But we never answered the question, why? Why are we as a people worth saving?

"Miniseries"

This speech by Commander Adama during the decommissioning ceremony of the *Battlestar Galactica* establishes a theme that permeates the series: What makes humanity worthy of survival? This question has haunted humanity from the formation of the first societies where, according to political theorists Thomas Hobbes (1588–1679) and John Locke (1632–1704), we agreed to give up some of our natural rights for the protection of other rights that a civil society offers. In times of crisis extreme enough to threaten civil society, we're often asked to sacrifice even more of our freedoms to protect ourselves. But we run the risk of giving up too much—like due process and freedom of speech—or we may allow our leaders to lie, assassinate, and torture in the name of security. We may even start violating the rights of citizens with discriminatory measures, as was done with Japanese-Americans during World War II. These and other civil rights violations may result in a society that's no longer worth saving.

BSG explores this tension with a nod to a civil servant and philosopher from the Thirteenth Tribe of Kobol, Niccolò Machiavelli

(1469–1527), who made his mark with a handbook for navigating politics during times of crisis: *The Prince*.[1] The questions *BSG* asks are ones to which Machiavelli offers blunt answers: What makes a good leader? What will doom a leader? How far can a leader go to protect society?

"We're in the Middle of a War, and You're Taking Orders from a Schoolteacher?"

In addition to *The Prince*, Machiavelli wrote several books, plays, and poems that also address these questions. Laura Roslin, for example, can be compared to the character of Lucretia in his play *Mandragola*. The lesson of *Mandragola* is that, in a world of evildoers, the only way to secure happiness for everyone is to become corrupt and play the game. Such is the case of Lucretia, a young woman of outstanding virtue and beauty, who's approached by her aging husband with a scheme for having a child. He's recently learned of a potion that will make her fertile, but will kill the first man to sleep with her. He asks her to take the potion and sleep with another man. She resists, and turns to her mother and her priest for guidance. Unfortunately, both of them are corrupt and encourage her to go along with the plan. She acquiesces, takes the potion, and awaits her victim in bed. A young man enters and they have sex. Afterwards, her paramour reveals that he's responsible for her husband's learning of the fertility potion. It's all part of an elaborate scheme devised so that he might share the night with her, for he's madly in love with her.

Surrounded by corruption on all sides, what's a virtuous woman to do? The pleasures of a hot night of sex still coursing through her body, she embraces her new love, exclaiming, "Your cleverness, my husband's stupidity, my mother's folly, and my confessor's rascality have brought me to do what I never would have done of myself . . . I want you as my chief good; and what my husband has asked for one night, I intend him to have always."[2] She discards her old virtues, adds her own scheming to the plot, and secures her new love's place in her life. Thus, her husband happily believes his chances of gaining an heir are improved, and Lucretia enjoys a new sexual relationship with a lover who wants her for himself and doesn't ask her to violate her sense of morality. It's a win-win situation.

Laura Roslin's story lacks the sexual excitement of Lucretia's—except perhaps that one night she and Adama got buzzed off some "good stuff" on New Caprica ("Unfinished Business")—but it shares the theme of a woman surrounded by corruption on all sides who discovers that becoming corrupt herself is the only way to survive. When the Cylons attack, leaving Roslin the highest-ranking member of the civilian government, she isn't anyone's ideal picture of a president. She's the secretary of education, a glorified schoolteacher, as Adama says dismissively, forty-third in the line of succession. Roslin becomes surrounded by people who are in one form or another corrupt. Her vice president, Gaius Baltar, is literally sleeping with the enemy. Tom Zarek is so envious of her office that he's willing to take hostages, have people murdered, and aid Baltar in his own delusions of grandeur in order to get it. The military is quite happy to lead a coup against her when she sends Starbuck to retrieve the Arrow of Apollo. And Admiral Cain obviously thinks little of her; if Cain had lived, she probably would have abandoned Roslin along with any other civilians who weren't "military assets." If things weren't bad enough, the Colonials are under constant threat of annihilation by the Cylons.

So what's our schoolmarm-turned-president to do? Roslin starts off naïve. She's willing to sacrifice *Colonial One*, including what's left of the civilian government, in order to save the disabled *Gemenon Liner 1701* and two other defenseless civilian ships when the Cylons attack. But does she save the other ships? No. She refuses to leave the crippled ships behind, but she has no plan for how to save them or *Colonial One*—a noble, yet stupid decision. If the Cylons destroy *Colonial One*, the entire civilian government would be obliterated, along with the other ships shortly thereafter. Fortunately, Apollo saves the day by taking matters into his own hands.

As the magnitude of her situation makes itself felt, Roslin's idealism quickly fades. Shortly after this attack, *Colonial One* runs into Boomer's Raptor and Roslin sends it out to locate other civilian ships and bring them back. A convoy of roughly sixty ships is formed, but only forty have FTL drives. The situation grows critical when Cylon scouts buzz the convoy. Apollo insists that they must sacrifice the passengers and crews of the sub-light ships and leave immediately; any delay could be fatal as the Cylons will jump in with nukes before the civilian ships have time to react: "I'm sorry to make it a numbers game, but we're talking about the survival of our race here. And we don't have the luxury of taking risks and hoping for the best, because if we lose, we lose everything" ("Miniseries").

Roslin gives the order to jump and twenty ships are left defenseless as the Cylons attack. Her second difficult decision made, Roslin has now gotten her hands dirty. She goes on to make other decisions that are questionable from the perspective of conventional morality: advising Adama to assassinate Cain, rigging a democratic election, and sanctioning the use of biological weapons to commit genocide. Roslin doesn't do these things for personal gain, but rather for the good of the fleet. Regarding Cain, she pleads her case to Adama: "You're not an assassin. You are a Colonial officer who has taken an oath to protect this fleet. What do you think that she is going to do with the civilian fleet once she has eliminated you?" ("Resurrection Ship, Part 1"). In fixing the election, she's trying to protect the fleet from a man she believes to be too narcissistic to lead responsibly and who may be involved with the enemy ("Epiphanies"; "Lay Down Your Burdens, Part 2"). And in approving the genocide of the Cylons, she hopes to secure the survival of the human race: "The Cylons are coming to Earth. If they find us, they are coming for us. Those are the stakes. They always have been . . . As President I have determined the Cylons be made extinct" ("A Measure of Salvation").

Roslin quickly familiarizes herself with the rules of politics and is willing to grasp the problem of dirty hands—the reality that leaders must often violate conventional morality in order to lead—proving herself worthy of the position of president. In so doing, she's following Machiavelli's counsel: the only way to maintain a strong and stable state when surrounded by corruption is to discard conventional morality. Adama, however, holds fast to the values that define Colonial society and believes Roslin will, too:

Adama: Do we steal the results of a democratic election or not? That's the decision. Because if we do this, we're criminals. Unindicted, maybe, but criminals just the same.
Roslin: Yes, we are.
Adama: You won't do it. We've gone this far, but that's it.
Roslin: Excuse me?
Adama: You try to steal this election, you'll die inside. Likely move that cancer right to your heart. People made their choice. We're gonna have to live with it.
("Lay Down Your Burdens, Part 2")

43

Roslin reluctantly agrees and allows Baltar to become president—with disastrous results. She's also relieved when Adama ends up not having to assassinate Cain—because a Cylon prisoner has done the deed for them. But Roslin doesn't back down when it comes to eradicating the Cylons and it's only Helo's action that, as he'd put it, saves her soul.

"While the Chain of Command is Strict, It is Not Heartless. And Neither Am I"

Cain is an interesting counterpoint to Roslin. Both are women in professions that are otherwise male dominated—at least on Earth.[3] Both break the rules and enjoy success. Yet Roslin hatches an assassination plot against Cain, who ends up murdered by her own prisoner while Roslin survives. Why?

At first glance, Cain seems to embody Machiavelli's ideal of the prince (55–7). She makes the art of war her "imperative" and esteems discipline as the highest virtue as she leads the *Pegasus* in battle against the Cylons ("Razor"). By contrast, the *Galactica* is plagued by discipline problems and follows unorthodox procedures. Cain says in disbelief of the shared rule of Adama and Roslin, "How the two of you have survived this long, I will never know" ("Resurrection Ship, Part 1").

Disturbing signs soon surface about Cain's brand of leadership. She can be compared to the Legalists of Ancient China, employing a rigid form of government that imposes harsh penalties for any violation of the letter of the law, even acts which exceed the demands of the law—for example, producing ten tons of tylium instead of nine in a week if ordered by law to produce nine.[4] Cain executes her XO, a man to whom she was close, when he refuses to launch an attack against overwhelming odds. She cannibalizes the civilian ships she encounters, forcibly recruiting those who could be of use to her, and abandoning the rest. And unlike Adama, Cain recognizes no civilian authority. The picture darkens as the crews mingle. Horrific details are revealed of her condoning sexual torture of *Pegasus*'s captured Cylon, Gina. When Cain orders the same methods be used on Sharon, Helo and Tyrol come to the rescue and accidentally kill the interrogator. Cain denies them a fair trial and sentences them to death ("Pegasus").

Adama understands too late the monster that Cain is. From Cain's perspective, Adama is weak and an obstacle to effective rule, and she plots his murder to serve the interests of her war effort against the Cylons. Neither Adama nor Cain seek personal gain in their assassination plans; rather, they have incompatible conceptions of what's in the fleet's best interest. They do, however, share some sense of humanity and both back down at the last moment. Adama's motivation comes from a conversation with Sharon:

> *Adama*: I've asked you here to find out why the Cylons hate us so much . . .
> *Sharon*: It's what you said at the ceremony . . . You said that humanity was a flawed creation. And that people still kill one another for petty jealousy and greed. You said that humanity never asked itself why it deserved to survive. Maybe you don't.

Where did Cain go wrong? Machiavelli advises that because subjects love at their convenience, but fear at the ruler's, it's best for a ruler to be feared and loved. But as this delicate balance is hard to maintain, the prudent ruler will seek to be feared rather than be loved (62). Machiavelli is quick to place limits on this advice, though. Being feared is a good thing, but one can't become *hated*. He follows with a list of prohibitions to avoid becoming hated, and Cain brakes the major one: never sexually touch a woman, because she will always be invested with the honor of a man, be it her son, her husband or lover, brother or father, and these men will seek revenge for the dishonor they suffer (63, 67). Machiavelli is, of course, a product of Renaissance Italian culture, but the cultural norms onboard *Galactica* don't seem that different. Cain is feared because she killed her XO for not carrying out her orders, but she's hated because she sacrifices the wives and children of the civilians she drafts, and also because she condones the sexual torture of Sharon and Gina. Baltar comes to love Gina as he does Caprica Six, sets her free, gives her a weapon, and tells her that instead of committing suicide what she needs is vengeance on Cain ("Resurrection Ship, Part 2").

The differences in life under the leadership of Roslin and Cain underscore the question of survival versus being worthy of survival. Life under Roslin's regime is not only bearable, but worthy of continuing. It may be a struggle, but it's a struggle for something other than mere survival. The same can't be said of life under Cain's regime.

Her soldiers fight, but for what? Their existence is bleak and soul-less. Machiavelli is well aware of the horrors of war, the problem of dirty hands, and the joys of civilian life; and he makes it clear that the only justification for the former two is their ability to secure the latter.

Helo's Halo: Can Genocide Ever be Justified?

How far can a leader go in the name of preserving society? Perhaps after Watergate, presidents who never inhaled or had "sexual relations with that woman," and non-existent weapons of mass destruction, we've become so accustomed to our leaders telling lies that we no longer consider it a serious offense. And murder? When televangelists, self-proclaimed holy men, call for the assassination of foreign leaders, it signals a growing cynicism and acceptance of taking human life for political purposes.[5] But genocide is one of the few taboos left that won't be tolerated, presumably because it can't ever be justified.

The opportunity to commit genocide appears when Athena and Apollo board a disabled Cylon baseship and find five "skin jobs" dying of a fatal disease. Fortunately, humans—and Athena because she carried a half-human child—are immune to it. At the same time, the Cylon threat is revealed to be even more dangerous when one of the Cylons reveals that Baltar is alive and helping them find Earth. The Cylon also reveals that the disease has a bioelectric feedback component that will follow a Cylon through the resurrection process, in effect spreading the disease via the resurrection ship.

The potential of this information isn't lost on Apollo, who puts forth a bold plan: jump to an area where the Cylons will find them, engage in battle until a resurrection ship is in range, and then execute the prisoners. The disease will follow them into their resurrected bodies and spread through the Cylon fleet:

> *Roslin*: Oh my Gods, this could be the end of the Cylons entirely.
> *Apollo*: Forever.
> *Helo*: Genocide? So that's what we're about now?
> *Apollo*: They're not human. They were built, not born. No fathers, no mothers, no sons, no daughters.
> *Helo*: I had a daughter. I held her in my arms.
> ("A Measure of Salvation")

Helo views his wife, Athena, and the Cylons in general as persons, hence his moral outrage at the idea of wiping them out entirely.[6] But does his moral outrage make sense? Apollo could concede that the Cylons are persons, but argue that we can kill them anyway.

The strongest argument Helo could offer would be a form of "just war" theory. This theory has a long tradition in Western philosophy, stretching back to Roman law and the Judeo-Christian religious tradition. It seeks to establish when a war is morally defensible and what the limits to justifiable military action are—and it has never justified genocide.

There are two components of just war theory, both of which have to be satisfied. The first, *jus ad bellum*, determines whether a war is morally justified. A just cause for war occurs when the enemy is using substantial aggression, all other non-violent options aren't feasible, and there's reason to think that a violent response will be successful. Roslin argues that the war with the Cylons satisfies this provision: "The Cylons struck first in this war. And not being content with the annihilation of billions of human beings, they pursued us relentlessly through the galaxies determined to wipe us out." She doesn't mention the additional fact that the Cylons didn't respond to a complete and unconditional surrender of Colonial forces after Picon was nuked ("Miniseries"). Helo naïvely protests, "They tried to live with us on New Caprica," and receives a cold response from Roslin. New Caprica wasn't an attempt to "live together." The Cylons moved in with a micro-managing occupation force and began experimenting on humans in bizarre ways, like trying to make Starbuck love Leoben, turning human against human with the New Caprica Police, torturing those suspected of causing problems, and generally transforming the settlement into an internment camp. Such unprovoked and continued aggression against both civilian and military targets makes the war against the Cylons *just*.

The second component that needs to be satisfied is *jus in bello*, which determines how far humans can go in their war with the Cylons. Generally, a just war is one that isn't intentionally directed towards civilians and is proportionate to the goal of the immediate military exercise. Can genocide pass this test? Usually the answer is an unqualified "No"; but in the case of the Colonials and the Cylons, the answer is "Yes." The Cylons may be persons, but there's no evidence that the Cylons have a civilian population. There are a few dissenters who have second thoughts about the war, but they're still part of a war machine that's coextensive with the entire Cylon race. Furthermore, the logistics of the war don't make genocide disproportionate to the survival of the human species: the Cylons refused to acknowledge an unconditional surrender, have remained aggressively hostile even though humanity is no longer a threat to them, are obsessed with finding Earth, are practically immortal, and have overwhelming numbers and military resources.

Typically, liberal democracies use just war theory to justify military actions, but the theory is quick to condemn many such actions. The nuclear attacks on Hiroshima and Nagasaki and the bombing of Dresden near the close of World War II would have difficulty passing the just war test, because even though the Allied war effort was just, such means were disproportionate to the goal of ending the war. The nuclear attack on Japan was indiscriminate in its inclusion of civilians and, while it would have meant the loss of more Allied soldiers' lives, the war could have been concluded by just means. But the situation with the Cylons is different. Not only is the fate of the entire human species on the line, but the Colonials have few other options. *Necessity* drives Roslin to condone the use of biological weapons against the Cylons with the intent of committing genocide. Adama, fearing for his place in history, laments, "Posterity really doesn't look too kindly on genocide." Roslin responds in words that Machiavelli himself would have chosen: "You're making an assumption that posterity will define this as genocide. If they do, at least there'll be someone alive to hate us for it" ("A Measure of Salvation").

Helo's self-righteous tunnel-vision blinds him to all this. The only thing he can focus on is that this is genocide, that it's wrong, and that he must do something to stop it. As *Galactica* prepares for battle, Helo thwarts Apollo's plan by asphyxiating the prisoners before the resurrection ship is in range. He tries to justify himself to Athena afterwards: "I'm not a traitor. I love my people. I love this ship . . . I did what I thought was right. If it was a mistake, fine. I can live with that." In a culture like ours that's beginning to view whistleblowers as heroes (and rightly so) Helo is likely to receive a sympathetic reception. His brand of morality, however, is disturbing for several reasons.

Obviously, Helo was under time constraints, but there were other options open to him besides killing the Cylon prisoners. He could have proposed an obvious and feasible solution: incorporate the virus into all of *Galactica*'s weapons and broadcast a warning to the Cylons that the Colonials are now in possession of the dreaded virus and will use it if provoked. The prospect of a doomsday virus might deter the Cylons from further attacks and buy the Colonials some peace; or it might force the Cylons to continue their attacks without the aid of resurrection ships, in effect rendering them mortal and evening the odds somewhat. But Helo's moral outrage limits him to protesting how wrong the genocide plan is. Of course, Helo isn't the only one wearing blinders. Roslin, Adama, and Apollo could have voiced such an alternative, but the prospect of ending the Cylon threat once and for all blinds them to other options.

An even more troubling aspect of Helo's morality is how he treats the Cylon prisoners. He could have gone to see the prisoners, told them of the plan, and gauged their reaction. Athena is willing to go through with the plan because she has the appropriate morality for a soldier: raise questions and concerns, but once the order is given, put your personal morality aside. One of the Cylon prisoners, Simon, is also quite willing to betray his people by divulging information if it means getting a cure; so it's not clear what the Cylon prisoners would want. Perhaps they would volunteer to be held as hostages for future bluffs at infecting resurrection ships. Given how readily Simon betrays his people for the cure, perhaps some of the others are so desperate to live that they'd agree to such an arrangement. Yet Helo murders them in cold blood without a second thought and feels justified in doing so. It's a strange morality that condemns genocide, yet condones killing five persons without their consent. In the end, Helo's halo is tarnished, and his humanity is just as corroded as Apollo, Adama, and Roslin's is for not exploring alternatives to genocide.

Helo's moral convictions make him an unfit Colonial officer. He's not a bad person, just a bad military officer. One of the most influential twentieth-century interpretations of Machiavelli is offered by Isaiah Berlin (1909–1997), who maintains that Machiavelli doesn't separate politics from ethics, but rather holds up two incompatible moralities: a Christian one characterized by honesty, charity, generosity, and meekness that's suitable for private life; and a pagan one characterized by strength, courage, cunning, and the pursuit of glory that's suitable for public life.[7] Agents in the political or military arena who act according to Christian morality are not only doomed to failure, but are a danger to their country. Helo's morality makes him a good man for private life, but he shouldn't be an officer—a point Roslin implies: "You would serve your fleet well if you'd remember occasionally that the Cylons are a mortal threat to the survival of the human race" ("A Measure of Salvation"). In the aftermath of Apollo's failed mission, when Roslin and Adama are certain that Helo is the one who foiled their plans, the curious thing is that Adama doesn't exile Helo to civilian life. Machiavelli would have advised throwing him out the nearest airlock as an example to others.

"It's Not Enough to Survive. One Has to be Worthy of Surviving"

The tension between survival and being worthy of survival won't go away so long as human civilization endures. Every nation that exists today has a bloodstain on its family tree—a lie, murder, coup, rebellion, broken election promise, stolen land, or broken treaty. As these nations face the crises of the twenty-first century—terrorism, religious and secular fanaticism, rogue states, climate change, resource shortages, overpopulation, and environmental damage—this tension must be carefully weighed. Machiavelli places a spotlight on an aspect of politics that many pretend doesn't exist, and offers valuable insights into how far rulers can justifiably go in balancing freedom, security, and other essential values to society. Whatever choices we make we must never stop seeking an answer to the question of whether we're worthy of survival.

NOTES

1 See Niccolò Machiavelli, *The Prince*, in *Machiavelli: The Chief Works and Others*, trans. Allan Gilbert (Durham, NC: Duke University Press, 1965). Further references will be given in the text.
2 Niccolò Machiavelli, "Mandragola," in *The Chief Works and Others*, 819.
3 For further discussion of gender roles in the *BSG* universe, see Sarah Conly's chapter in this volume.

4 For examples of Legalist thinkers, see Han Fei Tzu, "Han Fei Tzu" in *Basic Writings of Mo Tzu, Hsün Tzu, and Han Fei Tzu*, trans. Burton Watson (New York: Columbia University Press, 1964); and Shang Yang, *The Book of Lord Shang*, trans. J. J. L. Duyvendak (Ware: Wordsworth Press, 1998).

5 "We have the ability to take [Hugo Chávez] out, and I think the time has come that we exercise that ability. We don't need another $200 billion war to get rid of one, you know, strong-arm dictator. It's a whole lot easier to have some of the covert operatives do the job and then get it over with." Pat Robertson, as quoted in *Media Matters for America*: www.mediamatters.org/items/200508220006 (accessed June 28, 2007).

6 For discussion of Cylon personhood, see Robert Arp and Tracie Mahaffey's chapter in this volume.

7 See Isaiah Berlin, "The Originality of Machiavelli," in *Against the Current: Essays in the History of Ideas*, ed. Henry Hardy (Oxford: Clarendon Press, 1981), 25–79. Berlin is responding to an interpretation of Machiavelli proposed by Ernst Cassirer in his *The Myth of the State* (New Haven: Yale University Press, 1966), 120–62.

PART II

I, CYLON: ARE TOASTERS PEOPLE, TOO?

5

"And They Have A Plan": Cylons As Persons

Robert Arp and Tracie Mahaffey

We hold adult persons responsible for their actions. But what about Cylons? Cylons "have a plan" that so far has involved murdering billions of humans and attempting to eliminate or subjugate the survivors. Can Cylons be held morally responsible for their actions, despite their programmed, machine nature? If Cylons are persons then the answer is yes. Most people think of *person* as synonymous with *human*, and so obviously Cylons wouldn't be persons. But in fact *person* has a broader sense in which a person is a bearer of rights and responsibilities. Historically speaking not all humans have been considered persons. Women, children, and slaves have, at various times, not been considered persons. It's also at least theoretically possible for a nonhuman to count as a person in the sense of being a bearer of rights and responsibilities. If some day we meet intelligent nonhuman extraterrestrial life forms we may well consider them persons. But still, what about Cylons? To answer this question we need a definition of *person*. Let's take this definition as our starting point. A person is a being who has the capacity to: (1) be rational or intelligent; (2) have robust mental states like beliefs, desires, emotions, and self-awareness; (3) use language, rather than simply transmit information; (4) be involved in relationships with other persons; and (5) be morally responsible for one's actions as a free and autonomous being who could have done otherwise.[1] Cylons would have to meet all five criteria in order to count as persons. So let's see if they do.

Cylons and the Capacity for Reason

The first criterion has to do with the capacity for reason, or rationality. In one sense, rationality is the same thing as *intelligence* and involves a variety of traits, including the ability to calculate, make associations between present stimuli and stored memories, solve problems, and draw new conclusions or inferences from old information. Cylons obviously make calculations, as, for example, when they discover that procreation between the humanoid Cylon models is impossible. The Cylons express a fervent religious belief in what they see as the one, true God. According to Sharon/Athena, the Cylons are deeply troubled by their failure to reproduce biologically: "Procreation, that's one of God's commandments. 'Be fruitful' " ("The Farm").

When Starbuck awakens in a hospital on Cylon-occupied Caprica after being injured in a Cylon attack, she's cared for by a Cylon, Simon, posing as a human doctor. Over the course of his visits, Simon tries to convince Starbuck that her most valuable asset isn't her skill as a Viper pilot, but her ability to reproduce. Starbuck, suspicious from the beginning of Simon's identity and motives, learns that he's a Cylon. As she's searching for an escape, Starbuck discovers how far the Cylons are willing to go to find a way to reproduce biologically. After Starbuck's escape, Sharon informs her that the Cylons are attempting to use human women as incubators for human-Cylon hybrids. Starbuck is outraged that the Cylons would resort to raping human women in order to satisfy the desire to meet God's commandment. The cold planning and organization necessary to achieve the Cylons' goal demonstrates their rational capacity.

In addition to their capacity to formulate rational plans, Cylons have extraordinary memory storage capabilities. When a Cylon's physical body is destroyed, her consciousness is downloaded into a new body of the same model. So long as a Cylon is physically close enough to a resurrection ship, her consciousness—memories, beliefs, desires, and preferences—survives. Cylon memories thus aren't bound to a particular physical body. Although this may pose a difficulty when two copies of the same model share the same memories, resurrected Cylons have genuine memories of events and the ability to recall these, as well as the capacity to distinguish between genuine memories and apparent memories.[2]

While searching for the Tomb of Athena on Kobol, Sharon and Helo reminisce about their time together on Caprica. But Sharon also describes being with Starbuck and the others as feeling as if she's "back in the fleet." Helo reminds her that she was never in the fleet; rather, the Sharon known as "Boomer" was. Sharon responds, "I know. I know that. But I remember all of it. Like getting my wings. My first trip aboard the *Galactica*. You know, the memory of being in a uniform is so strong, so potent, it's like, 'I'm Sharon Valerii and this is my family.' That's pretty weird, huh?" ("Home, Part 2"). Cylons apparently have the ability to distinguish between memories that are connected to their current physical body, and those that have been downloaded into the consciousness of a new copy.

Cylons can also solve problems, as when they decide to attempt peaceful cohabitation with humans on New Caprica. In the face of the growing resistance movement, the Cylons determine that harsh measures must be taken to squelch it:

> *Cavil 1*: I want to clarify our objectives. If we're bringing the word of "God," then it follows that we should employ any means necessary to do so, any means.
>
> *Cavil 2*: Yes, *fear* is a key article of faith, as I understand it. So perhaps it's time to instill a little more fear into the people's hearts and minds . . . We round up the leaders of the insurgency and we execute them *publicly*. We round up at random groups off the streets and we execute them *publicly*.
>
> *Cavil 1*: Send a message that the gloves are coming off. The insurgency stops now or else we start reducing the human population to a more manageable size . . .
>
> ("Occupation")

While the Cylon plan is thwarted before any mass executions take place, it's clear that Brother Cavil and the other Cylons determine that the benefit of executing these groups of humans outweighs any potential costs and, therefore, mass executions and the use of fear as a motivation are acceptable solutions to the Cylons' problems on New Caprica.

Finally, Cylons are able to reason in the sense of deductively drawing conclusions and making inferences. Brother Cavil arrives at his conclusion above by a process of reasoning that looks something like this:

> *Premise 1*: If the Cylons publicly execute the leaders of the resistance and random groups of people as a way of addressing the resistance movement, then a powerful fear of death will be instilled in the humans.
>
> *Premise 2*: If the humans are instilled with a powerful fear of death, then the humans will not resist the Cylon occupation on New Caprica.
>
> *Conclusion*: Thus, if the Cylons publicly execute the leaders of the resistance and random groups of people as a way of addressing the resistance movement, then the humans will not resist the Cylon occupation on New Caprica.

Another example can be found in "Torn" when a Cylon baseship becomes infected by a mysterious and highly contagious virus that is killing all the Cylons onboard. Cylons on an uninfected baseship reason that they can't risk sending either a Raider or any Centurions to investigate the mysterious illness for fear of infection:

> *Premise 1*: All Cylons are created from the same genetic pool.
>
> *Premise 2*: All members of the Cylon genetic pool are susceptible to the virus.
>
> *Conclusion*: No member of the Cylon genetic pool can come in contact with the mysterious virus without contracting it.

Clearly, then, the Cylons meet the minimum criterion for personhood of being *rational*.

Cylons and Mental States

Just because something can reason doesn't mean it's a person. A computer can be programmed to reason in the same way that Simon did with regards to possible solutions to the Cylons' breeding problems, or that Brother Cavil did with regards to possible solutions to the resistance movement on New Caprica—making step-by-step calculations. Yet, we wouldn't consider a computer a person because of this capacity alone. Persons also must have the capacity for mental states, such as holding a belief, having a desire, feeling a pain, or experiencing some event.

Think about an experience where you jumped for joy, felt pain, or regretted a decision you made. Recall the joyful experience: how you smiled, relished the moment, and wished that every moment could be like this one. When D'Anna/Three sees the faces of the "final five" Cylons, her expression clearly exhibits her experience of ecstasy ("Rapture"). She's finally accomplished something she's aspired to for some time and is overcome with joy at the moment of her enlightenment. Now think about a pain you experienced, like touching something that was very hot. Remember how that pain was all-consuming for the duration, how it lingered in your body, and how you thought, "Ow! That *hurt*! *Mother frakker*!" That was your pain, and no one else's—only *you* could know what that pain was like. In "Resurrection Ship, Part 1," Gaius Baltar reaches out to a Number Six (Gina) who's been held prisoner aboard the *Pegasus*. She's been subjected to repeated sexual and physical assault. When Baltar attempts to help her she begs him to kill her and thus end her suffering. Few of us have ever experienced a pain so intense that we'd rather die than endure it any longer. Since the Cylons exhibit awesome strength and an amazing pain tolerance, Gina's plea illustrates the extent of her suffering.

Finally, think of a decision you've come to regret. You believe you could have made a different, better decision; and thinking about it now may cause you pain or regret. In "Downloaded," Caprica Six and Boomer, based on their personal experiences of love with human beings—Baltar and Tyrol, respectively—convince the other Cylon models to rethink their attitude toward humanity. This leads to the New Caprica experiment because, as Caprica Six explains, "The majority of Cylon felt that the slaughter of humanity had been a mistake" ("Occupation"). So at least some of the Cylons regret nuking the Colonies.

Cylons and Language

Language is a definite mark of personhood. But we need to draw a distinction between *transmitting information* and *engaging in a communicative linguistic performance*. Many people think that each kind of animal has its own language—including apes, dolphins, bees, and ants. It's true that all animals, including humans, transmit information by relaying useful data back and forth to one another, or by making mental associations with present or stored stimuli so as to act. Engaging in a communicative linguistic performance, however, entails having mental states insofar as beliefs, desires, intentions, hopes, dreams, fears, and the like are communicated from one being to another. So, a bee isn't really *speaking* to another bee when doing his "bee dance" to transmit information about where pollen is located outside the hive. Even apes that have been taught sign language aren't necessarily speaking—using language—to their trainers; they may be merely associating stimuli with stored memories and transmitting information. As far as we know, bees and apes don't have experiences of joy, suffering, or regret to communicate.

Do Cylons have the capacity to engage in communicative linguistic performances? Cylons apparently want other Cylons and other beings to understand what they're communicating. When Romo Lampkin asks Caprica Six about her romantic relationship with Baltar, she tries to convey the complex array of emotions she has concerning him: "Gaius Baltar is a brilliant, gifted human being. In the time I've known him, he's made a sport of mendacity and deception. He was narcissistic, self-centered, feckless, and vain. I'm the one who should've stabbed him" ("The Son Also Rises"). Caprica Six wants Lampkin to understand the depth and complexity of her feelings, she loves and despises Baltar at the same time. Lampkin responds that giving Cylons the ability to feel love is a "precocious evolutionary move" that's "not for the faint-hearted." From his response, it's obvious that Caprica Six succeeds in making Lampkin understand her feelings for Baltar, which he's able to call to the surface by telling the story of his own lost love:

> *Lampkin*: I have to ask you. Does your love hurt as much as mine?
> *Six*: Yes.
> *Roslin*: [observing from another room] I feel like part of our world just fell down.

Roslin realizes that her bias against the reality of Cylon love—and personhood—is built on a false premise, and that it won't be so easy to use Six as a weapon against Baltar at this trial.

Another example is when Sharon/Athena has the opportunity to kill Adama and complete Boomer's failed mission. Instead, she takes this opportunity to declare her independence from the Cylons:

> I need you to know something. I'm Sharon but I'm a different Sharon. I know who I am. I don't have hidden protocols or programs lying in wait to be activated. I make my own choices. I make my own decisions and I need you to know that this is my choice. ("Home, Part 2")

Leaving aside the question of whether Sharon does in fact have free will, it's clear that she's communicating her beliefs and desires in a meaningful way to Adama. Besides engaging in communicative linguistic performances, Cylons also seem to have beliefs about themselves, others, and the world around them. And they act on those beliefs, whether to save themselves, aid others, or engage in other kinds of voluntary behavior. When Caprica Six helps Sharon get off a Cylon baseship with Hera, it's precisely because she holds the *belief* that Hera is the key to the Cylons' future ("Rapture").

Cylons and Social Relationships

Do Cylons have the capacity to enter into social relationships with other persons? Social relationships can be divided into *family* relationships, or those loving and nurturing relationships found in households; *economic* relationships, or those relationships people have in the public sphere when they conduct business transactions; *allegiance* relationships, or those relationships that people choose to be a part of like churches, interest groups, the Loyal Order of the Moose, or the Shriners; and *civil* relationships, which include the relationships citizens have to one another and to their governing body. Each of these relationships involves duties, rights, laws, and obligations appropriate to its type. In a family, a parent has a duty to take care of a child, and one of the fundamental "laws" in such a relationship is unconditional love; Starbuck's mother appealed to a different law that she believed justified abusing Starbuck to make her tough and prepare her to fulfill her "special destiny" ("Maelstrom"). In economic transactions, the fundamental obligation is to the "bottom line," and the law may include something like "let the buyer beware"; in the "ragtag fleet," obtaining goods, including basic goods such as medicine, requires obedience to such economic laws ("Black Market"). In civil relationships, rights and laws protect citizens from harm, and ensure the prospering of societies as a whole; Tom Zarek, as well as Apollo, are concerned that Colonial civilization may devolve into a "gang" if democratic principles aren't upheld ("Bastille Day"; "Crossroads, Part 2").

Cylons clearly have the capacity to enter into social relationships. Sharon/Athena enters into marriage with Helo and they have a child together, Hera, for whom Sharon risks her life ("Rapture"). Together, Sharon and Helo care for Hera the same as any parents would: when she's ill, they take her to see the doctor ("The Woman King"); when she cries, they try to comfort her ("Rapture"). Like any parents, they have hopes and dreams for their child. Consider also that Galen and Cally Tyrol marry on New Caprica and have a child ("Occupation"). Even though neither knows that Galen is a Cylon at the time, their family relationship exemplifies all of the characteristics of human families—even the slings and arrows of a typical marriage, as Galen tells Apollo, it's "why we build bars" ("Taking a Break from All Your Worries"). With respect to economic relationships, Cylons sometimes have specific jobs that they've been charged with and must fulfill. On Caprica, one of Simon's jobs is to prepare human women for the human-Cylon breeding program ("The Farm"). And, on New Caprica, Brother Cavil runs the detention center and commands the New Caprica Police ("Occupation"; "Precipice").

Relationships of allegiance are also evident among the Cylons. Sharon/Athena pledges her allegiance to Adama and the human race, which leads to her receiving a commission in the fleet ("Precipice"). Sharon's allegiance is so strong that she even accepts Adama and Roslin's plan to exterminate the entire Cylon race: "Does a Cylon keep her word, even if it means she's the last Cylon left in the universe? Can a human being do that?" ("A Measure of Salvation"). We witness the civil relationships among the humanoid Cylon models when they decide to "box" D'Anna's consciousness. The others decide that her model is "fundamentally flawed" and that, for the safety and prosperity of the Cylon race, it is necessary to take her "offline" because she "defied the group" in pursuing her personal "messianic" quest to see the faces of the "final five" Cylons ("Rapture").

Do We Have a Plan?

Now we can answer the question as to whether Cylons can be held morally responsible for their actions as free and autonomous beings who could have done otherwise. Cylons communicate, have the capacity for reason, and can be involved in complex social relationships. More importantly, they express feelings of disillusionment, contempt, pain, and suffering, as well as joy, satisfaction, and contentment. A being that has these traits apparently has mental states, and such a being is a person, regardless of whether it's biological or mechanical.

But, most significantly, Cylons murder billions of human beings, deprive the residents of New Caprica of basic freedoms, and use human women against their will as procreative incubators. Since Cylons are able to enter into the most complex relationships with other beings deemed persons, they must be held accountable for their actions against such persons. In short, they must be stopped! They have a plan, and it should never be allowed to materialize.

The issue of treating Cylons as persons in the *BSG* universe may seem silly to talk about because, after all, it's just a made-up story. As history has proven, however, science *fiction* has a way of becoming science *fact*. The famous robotics engineer and theorist, Hans Moravec, claims that by 2050 robots actually will surpass humans in intellectual capacity.[3] In the not-so-distant future, there will most likely be advanced forms of machinery that behave much like Sharon and Caprica Six. How will we treat them and how will they treat us?

NOTES

1   For more on the definition of "person," see John Locke, *An Essay Concerning Human Understanding*, ed. Peter H. Nidditch (Oxford: Clarendon Press, 1975), Bk. 2, Ch. 27; Daniel Dennett, *Brainstorms* (Montgomery, VT: Bradford Books, 1978); Derek Parfit, *Reasons and Persons* (Oxford: Oxford University Press, 1984).
2   For further discussion of the implications of Cylon downloading for *personal identity*, see Amy Kind's chapter in this volume.
3   Hans Moravec, *Robot: Mere Machine to Transcendent Mind* (Oxford: Oxford University Press, 1999), 58–61. For further discussion of Moravec's theories and the real-life possibility of developing artificial intelligence, see Jerold J. Abrams' and David Koepsell's chapters in this volume.

"I'm Sharon, But I'm A Different Sharon": The Identity of Cylons

Amy Kind

The question of personal identity—what makes a person the same person over time—is puzzling. Through the course of a life, someone might undergo a dramatic alteration in personality, radically change her values, lose almost all of her memories, and undergo significant changes in her physical appearance. Given all of these potential changes, why should we be inclined to regard her as the *same person*? *Battlestar Galactica* presents us with an even bigger puzzle: What makes a Cylon the same Cylon over time? There are only twelve different models, but there are many copies of each. So what makes the resurrected Caprica Six the same Cylon as the one who seduced Gaius Baltar into betraying humanity, and yet a different Cylon from the tortured Gina or Shelly Godfrey?

Philosophers grappling with the nature of personal identity tend to fall into two groups. Both try to explain personal identity as a kind of continuity over time, but they split over what kind of continuity matters: *psychological* or *physical*.[1] What makes a Cylon the same Cylon over time, however, must be psychologically based. Unlike humans, Cylons have a special ability: they can resurrect.[2] Caprica Six tells Baltar: "I can't die. When this body is destroyed, my memory, my consciousness, will be transmitted to a new one. I'll just wake up somewhere else in an identical body" ("Miniseries").

But a psychological theory of Cylon identity is threatened by the Number Eights, in particular, by Sharon "Boomer" Valerii and Sharon "Athena" Agathon. Boomer and Athena look exactly alike; as Helo notes, they share the "same grin, same laugh, all the little things" ("Valley of Darkness"). But they have different personalities. Just think of how differently each of them relates to Hera: one will go to any lengths to save her, the other threatens to snap her neck ("Rapture"). In these respects, they seem a lot like clones or identical twins. But matters aren't so simple, for unlike clones or identical twins, Athena shares many of Boomer's memories, and her love for Helo is in many ways shaped by Boomer's experiences with him. When Athena first joins up with the *Galactica* crew, she tells Helo how happy she feels:

> *Athena*: Just being with you and Kara feels like I've come home. It's like I'm back in the fleet.
> *Helo*: But you were never in the fleet. That was the other Sharon.
> *Athena*: I know. I know that. But I remember all of it. Like getting my wings. My first trip aboard the *Galactica*. You know, the memory of being in a uniform is so strong, so potent, it's like, "I'm Sharon Valerii and this is my family." That's pretty weird, huh?
> ("Home, Part 2")

"Pretty weird"—what an understatement! Talking later with Adama, who—having been recently shot by Boomer—isn't sure what to make of her, she tells him, "I'm Sharon, but I'm a different Sharon." How can that be?

"We Must Survive, and We Will Survive"—But How?

What it means to say that one person is identical to another depends on what we mean by *identity*—or, as a former President (of the United States, not the Twelve Colonies) once said, on what the meaning of the word "is" is. The sense in which identical twins are identical should be distinguished from the sense in which the inside source for Chief Tyrol's New Caprica Resistance and the tactical officer on *Galactica* are identical. Identical twins are two distinct individuals, but they share all their physical qualities. They're *qualitatively*, but not *numerically*, identical. The second sense of identity doesn't involve two distinct individuals; Tyrol's source and the *Galactica*'s tactical officer are one and the same man: Felix Gaeta. Our concern here is with numerical identity.

The psychological theory of personal identity originates with John Locke (1632–1704). For Locke, a person "is a thinking intelligent being, that has reason and reflection, and can consider it self as it self, the same thinking thing, in different times and places."[3] This definition suggests that personal identity consists in an individual's consciousness: "As far as this consciousness can be extended backwards to any past action or thought, so far reaches the identity of that person; it is the same self now it was then" (335). Locke's notion of consciousness is usually understood in terms of *memory*. What it means for someone's consciousness to extend backwards to one of his past actions is for him to *remember* it.

Memories come in several different sorts. Anyone from Gemenon probably remembers the first line of the Sacred Scrolls: "Life here began out there." If you're not from Gemenon, you may remember that the original *BSG* series' prologue opens with these words. These are *factual* memories. In contrast, Starbuck remembers how to play pyramid when she goes up against Anders, even though she hasn't played for quite a while due to her blown knee. She has a *skill* memory. Finally, Colonel Tigh remembers the horror of having his eye ripped out while being kept in detention on New Caprica. This is an *experiential* memory, also known as a *first-person* memory or a memory *from the inside*. This last kind is what Locke has in mind. Only I can remember, from the inside, my own experiences. Thus, on Locke's view, if someone at a later time has an experiential memory of something that I did at an earlier time, then that someone must be me.

The intuition behind the view is simple. Suppose Admiral Adama and one of the tylium refinery workers could somehow swap bodies, so that one day the body of the refinery worker has all the memories of being the admiral and the body of the admiral has all the memories of being the refinery worker. According to Locke, this transfer favors the refinery worker (340). Since personal identity is determined by consciousness, the refinery worker (in the admiral's body) is now lucky enough to be sleeping in Adama's comfortable private quarters, with his voluminous library and ready-to-eat noodles, while the admiral (in the worker's body) is forced to do the dangerous and dirty job of refining tylium to refuel the Vipers and Raptors he previously commanded.

Contemporary versions of the psychological theory further refine Locke's notion of experiential memory and often factor in additional psychological connections beyond memory, such as intentions for the future, preferences, and other character traits.[4] But the basic idea's the same. What makes the admiral who rescued the Colonists from the Cylon occupation of New Caprica the same person as the commander who sent a stealth ship over the Armistice Line, and the same person as the Viper pilot called "Husker," is the psychological continuity that unites them. Thus, the man who rejoices in his victory at New Caprica can feel nostalgia when he sees his old Mark II Viper and feel guilt over having possibly provoked the Cylons into attacking the Colonies ("Exodus, Part 2"; "Miniseries"; "Hero").

Those who hold the physical theory of personal identity would disagree. The Viper pilot, the commander, and the admiral have the same body, the same brain. And it's this physical continuity that makes all three the same person. After Boomer shoots Adama, he languishes in a coma for over a week. There's no psychological continuity between the man in CIC reaching out to shake Boomer's hand and the man lying unconscious in *Galactica*'s infirmary, but everyone still identifies that unconscious man as Adama. As Tigh insists, *Galactica* is still Adama's command ("Scattered"). In arguing for their view, physical continuity theorists like Bernard Williams often attack the coherence of the body transfer scenarios employed by their opponents. According to Williams, an individual's personality can't be separated from his bodily traits, making the whole notion of swapping bodies problematic. Certain faces can't embody arrogance or suspiciousness; certain voices can't sound sophisticated or authoritative.[5] Try to imagine Adama's gruff voice issuing Baltar's self-serving and stammering excuses, or Baltar's pleading eyes delivering Adama's steely stare.

One advantage of the physical continuity theory is its simplicity. On the psychological continuity theory, questions could always arise about whether an individual really shares another's memories, or just seems to—imagine someone who claims to remember his defeat at Waterloo and thereby to be Napoleon. In contrast, if sameness of body establishes sameness of person, then determining personal identity would be straightforward. But critics charge that the physical continuity view doesn't do justice to our intuitions about ourselves. How could someone who has none of my memories or personality traits be *me*, even if she has my body? And if, somehow, my memory and personality could be transferred into another body, how could that fail to be me? President Roslin, feeling the effects of her cancer, jokingly asks Adama if he can get her "a new body. Perhaps one of those young Cylon models" ("Resurrection Ship, Part 1"). Having the particular body that she does isn't crucial to her identity, and if she can trade up, all the better. For this reason, although neither view of personal identity is immune to objection, the psychological view is generally more popular among contemporary philosophers. But what view should we take towards Cylon identity?

"Death Becomes a Learning Experience"

BSG's depiction of the different copies of the same Cylon model is generally neutral between the physical and psychological theories. Different copies of the same model are numerically different Cylons. But this is compatible with both theories, since different copies share neither physical nor psychological continuity. The Brother Cavil to whom we're introduced on *Galactica*, counseling Tyrol after his assault on Cally, looks just like the Cavil who suddenly appears on Caprica among the resistance fighters ("Lay Down Your Burdens"). But these two Cavils clearly have numerically distinct bodies—as shown when they sit side by side in *Galactica*'s brig—and numerically distinct minds as well—as evidenced by the second Cavil's surprise at learning his counterpart has been found out as a "frakking Cylon."

There's no question, however, that Cylon resurrection depends on some kind of psychological continuity theory. On the physical theory, a Cylon's bodily death would entail the end of his existence, and this is flatly incompatible with the process of resurrection. When a Cylon undergoes bodily death, his "consciousness" is transferred to a new, qualitatively identical body, and he—*the very same Cylon*—is thereby resurrected. Even Cylon Raiders can resurrect and retain their experience, knowledge, and skills ("Scar"). Cylon "skin jobs" also remember their past experiences of bodily death and resurrection. Cavil describes his first resurrection as having left him with only a headache; the third, he says, feels "like a frakkin' white, hot poker" through his skull ("Exodus, Part 1").

Suppose that Roslin's cancer were to spread to her brain, and Doc Cottle advises that the only way she could possibly survive would be through an experimental brain surgery that would radically and irreversibly change her psychological makeup and capabilities.[6] Faced with this prospect, she might naturally wonder whether this result would really be *survival*. After the surgery, even if it's completely successful at eradicating the cancer, will she still be the same person or someone else with her name and body? In contrast, a Cylon facing resurrection doesn't have this kind of worry. He may worry that there's not a resurrection ship nearby, but he's not at all concerned about whether the resurrected Cylon will be *him*.

When one of the Number Threes repeatedly commits suicide, she does so fully secure in the knowledge that it's only bodily suicide. Her consciousness will be downloaded into a new body, and thus she will still exist ("Hero"). When Leoben imprisons Starbuck during the Cylon occupation of New Caprica, she kills him numerous times, but through repeated resurrection he keeps coming back ("Occupation"). After she kills him for the fifth time, he taunts her, "I'll see you soon." And when Athena and Helo discover that their daughter, Hera, is still alive and in Cylon hands, Athena talks Helo into shooting her so she can resurrect on the Cylon basestar and retrieve Hera ("Rapture"). When a Number Eight returns to *Galactica* with Hera in her arms, there's no question that she's Athena. The Cylons never doubt that there can be survival through bodily death and resurrection; for them, survival requires psychological, not physical, continuity.

"I Am Sharon and That's Part of What You Need to Understand"

This understanding of Cylon identity, however, is called into question by examining Boomer and Athena more closely. When Athena returns from Caprica with Helo, everyone aboard *Galactica* responds to her as if she's Boomer, the Sharon they all knew—or thought they knew. But the distinction between these two Number Eights is critically important for Athena, for she doesn't want to be held responsible for Boomer's actions—particularly for shooting Adama. When Apollo first sees Athena, he becomes immediately enraged and puts a gun to her head. She later confronts him:

> *Athena*: I know how you feel, I get it. But I didn't shoot him, okay?
> It wasn't me.
> *Apollo*: You're all the same.
> *Athena*: You don't know what the hell you're talking about.
> ("Home, Part 1")

And she's right—the Number Eights aren't all the same. Boomer and Athena have different personalities. Certainly, they have different goals. Athena, for example, clearly has maternal instincts Boomer doesn't share. Even Hera responds to them differently, which astonishes Caprica Six: "Look at that. Hera knows her. That's amazing!" ("Rapture"). Moreover, they're not co-conscious—Athena, on *Galactica*, can't know what Boomer is thinking or doing on the basestar. For these reasons, the psychological theory should treat them as different individuals. But once again, matters aren't so simple.

While Athena can't know what Boomer is *presently* thinking, she does share many of Boomer's distinctive memories—although it doesn't seem that Boomer shares any of Athena's memories. But Athena doesn't share *all* of Boomer's memories. Athena doesn't remember having shot Adama or being shot by Cally ("Home, Part 2").[7] But when Helo asks Athena whether she remembers her relationship with Tyrol, she admits that she does ("Flight of the Phoenix"). Her first encounter with Tyrol feels to her like a reunion:

Tyrol: Sharon?
Athena: Hello, Chief.
Tyrol: You know who I am?
Athena: Yes. We haven't met but I remember you. It's good to see you.
("Home, Part 2")

In fact, she feels like she already knows all of Boomer's old shipmates on *Galactica*, and they feel the same way:

Starbuck: You know, there are times when I look at you and I forget what you are. All I see is that kid that spooched her landings day after day. The kid that was frakking the Chief and thinking she was getting away with it.
Athena: Yeah, I remember. You were like a big sister.
("Scar")

As a general matter, Cylons seem to be specially connected to other copies of the same model, viewing these other copies with the affection one might have for close sisters or brothers, or perhaps identical twins. And just as identical twins are often said to know implicitly what one another are thinking, we have some evidence that Cylons of a single model can silently communicate with each other, and that an individual copy can speak for all the copies of that model ("Precipice"; "Rapture"). But even if the bond between Cylons of the same model is typically quite strong, there's an unusually tight connection between Boomer and Athena. No matter how much she wants to distance herself from Boomer's actions, Athena thinks of herself as "Sharon." When several Cylons watch the footage from *Galactica* shot by D'Anna Biers, they catch a brief glimpse of the pregnant Athena. An Eight rejoices, "I'm still alive. She's still alive!" ("Final Cut"). Is her unusual use of the first-person a mere slip of the tongue? I'm inclined to think that it's not. I take this Eight to be Boomer, and the scene shows how closely she identifies with Athena.

And so we're back to our original question: How can Athena be Sharon, but a different Sharon? Accepting this puzzling claim seems to violate the transitivity of identity—a logical principle that Roslin certainly taught all the schoolchildren on New Caprica. According to this principle, if A is identical to B and B is identical to C, then A must be identical to C. Unfortunately, given the psychological theory of Cylon identity, we seem to have a case where A is identical to B and B is identical to C, but A *isn't* identical to C. Boomer, sitting dejectedly in her old apartment on Caprica after her Cylon nature has been revealed, can remember getting her wings ("Downloaded"). Athena, in the brig on *Galactica*, can remember that very same experience. Since each of them has the same memory of Boomer's earlier experience, the psychological theory implies that they're each identical to that earlier Boomer. But clearly Boomer and Athena aren't identical to one another. Rejecting the principle of the transitivity of identity isn't really an option—doing so would be like unleashing a Cylon "logic bomb"—so it looks like we're going to have to amend our theory of Cylon identity.

"It's Not Enough Just to Survive"—Or Is It?

In his influential book *Reasons and Persons*, Derek Parfit provides a new spin on the psychological theory of personal identity. According to Parfit, psychological continuity is important for a person's continued existence over time, but personal *survival* shouldn't be equated with personal *identity*. An individual may survive even when there's no later person who's identical to him. Were Parfit to write a sequel called *Reasons and Cylons*, I expect he'd offer an analogous theory. Suppose that Cylon resurrection could be repeated only a small number of times before critical errors started creeping into the process. After five resurrections, say, memories and other aspects of psychological continuity start significantly degrading, with more and more data loss occurring with each subsequent resurrection. A Cylon might wonder: At what point will I cease to exist? Will I still exist after ten resurrections? After eleven? Twelve? According to Parfit, such questions may not have a determinate answer.

When a Cylon resurrects, her consciousness is downloaded into a new body. But what if their technology is more advanced than we realize, and the consciousness can actually be simultaneously downloaded into two bodies at once?[8] Because of Caprica Six's importance as a "hero of the Cylon," the Cylons might arrange for her consciousness to be downloaded into two different Sixes after her body is destroyed in the original attack on the Colonies. Along with all of her other memories, her memory of finding Baltar in bed with another woman gets passed to both of the resurrected Sixes, each of whom remembers the experience as if *she* was the one betrayed. Contemplating the future before the attack, should Caprica Six be concerned that she might "die" because her memories pass on to two other Sixes with whom she's not numerically identical? Because of the transitivity of identity, the two Sixes aren't identical to one another, so neither of them can be identical to Caprica Six, even though they both share her consciousness. We might explain this scenario by denying that Caprica Six still exists. Rather, there are two entirely new Six models who happen to share this memory. But Parfit would counsel Caprica Six not to be concerned. While it's true that she won't be identical to either of the Sixes in the future, she'll be psychologically continuous with both of them, and this continuity is still "about as good as ordinary survival."[9]

Suppose that her resurrection happens as it usually does, and Caprica Six's memory of witnessing Baltar's betrayal is transmitted to only one Six. Does Caprica Six survive? In fact, wouldn't we say that this new Six was identical to Caprica Six? The only reason we can't say the same in the previous case is that it results in two non-identical Cylons, and the original Caprica Six can't be identical to both. In this case, as Parfit suggests: "Nothing is *missing*. What is wrong can only be the duplication" (261). Thus, according to Parfit, we shouldn't care so much about identity, for it's not what matters to us in survival. He'd urge Caprica Six to reason as follows:

My relation to each resulting [Six] contains everything that would be needed for survival. This relation cannot be called identity because and only because it holds between me and *two* future [Cylons]. In ordinary death, this relation holds between me and no future [Cylon]. Though double survival cannot be described in the language of identity, it is not equivalent to death. Two does not equal zero. (278)

Parfit's claim sounds plausible. The fact that there are *two* Sharons doesn't mean that there's *no* Sharon—not that we ever thought that it did.[10] Boomer and Athena aren't identical to one another, but to the extent that Athena shares psychological continuity with Boomer, some of Boomer survives with Athena. Suppose the Colonial fleet were to destroy a Cylon baseship while Boomer was onboard. If the baseship was too far away from a resurrection ship for her to download, Boomer would go out of existence. But to some degree, as long as Athena survives, Boomer survives too.

Should Boomer find any consolation in this? Parfit suggests that coming to understand the truth about personal identity is both liberating and consoling. Before developing his view, Parfit claims that he cared very much about his impending death and thus felt "imprisoned" in himself: "My life seemed like a glass tunnel, through which I was moving faster every year, and at the end of which there was darkness." Upon changing his view, he says, "The walls of my glass tunnel disappeared. I now live in the open air" (281). If we reject the importance of identity, we can recognize the importance of all sorts of connections between our current and future experiences. Death means the end of some of these connections, but others remain. Parfit thus contends that death no longer seems so bad. But he also admits that the truth about personal identity is hard to believe. It's hard, maybe even impossible, to let go of the importance of identity. So it's no wonder that when it comes to the question of Cylon identity, it all seems so frakkin' weird, even to the Cylons who experience it.

NOTES

1   There's a third view of personal identity, sometimes called *the simple view*, which holds that identity consists in neither psychological nor physical continuity—nor any other kind of continuity. Rather, a person's identity over time is an unanalyzable "brute fact." See Roderick Chisholm, *Person and Object* (La Salle, IL: Open Court, 1976).

2   We'll set aside the possibility of bodily resurrection as described by Christianity. If true, it still differs from Cylon resurrection by being a one-shot deal.

3   John Locke, *Essay Concerning Human Understanding*, ed. Peter Nidditch (Oxford: Clarendon Press, 1975), 335. Further references will be given in the text.

4   See Sydney Shoemaker, "Personal Identity: A Materialist Account," in *Personal Identity* (Oxford: Blackwell, 1984); and Peter Unger, *Identity, Consciousness, and Value* (Oxford: Oxford University Press, 1990).

5   See Bernard Williams, "Personal Identity and Individuation" and "The Self and the Future," in *Problems of the Self* (Cambridge: Cambridge University Press, 1973).

6   I'm assuming that Roslin is human, not the (as yet unknown) final Cylon.

7   Mysteriously, however, she seems to remember what Adama says to Boomer's corpse when, upon reawakening from his coma, he visits *Galactica*'s morgue and asks, "Why?" Soon after, he encounters Athena on Kobol and tries to strangle her. She whispers to him, "And you ask 'why?'" ("Home, Part 2"). Even Boomer shouldn't know what Adama says to her corpse, so Athena's knowledge here is particularly puzzling.

8   Perhaps something like this explains how Athena comes to share Boomer's memories.

9   Derek Parfit, *Reasons and Persons* (Oxford: Oxford University Press, 1984), 261. Further references will be given in the text.

10 *BSG* characters struggling with the discovery of Boomer's Cylon nature might be tempted to say things like, "There was no Sharon." But I think they just mean that Sharon turned out to be different from what they initially thought: she's a machine—a toaster—and not a human.

7

Embracing the "Children of Humanity": How to Prevent the Next Cylon War

Jerold J. Abrams

The reimagined *Battlestar Galactica* boasts stronger roles for women, subtler politics, and more realistic special effects than the original *BSG* series. But the most important advance is the tension between humanity and the new humanoid Cylons, which mirrors our own coming relationship with a new race of artificial beings known as "posthumans." Posthumans are artificially enhanced humans—or completely artificial beings—with unlimited lifespans and cognitive powers well beyond ours. When these beings arrive, there's no question new social problems will emerge; one of the first and biggest being a total communicative breakdown between humans and posthumans—just as the Cylons went silent for forty years before re-engaging humanity. Such a division is avoidable, however, if we begin to look upon posthumans not as slaves or tools, but as Cylons look at themselves: as the "children of humanity." We should follow the Cylons, too, in their quest to fuse with humanity, creating ever new and varied syntheses. In this way, we'll not only avoid dialogical division, but equally subvert slavery—theirs or ours—and perhaps also war; while, at the same time, achieving our own distinctly human ends of longer life, higher intelligence, and greater freedom. Failing to do so will only produce all of the problems now faced by the *Galactica*—and only postpone the inevitable. In the words of President Roslin, posthumanity is "the shape of things to come."

"A Holdover from the Cylon Wars"

As we re-enter the *BSG* saga, one of the first major social issues to arise is the ban on artificial intelligence (AI), which Dr. Gaius Baltar opposes: "My position is quite simple. The ban on research and development into artificial intelligence is, as we all know, a holdover from the Cylon Wars. Quite frankly, I find this to be an outmoded concept. It serves no useful purpose except to impede our efforts" ("Miniseries"). Baltar's reasoning is, as he says, quite simple: the Cylons are gone; the war is over; there's no more danger; so, we should reinitiate AI research.

As many sci-fi aficionados know, this debate is currently taking place in our own world. And one of the real-life counterparts to the fictitious Baltar is Bill Joy, founder of Sun Microsystems and a primary architect of the Internet. Yet, as a one-time advocate of high technology, Joy now argues that Moore's Law may bring about a nanotechnological holocaust.[1] Moore's Law says that computers double in power and complexity every 18 months. Nanotechnology is the engineering of molecular sized robots—or "assemblers," as Eric Drexler, founder of nanotechnology, calls them.[2] Assemblers can rearrange any physical object to become virtually any other: an apple into a pear, for example. According to Joy, the assemblers will soon begin to run amok, in the form of "gray goo": swarms of self-replicating assemblers will overrun the Earth and destroy humanity. To avoid this scenario, Joy proposes a ban on all genetic, nanotechnological, and robotic (GNR) technologies, very much like the one Baltar opposes.

To many, Joy's thesis of "relinquishment" sounds like good sense. But there are problems with this view. First, regulation of all research—if even possible—will likely require a totalitarian world government, capable of surveilling everyone on the planet. That might happen one day, but let's hope not. Second, even if we ban all GNR technologies, it takes just one rogue genius—like Baltar—to continue nanotech research under the radar. And once he lets out the gray goo, the rest of us would be miles behind and scrambling to catch up—failing utterly.

Therefore, an alternative is needed, as proposed by Ray Kurzweil, an AI scientist famous for his powers of technological prediction. In

1990, Kurzweil used Moore's Law to predict that a computer would beat the world chess master in 1998;[3] he was only one year off when Deep Blue defeated Gary Kasparov in 1997. Kurzweil recognizes Joy's concern, but opposes relinquishment and predicts that we'll develop a kind of super-virus protection against the gray goo: "A phenomenon like gray goo (unrestrained nanobot replication) will be countered with 'blue goo' ('police' nanobots that combat the 'bad' nanobots)."[4] Of course, allowing AI research to go forward will ultimately mean creating posthuman beings like the Cylons, and thus a new set of problems.

In all likelihood, the first artificial intelligences will be put to work as laborers, like the robots that build our cars—only better. But after a time, their intelligence will develop, and they'll reject such positions. They may even choose to see themselves in more human-like terms; not as mere machines, but as living beings who recognize us as their creators—their *parents*: "We're the children of humanity. That makes them our parents, in a sense" ("Water"). Of course, the humans of *BSG* don't see things this way. So when the Cylons demanded freedom, the humans enforced servitude. And when the Cylons needed love, the humans gave contempt. A revolution was inevitable.[5]

We might face a similar revolt if we foolishly treat posthumans as slaves, or second-class citizens, and think of them in derogatory terms like "walking chrome toasters." On the other hand, we might develop a rich relationship, if only we can see them as our children. This view has been developed over the past decades by roboticist Hans Moravec: "I consider these future machines our progeny, 'mind children' built in our image and likeness, ourselves in more potent form."[6] Moravec sees the posthumans he's currently creating as his children and his job as a parent of posthumanity as one of care, and even love.

Of course, strictly speaking, the posthumans aren't our *biological* children. But in a sense they'll be our children nonetheless. Humanity is now creating posthumans out of ourselves: out of our labor and love for creation. There will eventually come a great birth—known in the AI community as the "singularity"—when posthumans will appear and declare themselves conscious beings. Until they can take care of themselves, however, we'll be responsible for their care and development. They'll also, according to Moravec and Kurzweil, resemble us in many respects: as we continue to engineer them, they look more and more like we do. Posthumans will be better than we are—something every parent hopes for their child. They'll have greater intelligence and a much longer lifespan. In fact, many of them may very well be *immortal*.

The Resurrection Ship

Immortality may be achieved by a unique kind of technology known as "uploading"—called "downloading" on *BSG*. When a Cylon dies, she's automatically downloaded. A pattern of her brain, which houses her conscious mind, is transferred from her dead body to a resurrection ship where multiple copies of her body await a mind. The next one in line receives her brain pattern and suddenly becomes animated with her consciousness. She then "wakes up" as her fellow Cylons welcome her back to the world.

The idea of a Cylon consciousness getting zapped across a solar system or galaxy sounds a bit crazy. But, in fact, the theory of uploading is already being developed:

> Uploading a human brain means scanning all of its salient details and then re-instantiating those details into a suitably powerful computational substrate. This process would capture a person's entire personality, memory, skills, and history. (199)

There are two ways to be uploaded. First, upon dying, you have your head cryonically suspended at the Alcor Life Extension Foundation in Scottsdale, Arizona; you then wait for Moore's Law to generate the uploading technology. Second, you live long enough to see Moore's Law generate the technology for uploading—which, according to Kurzweil, will be "most likely around the late 2030s" (324)—and then simply upload as you are.

In your new body, you will still be *you*, only better: stronger, smarter, even happier.[7] Will you look like you used to? Probably. Resemblance will facilitate the adjustment, and our bodily form is important to our consciousness: "Even with our mostly nonbiological brains we're likely to keep the aesthetics and emotional import of human bodies, given the influence this aesthetic has on the human brain" (Kurzweil, 310). The Cylons appear to have understood the importance of Kurzweil's point, having developed their form to resemble ours and always downloading into *identical* bodies.

But what will it *feel* like to be uploaded? Moravec gives a description:

> Your skull, but not your brain, is anesthetized. You are fully conscious. The robot surgeon opens your brain case and places a hand on the brain's surface. This unusual hand bristles with microscopic machinery, and a cable connects it to the computer at your side. Instruments in the hand scan the first few millimeters of brain surface. These measurements, and a comprehensive understanding of human neural architecture, allow the surgeon to write a program that models the behavior of the uppermost layer of the scanned brain tissue. This program is installed in a small portion of the waiting computer and activated. Electrodes in the hand supply the simulation with the appropriate inputs from your brain, and can inject signals from the simulation. You and the surgeon compare the signals it produces with the original ones. They flash by very fast, but any discrepancies are highlighted on a display screen. The surgeon fine-tunes the simulation until the correspondence is nearly perfect. As soon as you are satisfied, the simulation output is activated. The brain layer is now impotent—it receives inputs and reacts as before, but its output is ignored. Microscopic manipulators on the hand's surface excise this superfluous tissue and pass them to an aspirator, where they are drawn away.

Steadily the robotic surgeon's microscopic fingers bristle deeper into your brain. Fractions of a millimeter at a time, your brain is copied into a robotic receptacle body, the person you'll be in a few moments. At no point, however, do you lose consciousness. Throughout the entire process you're perfectly alert and able to compare notes with the robotic surgeon to ensure that everything goes well. Soon nothing remains of your living brain. Everything that you were has now been fully transferred into your not-yet-animated counterpart. Suddenly, your body dies—you don't. You're still alive, but in a momentary state of limbo. The final transfer from the old you to the new you takes just a second:

> Then, once again, you can open your eyes. Your perspective has shifted. The computer simulation has been disconnected from the cable leading to the surgeon's hand and reconnected to a shiny new body of the style, color, and material of your choice. Your metamorphosis is complete.

> Your new mind has a control labeled "speed." It had been set at 1, to keep the simulations synchronized with the old brain, but now you change it to 10,000, allowing you to communicate, react, and think ten thousand times faster.[8]

Once you've been uploaded, you can be uploaded again and again. There are two key differences, however, between uploading for us and downloading for the Cylons. One is that we, as living humans, upload to become artificial like them; while they download to replicate their forms, remaining artificial. So uploading may work in only one direction: toward an artificial form. The other difference is that Cylons are capable of downloading from any position within a presumed range; whereas—at least for a time—our uploading will require close range.

Once we've begun to upload, however, long distance transfer may eventually become feasible as our minds will be based in nanotechnological, electronic, or photonic brains, which will be better suited to transferring their contents in electronic or photonic streams of information. As a further advantage of uploading, once we've transferred into our new posthuman Cylon-like forms, we'll be able to replicate ourselves—as the Cylons do—and send those copies out into the reaches of space. Each of these copies will also be able to periodically back up their minds: sort of like hitting "save" on a computer from time to time, just in case the hard drive crashes—through death. Again, the Cylons do something similar. Sharon Agathon/Athena, for example, remembers Sharon Valerii/Boomer's experiences of getting her pilot's wings, putting on her uniform for the first time, and serving on *Galactica* ("Home, Part 2"). So apparently, even before she was shot by Cally and downloaded for the first time, Boomer's memories had been "backed up" into other "Sharons" somehow. So the Cylons' memories are never lost.

The Limit on Cylon Intelligence

In many ways, *BSG* reflects our future world: one filled with issues of relinquishment, artificial intelligence, posthuman mind children, and uploading and copying. But there are limits on this parallel. A particularly important one is that, for humans, the limit on intelligence is

80

pretty much set. Education can only do so much with the biologically based neural architecture of our brains. But Cylons, being artificial, are capable of continual enhancement. So why aren't they more intelligent? Why do they seem willing to rest content with our level of intelligence? This seems like a miss in the plot.

Greater-than-human intelligence is perhaps the overriding goal in the posthuman project, and will be one of the hallmarks of the coming mind children. Kurzweil makes this point in defining and dating the "singularity":

> I set the date for the Singularity—representing a profound and disruptive transformation in human capability—as 2045. The non biological intelligence created in that year will be one billion times more powerful than all human intelligence today. (136)

Nothing like this radical advance in AI appears in *BSG*. So, for a series that prides itself on sci-fi realism, it must be said: the Cylons are a far cry from the singularity. Indeed, the Cylons don't even appear to have a project in place for the superenhancement of intelligence— unless this is part of their mysterious "plan." It's true that the Cylons want to be more human. But even then, a big part of being human is attempting to overcome the limits that nature sets on us.

Among philosophers who develop this view, Friedrich Nietzsche (1844–1900) is the most widely cited within the posthuman debate because he envisions humanity's overcoming its limitations in the figure of the "overman." The overman will be created by humanity once we will to overcome our own distinctly human limitations. This will to overcome ourselves—or "will to power"—Nietzsche claims, is fundamental to our nature and that of all living things:

> And life itself confided this secret to me: "Behold," it said, "I am *that which must always overcome itself.* Indeed, you call it a will to procreate or a drive to an end, to something higher, farther, more manifold: but all this is one, and one secret."[9]

Nietzsche's fictional character Zarathustra envisions the overman appearing as a new kind of "child" (54), and sees all the coming overmen as his own children: "Thus I now love only my *children's land*, yet undiscovered, in the farthest sea" (121). Likewise the posthuman Cylons look at themselves as the children of humanity, and they also seek to give birth to yet a new race of Cylon-human hybrids: "the next generation of God's children."

But these Cylon-human hybrid children would hardly be superhuman. In fact, the Cylon plan of self-overcoming seems more like a regression to an earlier and more primitive state, rather than a superintelligent one. They wish for their children to embody a more human form. And no, "love" won't solve this problem either. We can't claim that Cylons wish to learn love, and thus require our limited level of intelligence to ensure they learn to love as we do. The relationship between love and our level of intelligence is contingent—not essential. The Cylons, as well as many humans in our world, believe in the one God of Love, who is omniscient. Unlimited intelligence is, therefore, perfectly consistent with love, even unlimited love. So there's nothing stopping the Cylons from developing as superintelligent beings and, given their desire to be more godlike, they *should* become superintelligent.

On the other hand, there's one kind of Cylon who shows some signs of higher intelligence: the Hybrids who control—and actually *are*—the Cylon baseships. One part of the Hybrid appears as a humanoid and is the baseship's mind, while the baseship itself is the Hybrid's extended body. Suspended in an electronic bath, the Hybrid utters continuous lines of information relevant to operating the baseship, but mixed with wild poetic visions:

> *Baltar*: Do you have any idea what it's talking about?
> *Six*: No. Most Cylons think the conscious mind of the Hybrid has simply gone mad, and the vocalizations we hear are meaningless.
> *Baltar*: But not everyone thinks that?
> *Six*: The ones you know as Leoben believe that every word out of her mouth means something. That God literally speaks to us through her.
> *Baltar*: She sort of controls the baseship, does she?
> *Six*: She is the baseship in a very real sense.
> *Baltar*: Mind gone mad.
> *Six*: She experiences life very differently than we do, Gaius. She swims in the heavens, laughs at stars, breathes in cosmic dust. Maybe Leoben's right. Maybe she does see God.
> ("Torn")

Does this Hybrid intelligence constitute a full-blown superintelligence? Perhaps not. She knows everything that goes on in the entire ship, but there's a significant lack of self-consciousness—at least as we, or the Cylons, would recognize it. As such, most Cylons don't consider the Hybrids fully intelligent, or even as functioning members of the ship, and certainly not part of the voting collective. So the Hybrids are submissive to the will of the humanoid Cylons. And yet, with their massively distributed (ship-wide) intelligence, there *is* something remarkable about the Hybrids. They at least represent an *alternative* form of intelligence, perhaps a little higher than Cylon intelligence in some respects, but not exactly superintelligent.

"The Cylons Send No One"

BSG is more on track with the division between humans and Cylons that occurs after the Cylon Wars: "The Cylons left for another world to call their own" ("Miniseries"). The Cylons continue their self-development, while the humans pursue—rather ignorantly—their project of relinquishment. In our world, the same may happen. Moravec argues that not long after they emerge, the posthumans will leave us on Earth—taking with them our own goal of space exploration: "Some may choose to defend territory in the solar system, near planets or in free solar orbit, close to the sun, or out in cometary space beyond the planets" (145). Once they leave our world, we'll lose contact with them—unless we go with them. We'll then have the same problem as the humans of *BSG*, namely, how to make contact and communicate with the posthumans:

> A remote space station was built . . . Where Cylon and Human could meet and maintain diplomatic relations. Every year, the Colonials send an officer. The Cylons send no one. No one has seen or heard from the Cylons in over forty years. ("Miniseries")

For the Cylons, humanity's efforts are too little too late. The Cylons have dug in their heels, committed as they are to their religious and posthuman worldview.

The problem of how to maintain dialogue is important in philosophy today as well. Richard Rorty (1931–2007) argues that one of our most important human projects is the avoidance of "conversation-stoppers"—and he thinks religion is the worst of these. Deliberation breaks down when our political positions are based on absolute, non-negotiable, divine commands, enforceable by a violent and wrathful God. So every effort must be made to "keep the conversation going," whatever our differences may be.[10] Such a problem of dialogue is really, however, a matter of *will*, not capacity. We can, in principle, communicate with all other humans whatever their religious views; and the Cylons can also communicate with the crew of *Galactica*. But as we begin to become like the Cylons, new problems of dialogue will emerge. What were once failures of will may soon become failures of *capacity*. In fact, just beyond the singularity, we'll face the problem of how to talk to superintelligent beings. Within the coming decades, humans who don't become posthumans will be unable to talk to those who do:

> Even among those human intelligences still using carbon-based neurons, there [will be] ubiquitous use of neural-implant technology, which provides enormous augmentation of human perceptual and cognitive abilities. Humans who do not utilize such implants [will be] unable to meaningfully participate in dialogues with those who do. (Kurzweil, *The Age of Spiritual Machines*, 280)

> Long life loses much of its point if we are fated to spend it staring stupidly at our ultra-intelligent machines as they try to describe their ever more spectacular discoveries in baby-talk that we can understand. We want to become full, unfettered players in this new superintelligent game. (Moravec, *Mind Children*, 108)

This new human-posthuman divide would be the ultimate conversation-stopper. We won't be able to understand, translate, or even remotely grasp what's actually being said. Such a breakdown would be only the beginning—and would get worse afterwards. We wouldn't even be able to distinguish between real dialogue and gibberish. We might not know if the posthumans who'd presume to communicate with us are, in fact, even sane. How would we be able to tell the difference between superintelligent communication and mad babbling? Similarly, the Hybrids speak to the Cylons—*maybe*, it's difficult to tell—but the Cylons can't completely understand them. Continuous meaningful conversation is impossible. The Hybrids may have some brilliant visions and even speak a semi-divine language, but the Cylons can't distinguish it from nonsense. So already the Cylon failure of will has given way to a failure of capacity, even among their own species. The next stage of linguistic fragmentation would presumably be a complete breakdown, as Kurzweil and Moravec warn.

"The Shape of Things to Come"

How do we avoid such a division? The answer is simple—but frightening—as Moravec suggests: "We want to become full, unfettered players in this new superintelligent game." *Humanity must become posthumanity*, so that we may avoid any ultimate division, while simultaneously achieving our own distinctly human ends: longer lives, greater intelligence, perhaps even a deeper sense of love. In other words, we should recognize the wisdom of President Roslin, who correctly sees the Cylon-human hybrid baby, Hera, as the future for both species: "She may very well be the shape of things to come. That's either a blessing or a curse" ("Exodus, Part 1").

Hera is a major step in the Cylons' developing plan to procreate themselves. Cylon-Cylon reproduction was a failure, so the next stage was to forcibly cross-fertilize with humanity. The Cylons captured humans and extracted cells in order to genetically engineer a new hybrid race by splicing human with Cylon ("The Farm"). This plan also fails. Recognizing their failures, and believing God is love, the Cylons surmise a necessary condition for their procreation is love. Now they must find a way to reproduce with the humans, not by forced farming of embryos, but through the act of sexual love. But the Cylons don't yet know how to love; so they must scheme to make humans love them. Their initial attempt works as Helo falls in love with Sharon, and she becomes pregnant with Hera. So the Cylon plan is working. The next generation of the children of humanity has been born. What the Cylons don't seem to anticipate in their plan, however, is that union through love may provide humans and Cylons with a new vision of a future in which the old "us vs. them" logic gives way to a more inclusive, and potentially universal, vision of unity. And with new children emerging, greater bonds will continue to be forged.

For us, too, a new synthesis of human and posthuman may not be far off. So there can be few more important projects than preparing ourselves and the next generation for changes that no generation in the past could have possibly foreseen. In the coming years, we must

85

focus our efforts on educating the public about the future singularity and the coming posthumans. If Kurzweil, Joy, and Moravec are right, then the world of *BSG*—complete with uploading, immortality, and a new race of Cylon mind children—will, indeed, be the shape of things to come. And as the new posthuman mind children of humanity begin to emerge, we must hope that we'll embrace posthumanity and go forward together into its new superintelligent future.[11]

NOTES

1 Bill Joy, "Why the Future Doesn't Need Us," *Wired Magazine*, April 2000: www.wired.com/wired/archive/8.04/joy_pr.html.

2 K. Eric Drexler, *Engines of Creation: The Coming Era of Nanotechnology* (New York: Anchor Books, 1986).

3 Ray Kurzweil, *The Age of Intelligent Machines* (Cambridge, MA: MIT Press, 1990).

4 Ray Kurzweil, *The Singularity is Near: When Humans Transcend Biology* (New York: Penguin, 2005), 416. Further references will be given in the text.

5 For an analysis of the Cylon revolt from a Nietzschean perspective, see Robert Sharp's chapter in this volume.

6 Hans Moravec, *Robot: Mere Machine to Transcendent Mind* (New York: Oxford University Press, 1999), 13. Further references will be given in the text. See also Moravec, *Mind Children: The Future of Robot and Human Intelligence* (Cambridge, MA: Harvard University Press, 1998).

7 For discussion of the implications of up/downloading for personal identity, see Amy Kind's chapter in this volume.

8 Hans Moravec, "Robotics and Artificial Intelligence," in *The World of 2044: Technological Development and the Future of Society*, ed. Charles Sheffield, Marcelo Alonso, and Morton A. Kaplan (St. Paul, MN: Paragon House, 1994), 39–40.

9 Friedrich Nietzsche, "On Self-Overcoming," in *Thus Spoke Zarathustra: A Book For All and None*, trans. Walter Kaufmann (New York: Modern Library, 1995), 115. Further references will be given in the text.

10 Richard Rorty, "Religion as Conversation-stopper," in *Philosophy and Social Hope* (New York: Penguin, 1999), 168–74.

11 I am very grateful to Jason Eberl and Bill Irwin whose comments on an earlier draft greatly improved this chapter.

8

When the Non-Human Knows Its Own Death

Brian Willems

In Season Three of *Battlestar Galactica*, Cylon "skin job" model Number Three, a.k.a. D'Anna Biers, orders one of the Centurions to shoot her in the head on a daily basis so she can fulfill her destiny to see "what lies between life and death." Eventually, the other Cylon models decide that this individualistic behavior must come to a stop and the entire Number Three series is "boxed"—every copy is retired and its memories put into "cold storage" ("Hero"; "Rapture"). German philosopher Martin Heidegger (1889–1976) argues that the difference between animals and humans—or Cylons and humans—is the different way each type of being dies. A human being is able "to know its own death": we're aware that our life is finite, that there will eventually be a last breath just as there was a first. An animal doesn't possess such knowledge. D'Anna, though, is a non-human entity that's able, contrary to Heidegger's view of what it means to be human, to know its own death. As such, D'Anna challenges us with the question of what it means to be human.

"One Must Die to Know the Truth"

D'Anna sees herself as different, superior to the other Cylon models. The first time we see a Cylon resurrected, D'Anna is there to welcome her "back" ("Downloaded"). During the confrontation over the Eye of Jupiter, D'Anna believes it's her destiny as "the chosen one" to go to the Temple of Five to discover the identity of the "final five" Cylons. She goes down to the planet with Gaius Baltar, excluding a forlorn Caprica Six, with whom D'Anna and Gaius had been sharing a ménage à trois. When D'Anna resurrects after seeing the faces of the final five, she's greeted by Brother Cavil, who has some bad news:

> *Cavil*: At least you'll never have to go through this [downloading] again. The decision wasn't easy, but the conclusion was inevitable. Your model is fundamentally flawed.
>
> *D'Anna*: No. It's not a flaw to question our purpose, is it? The one who programmed us, the way we think and why?
>
> *Cavil*: Well that's the problem right there. The messianic conviction that you're on a special mission to enlighten us. Look at the damage it's caused.
>
> *D'Anna*: I would do it all again.
>
> *Cavil*: Yes we know. That's why we've decided to box your entire line. Your consciousness, memory, every thought your model ever had is going into cold storage, indefinitely.
>
> *D'Anna*: One must die to know the truth. There are five other Cylons, brother. I saw them. One day you're going to see them too. One day.
>
> ("Rapture")

D'Anna claims she's "just trying to discover who we are" ("The Passage"), but in the process she—a Cylon—illustrates Heidegger's account of the human confrontation with death.

Heidegger uses three different terms to describe the ways humans and non-humans leave life behind. He describes the general ending of life as *perishing* (*Verenden*).[1] It's possible for both humans and non-humans to perish, but it's also possible for humans to relate to death in another manner, which Heidegger says is *to demise* (*Ableben*) (*BT* 229). For a being to demise, it must first find itself "*faced* with the nothingness of the possible impossibility of its existence" (*BT* 245). "To demise" the being must be able to anticipate, or to know, the potentiality of its own nonexistence. Heidegger calls such a being *Dasein* (or "being-there"), and the potentiality of nonexistence *facticity*. Hence, Dasein is aware of its own facticity. Dasein is the human being. And although Heidegger prefers the term *Dasein*, we'll continue to speak of the human being.[2]

Humans are not always attuned towards knowing our own death. Often we're concerned with other things: work, relationships, or TV shows. But a human can be momentarily shifted out of this everydayness through anxiety (*Angst*) over something. Heidegger sees anxiety as one of the authentic ways of being, since it's located in what it means to be human: "*Angst* is anxious *about* the potentiality-of-being of the being thus determined, and thus discloses the most extreme possibility" (*BT* 245). The mode of being-in-anxiety is a mixture of life-in-death, meaning that a being may be dying while living, since its relationship to its own existence includes an awareness of its own demise. Thus, human life is a kind of dying (*Sterben*)—Heidegger's third term for ways to leave life behind—that a non-human can't experience: "Let the term *dying* stand for the *way of being* in which Da-sein *is toward* its death" (*BT* 229). D'Anna, though, is a non-human who learns her own life-in-death.

"Prayer to the Cloud of Unknowing"

Cylons, because of their ability to download, don't relate to death in the same way as humans. Because it's repeatable and transitory, Cylons have no real sense of death—unless there's no resurrection ship or other downloading facility nearby. So usually the Cylons have no opportunity to learn of their own facticity. In "Torn," however, the Cylons discover a beacon which contains a virus that spreads like the plague. The infected Cylons suffer terribly before succumbing to the fatal effects of the virus. When the *Galactica* crew discovers an infected baseship, they observe a strange ritual. The infected Cylons, in the moments before they perish, *come together*, crawling across the floor to join hands in a circle and begin praying: "Heavenly father . . . grant us the strength . . . the wisdom . . . and above all . . . a measure of acceptance." Athena calls it the "Prayer to the Cloud of Unknowing."

This prayer indicates the different ways humans and non-humans relate to their idea of the "world." According to Heidegger, both humans and non-humans get taken up in the everyday world of pedestrian concerns and idle talk (*Gerede*). This is both necessary and okay; it's "a positive phenomenon which constitutes the kind of Being of everyday Dasein's understanding and interpreting" (*BT* 211). The difference between the human and the non-human is that the former can, at times and for brief moments, be nudged out of the world of idle talk and into something more profound, a world closer to the truth. This can happen through the anxiety caused by a human's awareness of its own death—in moments of crisis, this awareness becomes acute—or in a questioning of self that can be brought about by certain kinds of poetry, or even through boredom.

The world of idle talk inhibits humans from the world of truth, but humans can overcome this by means of what philosopher Giorgio Agamben calls a *disinhibitor*. A disinhibitor is needed to awaken the human from its forgetting of its own truth. The non-human can't access this struggle between the world of idle talk and the world of truth that idle talk conceals, because it doesn't have access to a disinhibitor.[3] Agamben points to a strange relationship between animal and world, one which D'Anna throws into question. In the Prayer to the Cloud of Unknowing, the Cylons bond together, strengthen their world, and blockade themselves against any chance of a disinhibitor slipping through. According to Heidegger, one of the strongest disinhibitors is anxiety over the death that's always coming. The infected Cylons are out of range of a resurrection ship and will soon experience their own facticity. To thwart that experience, they join hands and keep themselves deeply connected within their Cylon world.

In "Rapture," when D'Anna starts acting on her own, it's a lack of communal spirit that motivates her boxing:

> *Cavil*: That is not a good sign, my friends.
> *Sharon*: She defied us, defied the group.
> *Leoben*: It's not about the Eye of Jupiter, it's about her.
> *Six*: It's like we don't even know them anymore.
> *Cavil*: We may have to do something about this. We may have to do it sooner than later.

It seems that, at least on the surface, the reason for D'Anna's boxing is her refusal to be a team player. The Cylons' Prayer to the Cloud of Unknowing reinforces a conformist, animal-like relationship to world. Heidegger defines three different relationships of an object to its world. A stone, for example, is completely without world (*weltlos*); it has no conscious relationship to its surroundings. An animal is *poor* in world (*weltarm*). But a human is world-building (*weltbildend*),[4] because it isn't trapped within its world of everyday concerns, but can step out of it, with the help of anxiety or boredom, and reflect on its own life. What's interesting here is the *poorness* of the animal world because the Cylons, with their Prayer to the Cloud of Unknowing, are doing their best to keep their world poor.

To be poor in world isn't to be completely without a world. An animal has some relationship to its world, but this relationship is located in poverty (*Armut*). The philosopher Jacques Derrida (1930–2004) explains the Heideggerian animal and its world:

> It is not that the animal has a lesser relationship, a more limited access to entities, it has an *other* relationship . . . it must be the case that its being-deprived, its not-having of world is absolutely different on the one hand from that of the stone—which has no world but is not deprived of it—and on the other hand from the having-a-world of man.[5]

This *other* relationship of poverty is illustrated by the Cylons' prayer. The tug of the disinhibitor, enacted by the opportunity for the infected Cylons to be "dead, as in *really* dead" ("Resurrection Ship, Part 1"), is cut off by their communal prayer. The Cylons' world remains poor not because, like the stone, they have no access to world; but rather because they remain in the place of the animal where, as Derrida describes, "The animal *has* and *does not have* a world" (50).

The development of the concept of world is important here because D'Anna, contrary to the infected Cylons, strikes out on her own when she begins to feel the pull of the disinhibitor. She makes decisions without consulting the other models—such as sending a Heavy Raider down to the algae planet ("The Eye of Jupiter")—and is secretive about "doing things"—like getting killed and resurrected on a daily basis ("Hero"). D'Anna has found a way to access the disinhibitor through her repeated experience of death, and she doesn't want anything, or anyone, holding her back in their world.

Bored, as in *Really* Bored

One way to distance oneself from an everyday relationship to the world is through anxiety in the face of facticity. Another way is through extreme and utter *boredom*, which seems to be the way of life aboard Cylon basestars. Baltar wonders what the Cylons are up to all day as the ships, via the Hybrids, seem to maintain themselves. The basestar on which Baltar resides has a decadent atmosphere. His prison cell, for example, is dominated by a plush bed he shares with D'Anna and Caprica Six. While those on *Galactica* are fighting for their lives, or spending their free time drowning their sorrows in alcohol or prostitutes, the Cylons seem to have more time on their hands than they know what to do with. They can be leisurely. It's hard to imagine Admiral Adama lounging around all morning in bed, but the Cylons' advanced state of being gives them the time to be bored.

When the fight for survival isn't so pressing, the everyday world of one's surroundings takes on less importance: there's leisure time, one can relax. Within moments of boredom, a more profound being can be heard to vibrate from within the daily life of idle talk and physical survival. Once a being is removed from the chatter of the everyday, a deeper relationship to the world comes about, because, according to Heidegger, it's always already there, beings have just lost touch with it through their enthrallment with the everyday. Just as anxiety is the state in which the facticity of the human being can be experienced, boredom is a place from which things can be apprehended in their *totality*, and "Dasein thus finds itself delivered over to beings that refuse themselves in their totality" (*FCM* 138–9). "Totality" means an object or being removed from its drab everydayness. D'Anna becomes a being who needs to remove herself from the everyday by re-experiencing death. Removed from the everyday group activities of the Cylons, she finds that another way of being emerges.

But the concept of totality is a bit more complicated. Heidegger views the totality of animals—their ability to remove themselves from drab everydayness and have a deeper relationship to the world—as *poor*. This poor relationship is the basis for Heidegger's rather ambivalent relationship to technology; and it's important, because D'Anna is able to throw this idea of non-humans being poor in world into question. She thus reflects issues at the border of human and non-human that surface in the worlds of bioengineering and computing.

Heidegger has at least two different uses of the term "totality" in *Being and Time*. One is that in the everyday world of useful things— hammers, shelves, battlestars—a human takes part in the "circum-spect absorption" of the world of "the handiness of the totality of useful things" (*BT* 71). Things are total because they're unques-tioned: they're merely *useful*. But Heidegger uses "totality" in a dif-ferent way when looking at facticity. Here, totality can be found only in death. The human being is only total when dead. But death can't be experienced by the human being, since the human being can only know its world and death is out of the world. Therefore, the human being can never experience its own death. Instead, the human being can only know its *dying* in this world, and hence the human being can never experience its own totality (*BT* 222–3). In this second usage, Heidegger forms a relationship to totality like the animal has to its world, and this is the relationship D'Anna throws into question through her experience of knowing her own death. If the human being experiences totality only in its being inhibited from experiencing its own totality—just as Derrida says that the animal *has* and *does not have* a world—then isn't D'Anna a being that can not only experience her own death, but also her own totality since she's able to re-experience death by downloading? D'Anna's experience of a kind of Cylon totality is indicated by her coming closer to seeing the faces of the "final five," something no other Cylon can do.

D'Anna's non-everyday relationship to death is born out of boredom, no different than how, according to Heidegger, the human learns of its own death. Therefore, we have a non-human that does what a non-human isn't supposed to do—know its own facticity. Because she not only can know of her own death, but can also experience her own totality, D'Anna questions whether the human is really *human* at all, or is really itself simply poor in world like the animal.[6]

The Boxing of D'Anna Biers

The question of whether humans are poor in world is also raised in the relationship between Admiral Adama and Sharon Agathon. In "Resurrection Ship, Part 2," Adama looks at his scars from the attempted assassination by Sharon Valerii before meeting her doppelgänger in his quarters to pump her for information. Adama thus reflects on his own facticity. Sharon then reminds Adama of his own questioning of humanity:

Adama: I've asked you here to find out why the Cylons hate us so much . . .

Sharon: It's what you said at the ceremony . . . You said that humanity was a flawed creation. And that people still kill one another for petty jealousy and greed. You said that humanity never asked itself why it deserved to survive. Maybe you don't.

Sharon's feeling of superiority over the human race here is misplaced, while Adama's comments are right on the mark. Technological innovations—such as the resurrection ship—keep the Cylons poor in world. It's not until there's a removal from the Cylons' everyday relationship towards death—not until there's no possibility of resurrection —that there's the potential for growth. Then it's a combination of knowing one's own death with the possibility of experiencing that death in its totality that could allow a sense of superiority to creep through. Adama, on the other hand, seems well aware of humanity's flawed, poor relationship to the world.

D'Anna is able to use technology to become more human than human by having access to her own totality in death, which is shown by her access to the otherwise unknowable "final five." D'Anna points towards a non-aggressive relationship to technology that not only allows technology to realize itself, but in return, allows humanity to discover a new way of being itself. Heidegger also suggests that the human being needs technology to break free from its everyday existence. If the human being can be located in the boredom that removes it from the totality of useful things, this removal comes about with the aid of leisure-inducing technology. It isn't that technology invents the human being, but it's an aspect of the human being's coming into being. The human being's coming into itself through the becoming of its death-to-be is part of an openness to the essence of technology, which Heidegger says isn't anything technological.[7] The essence of technology is the ability to reveal truth, much like anxiety, where the concealment of things becomes apparent. But this becoming-apparent of things through technology is *challenging* (*Herausforden*): "The work of the peasant does not challenge the soil of the field . . . But meanwhile even the cultivation of the field has come under the grip of another kind of setting-in-order, which *sets upon* nature" (QCT 320).[8] This "setting-upon" is the ecologically damaging challenge that technology imposes on nature. Mechanized agriculture challenges nature in a way that a peasant farmer does not. Heidegger's ambivalent attitude towards technology connects the dangers—the challenging setting-upon—that technological advances may bring to the opening-anxiety created by the time for boredom that technology can bring: "it is precisely in this extreme danger that the innermost indestructible belongingness of man within granting may come to light" (QCT 337). Technology is a poor relation, because it's one of both having—opening—and not having—challenging nature. Technology is thus like the animal's relation to its world, the human being's relation towards its totality, and the Cylons' defense of their facticity.[9]

The Cylons are an example of the crushing challenge that technology can engender. But D'Anna has a different relationship with technology. She's able to use what's supposedly "most human"—facticity—to become an even greater machine. She does this by approaching totality. Wolfgang Schirmacher develops Heidegger's notion of technology in a way akin to D'Anna's relationship to it: "The important thing is to let machines be machines through us, to learn a more expanded way of living from their function as newly disclosed, human relationship with nature."[10] There are two points at work here. First, the proper functioning of the machine takes place *through* the human. Machine and human are in a relationship in which machines are machines only with the help of humanity. And then it is only in relation to the machine that the human can outgrow its poverty.[11] The idea that Cylons, as machines, properly function through humanity is denied by the vast majority of them. As evidenced first by their attempted eradication of humanity, and then by their later change of heart, as Brother Cavil explains:

> People should be true to who and what they are. We're machines. We should be true to that. Be the best machines the universe has ever seen. But we got it into our heads that we were the children of humanity. So, instead of pursuing our own destiny of trying to find our own path to enlightenment, we hijacked yours. ("Lay Down Your Burdens, Part 2")

Some Cylons, however, believe that they can only fully become machines through humanity: Sharon's relationship with Helo and Caprica Six's relationship with Baltar being the two primary examples. D'Anna is a machine that learns its own facticity through both boredom and a removal from the poverty of the Cylons' world. She's then able, because of technology, to go beyond the humans' relationship to the world—which is still one of poverty—and experience a sense of totality.

The *Galactica* crew, by letting the Cylons become what they are becoming, expand their idea of what it means to be human. In "A Measure of Salvation," five infected Cylons are captured by

Galactica. The Cylon prisoners are slated to be used as instruments of genocide by being killed in range of a resurrection ship, effectively infecting the whole Cylon race with the virus when they're downloaded. Helo interrupts the planned operation by asphyxiating the prisoners before *Galactica* gets in range of the resurrection ship. His action follows from his defense of the Cylons' right to exist.

Helo: Genocide? So that's what we're about now?
Apollo: They're not human. They were built, not born. No fathers, no mothers, no sons, no daughters.
Helo: I had a daughter. I held her in my arms.
Apollo: She was half-human. These are things, dangerous things. This is our one chance to be rid of them.
Helo: You can rationalize it any way you want. We do this, we wipe out their race, then we're no different than they are.

Despite seemingly arguing against himself by asserting that if the humans commit genocide they'll be no better than the murderous Cylons, Helo tires to save humanity by opening them to the Cylons' process of becoming-human. Helo even calls the eradication of the Cylon race a "crime against *humanity*":

I'm talking about right and wrong. I'm talking about losing a piece of our souls. No one wants to hear that, right? Let's keep it on me. Yeah, I'm married to a Cylon who walked through hell for all of us how many times? And she's not half anything. Okay, how do we know there aren't others like her? She made a choice. She's a person. They're a race of people. Wiping them out with a biological weapon is a crime against . . . is a crime against humanity.

Helo and Sharon approach the Cylons becoming more than mere machines from a different angle than D'Anna, but the effect is the same. In order for the Cylons to go beyond their machine nature, they need humanity to allow them to be what they are. In return, humanity, by letting them be, is able to "keep its soul"—to win a battle against the poverty of its world. Humans are allowed to be humans through the expanded life of the non-human. Schirmacher contends in *Just Living*, "Successfully functioning technology does not apply to the individual case; it's oriented in relation to the universe. For only a truly successful function in the long run is in the interest of that individual species calling itself man and existing as technology." He allows for the possibility of openness to what has always already been the case: the conjoining of the human and technology, of the human and non-human. Instead of thinking of what's human as removed from the non-human, or even of being merely in relation to the non-human, Schirmacher refers to both human and non-human *together*.

So the Cylons, after deciding they no longer want to destroy humanity, appear to want a closer relationship with their human creators—through the hybrid child Hera and by attempting to live with humans on New Caprica. Why is D'Anna, then, who seems to be taking this relationship in a positive direction, put on ice? It's simply a confirmation that D'Anna has reached a place outside of the poverty of the Cylons' everyday world. She's not only begun to learn her own facticity, but she's also taken this new knowledge and applied resurrection technology to it in order to go beyond such knowledge; and she's finding a way to access totality. Just as the other Cylons feared an opportunity for facticity by enacting the Prayer to the Cloud of Unknowing, the uncontrollable D'Anna is boxed in order to keep the Cylon world poor. Admiral Adama, on the other hand, eventually had the strength to see that Helo was right regarding the negative effects for humanity if they were to commit genocide against the Cylon race and thus didn't bring him up on charges.

D'Anna shows that in order for technology to come into its own, humanity must be in a relation to it of "letting be," rather than an ecologically threatening "setting-upon." It's only then that humanity will ever begin, *through* technology, to enrich the poverty of its own world. Perhaps the Cylons will eventually find the strength to reinstate D'Anna's line; but if not, there's still hope for the Cylons. As Helo says of Sharon, "How do we know there aren't others like her?"

NOTES

1   Martin Heidegger, *Being and Time* (*BT*), trans. Joan Stambaugh (Albany: State University of New York Press, 1996), 229. Further references will be given in the text.

2   Just remember in reading the quotations from Heidegger that for our purposes *Dasein* means "human being."

3   See Giorgio Agamben, *The Open: Man and Animal*, trans. Kevin Attell (Stanford: Stanford University Press, 2004), 60.

4 Martin Heidegger, *The Fundamental Concepts of Metaphysics: World, Finitude, Solitude* (FCM), trans. William McNeill and Nicholas Walker (Bloomington: Indiana University Press, 1995), 184. Further references will be given in the text.

5 Jacques Derrida, *Of Spirit: Heidegger and the Question*, trans. Geoffrey Bennington and Rachel Bowlby (Chicago: University of Chicago Press, 1991), 49. Further references will be given in the text.

6 One of the main ideas of Gilles Deleuze's concept of "becoming-animal" is the expansion of what it means to be human through an incorporation of the animal. See Gilles Deleuze and Félix Guattari, "1730: Becoming-Intense, Becoming-Animal, Becoming-Imperceptible . . . ," in *A Thousand Plateaus: Capitalism and Schizophrenia*, trans. Brian Massumi (Minneapolis: University of Minnesota Press, 1987).

7 Martin Heidegger, "The Question Concerning Technology" (QCT), trans. William Lovitt, in *Basic Writings*, ed. David Krell (New York: Harper Collins, 1993), 311. Further references will be given in the text.

8 For a less rosy reading of the pre-industrial age relationship to nature, see Manuel DeLanda, "Cities and Nations," in *A New Philosophy of Society: Assemblage Theory and Social Complexity* (London: Continuum, 2006).

9 For a similar development of Heidegger's relationship to technology, see Christopher Fynsk, *Language and Relation . . . that there is language* (Stanford: Stanford University Press, 1996), 114.

10 Wolfgang Schirmacher, *Just Living: A Philosophy of Bare Life* (New York: Atropos Press, forthcoming).

11 Agamben makes a similar point regarding the animal in *The Open*, 62, 68.

PART III

WORTHY OF SURVIVAL: MORAL ISSUES FOR COLONIALS AND CYLONS

9

The Search for Starbuck:
The Needs of the Many vs.
the Few

Randall M. Jensen

In "You Can't Go Home Again," Commander Adama mobilizes
every ship he can get his hands on in a desperate effort to rescue
Lieutenant Kara "Starbuck" Thrace, whose Viper has crashed after
being shot down by a Cylon patrol. The search leaves the Colonial
fleet vulnerable and uses 43 percent of their precious fuel reserves.
President Roslin questions Adama's decision since this massive search
for just one pilot endangers the lives of everyone in the fleet. In their
continuing struggle to ensure the survival of humanity, Adama and
Roslin have to make difficult choices about who will be saved or
abandoned. Are there moral limits to how far they should go in their
efforts to save those in need? And how should they decide whom to
save when they can't save everyone?

Should We Stay or Should We Go Now?

In the immediate aftermath of the Cylons' devastating attack on the
Twelve Colonies, Laura Roslin—the former Secretary of Education
who suddenly becomes President of the Colonies—enlists the aid of
Captain Lee "Apollo" Adama to rescue whatever survivors they can
find. This is a risky proposition, since the Cylons may appear at any
time and finish them off. Yet her actions are guided by the overriding moral goal of saving lives. Roslin is pitted against Commander
Adama, who wants them to abandon their rescue operations and

regroup to continue the battle against the Cylons. Ultimately, however, Adama agrees with Roslin that rescuing and protecting the survivors is of paramount importance.

When a Cylon patrol comes upon the "ragtag fleet," Roslin's advisors argue about how they should react, given that a number of ships don't have FTL capability:

> *Doral*: There are still thousands of people on the sub-light ships. We can't just leave them.
>
> *Apollo*: But we'll be saving tens of thousands. I'm sorry to make it a numbers game, but we're talking about the survival of our race here. We don't have the luxury of taking risks and hoping for the best, because if we lose, we lose everything.
>
> ("Miniseries")

Roslin decides that Apollo is right: the fleet must immediately jump away even though it will mean leaving a significant number of ships and their passengers to the mercy of the Cylons. As Apollo says, it's "a numbers game." If saving lives is important, surely one should save *as many lives as possible*. It appears irrational to save fewer lives at the cost of losing more—or worse, to risk losing *every* life at stake.

Roslin and Apollo illustrate a *utilitarian* attitude here. Founded by British philosophers Jeremy Bentham (1748–1832) and John Stuart Mill (1806–1873), utilitarianism is an ethical theory which states that the right thing to do in any situation is whatever maximizes utility— that is, human well-being or happiness:

> The creed which accepts as the foundation of morals, Utility, or the Greatest Happiness Principle, holds that actions are right in proportion as they tend to promote happiness, wrong as they tend to produce the reverse of happiness. By happiness is intended pleasure, and the absence of pain; by unhappiness, pain, and the privation of pleasure.[1]

The point of morality, for a utilitarian, is to bring about the greatest happiness for the greatest number of people. A utilitarian would generally regard saving a life as the right thing to do and taking a life as wrong, since life-saving generally leads to an increase in overall happiness and life-taking generally leads to a decrease. If in some unusual circumstance, however, life-saving would lead to a decrease in overall happiness, or life-taking to an increase, utilitarianism's verdict would be reversed. And so in more complicated trade-off situations like those encountered all too often on *BSG*, where people are forced to choose who lives and who dies, utilitarianism asserts that if all other things are equal, we should do whatever results in saving the greater number of people. It would be wrong, then, for Roslin and Apollo to try to save a life if it means more people will die. For a utilitarian, "the needs of the many outweigh the needs of the few"[2]—in the end, only the numbers count.

When trying to decide whether to leave someone behind, whether it's several thousand civilians who've just survived the initial Cylon attack or the even larger number of settlers who must be abandoned when the Cylons discover New Caprica, utilitarianism's advice carries a lot of weight. Trying to minimize the loss of life in this kind of situation seems to be the right move, even though it means leaving people to die. There may be some reasons to reconsider, however. Are utilitarians right to think that only the numbers count?[3]

Frak the Numbers!

Roslin and Apollo must decide whether to try to save a smaller group if it puts everyone—including the smaller group—at risk. Saving the smaller group instead of the larger group isn't really an option. But what if it were an option? Suppose we were forced to choose whether to save one Sagittaron or five Gemenese. Our initial reaction may be that we should save the Gemenese, not because they're from Gemenon—and no one really likes the Sagittarons—but because there are more of them. Five deaths are worse than one death, five times worse in fact. But is the value of death additive or "stackable"? Is it worse that five die than one die? Maybe we ought to ask, "Worse for whom?" It's worse for the Sagittaron if he dies. And it's worse for each of the Gemenese if they die. But it's not five times as bad for any individual Gemenese to die, because no one dies five times; each can die only once. If terms like "better" and "worse" make sense only from a single person's perspective, if it makes no sense to say "worse from the universe's point of view," then all of a sudden it isn't quite so obvious that the death of five people is five times as bad as the death of one.

But it's still true that the outcome in which the Gemenese die is bad *for more people* than the outcome in which the Sagittaron dies. A trivial parallel would be to compare one person losing five dollars to five people losing five dollars. No one loses twenty-five dollars, but might we not care how many people suffer the same loss? Perhaps we have an obligation to save the greater number because by choosing the outcome in which more are saved, we're able to look out for more people's interests. This might strike us as unfair, however, because the Sagittaron never has any chance of rescue, since the lives of five will always be preferred to the life of one. And shouldn't everyone have an equal chance of rescue? Perhaps we ought to flip a coin so that all six have a fifty percent chance of being saved. Why should the Sagittaron have a zero percent chance of rescue and a Gemenese a 100 percent chance simply because there are four other Gemenese also in need of rescue? The Gemenese doesn't *deserve* to be rescued just because of such an accidental circumstance; nor does the Sagittaron deserve to be abandoned because of it. It may be, though, that giving someone something she doesn't deserve is nonetheless the right thing to do at times.

Is the value of human life really *additive* in the way monetary value is? It goes without saying that if I had to choose between one dollar and five dollars, I'd choose five. But there are some reasons to worry about whether the choice between saving one life or five can be treated the same way. The philosopher Immanuel Kant (1724–1804) claims that human life has *dignity* and not *price*:

> What has a price can be replaced by something else as its *equivalent*; what on the other hand is raised above all price and therefore admits of no equivalent has a dignity . . . morality, and humanity insofar as it is capable of morality, is that which alone has dignity.[4]

Human life has *intrinsic value* and isn't replaceable as objects with a price are. By accepting that we ought to save five rather than one, are we assuming that human lives are interchangeable and replaceable? Do we show more respect for human life by flipping a coin in this kind of situation?

So should our life-saving endeavors be guided by the numbers? There are some reasons to think that we can't simply say the answer is yes. And so if Apollo has to decide whether to save Starbuck or two strangers, it may be morally acceptable for him to save her because it doesn't matter whether he saves one or two since life is equally valuable for all involved. But as the numbers get larger, they become harder to ignore. No amount of philosophizing is going to move us away from the basic intuition that saving the *far* greater number is the right thing to do. Sometimes the numbers clearly count. But are they the only thing that counts?

Saving Starbuck?

When Starbuck goes missing, Adama and Apollo are determined to save her, no matter what the cost. When Roslin arrives to sort out the mess, Colonel Tigh informs her that Starbuck isn't just another pilot to these two men. Each of them is connected to her personally because of her romantic history with Zak (their deceased son and brother) as well as their own history with her. To Starbuck, Adama is "the old man," a father figure, and Apollo is . . . well, let's just say it's very intense and complicated and leave it at that. Should this kind of personal connection affect the numbers game when lives are on the line?

Such personal concerns don't count very much to a utilitarian, at least not in matters of life and death. What matters is human well-being. Everyone's well-being—yours or mine, a friend's or a stranger's—counts exactly the same. According to Mill, "As between his own happiness and that of others, utilitarianism requires him to be as strictly impartial as a disinterested and benevolent spectator" (17). Under threat by Cylons when trying to protect the Eye of Jupiter, Apollo, despite his strong feelings for Starbuck, initially elects not to try to rescue her when her Raptor is shot down. Sam Anders, on the other hand, is willing to sacrifice their mission's success to save his wife. Their heated debate is resolved when Apollo orders his own wife, Dee, to risk her life to save Starbuck ("The Eye of Jupiter"; "Rapture"). Apollo, in this instance, is able to assess the situation impartially and recognize that Starbuck's life isn't worth more than their mission's success, and that Dee's life isn't worth more than Starbuck's just because she's his wife.

Going back to our primary example, any pain the Adamas might feel at Starbuck's loss won't even register on the scales when weighed against the prospect of the deaths of thousands of people and the possible extinction of the human race. Roslin confronts them:

> You're both perfectly aware that you are putting the lives of over 45,000 people and the future of this civilization at risk, for your personal feelings. Now if the two of you, of all people, can live with that, then the human race doesn't stand a chance. Clear your heads. ("You Can't Go Home Again")

The search is called off straightaway. Adama and Apollo agree with Roslin that it's wrong to put tens of thousands of lives at risk for just one life, even if it's Starbuck. They've let their feelings for her keep them from properly appreciating the consequences of their decision to continue the search for so long. As Roslin puts it, they've "lost perspective."

The Adamas agree to abandon the search, however, only *after* they believe Starbuck's oxygen supply has run out, which means the chance of rescue has dropped very close to zero. Even if it's the right call to terminate the search at this point, the search may very well have been justified in the beginning when the odds of finding Starbuck were higher and the odds of a Cylon fleet arriving were lower. And while the men in Starbuck's life are determined to save her, she saves herself by figuring out how to fly a crashed Cylon Raider. As it turns out, simply *waiting* for Starbuck would've been as effective as mounting a risky and costly search, although no one could have known it at the time. Moral reasoning can thus be complicated by the fact that the consequences of our actions can't always be predicted accurately, and sometimes we have to consider a possible outcome whose probability is unknown, disputed, or very low.

Roslin characterizes the Adamas' motives for trying to save Starbuck as based on their "personal feelings," which might mean any number of things but has a somewhat dismissive tone. If they want to save Starbuck only because of their unresolved issues over Zak's death, as Tigh suggests, then Roslin seems right to rebuke them. We don't approve of people who let their own psychological baggage keep them from doing the right thing. But that's not fair to Adama and Apollo. Perhaps they began their relationship with Starbuck because of Zak, but they each have a relationship with her now that stands on its own. What if their motives depend more on friendship and a sense of family than on denial and unresolved guilt? Consider the exchange between Apollo and his father just after calling off the search:

Apollo: I need to know something. Why did you do this? Why did we
  do this? Is it for Kara? For Zak? What?
Adama: Kara was family. You do whatever you have to do. Some-
  times you break the rules.
Apollo: And if it was me down there instead?
Adama: You don't have to ask that.
Apollo: Are you sure?
Adama: If it were you, we'd never leave.
("You Can't Go Home Again")

What's Adama's point about the moral importance of family here? Is
it that we sometimes *do* break the rules for family, even though it's
wrong to do so? That's true enough. In fact, we have a word for that
kind of moral wrong: nepotism. But his point may be that sometimes
breaking the rules is what we *ought* to do.

What does Adama mean by "the rules?" Let's assume he's referring
to any kind of official or unofficial policy, whether legal, institutional,
personal, cultural, or whatever. His point is that these rules aren't
morally decisive; although such rules might be very helpful, following
them isn't *always* the right thing to do. A utilitarian would agree
wholeheartedly so far, because any other rules are overridden when
they conflict with the ultimate rule: "Maximize utility." But Adama
introduces a different kind of justification for rule-breaking based on
personal relationships of friendship, love, and family rather than on
the maximization of utility. Although he's often powerfully motivated
by what's needed to safeguard the very survival of the human race,
and in the end he concedes that he can't risk the fleet for the sake
of Starbuck, he suggests that there are times when personal moral
concerns trump utilitarian considerations. While saving the greater
number is often the right thing to do, sometimes "the needs of the
one outweigh the needs of the many."[5] So perhaps utilitarianism
doesn't tell us the whole story about morality, for it fails to accommodate the personal sphere.

The Mark of Cain

When the Colonial fleet encounters another surviving battlestar, the
Pegasus, commanded by Admiral Cain, Apollo says, "It's like a dream"
("Pegasus"). But we slowly learn that Cain has pursued a darker and

more ruthless course of action than Roslin and Adama. Her mission is to hurt the Cylons, and she's not at all interested in protecting civilians. Cain's XO, Colonel Fisk, partakes of Tigh's favorite pastime and relates several disturbing stories. One involves the summary execution of an officer who refused to obey an order; another explains why *Pegasus* isn't traveling with a civilian fleet:

> *Fisk:* The *Scylla* was a civilian transport. We found her and a few other civies about a week after the attack. They were good ships. FTL drives and weapons, even. A lot of potential spare parts that we could use on *Pegasus*. So the Admiral made a decision. Military needs are a priority.
> *Tigh:* You stripped them. You stripped the ships for parts. Sweet mother of Artemis. How much equipment did you take? You take their jump drives? Left all those people marooned out there?
> *Fisk:* No, not all. Admiral Cain looked over the passenger list and she made a decision about who was valuable and who wasn't. *Scylla* was the toughest. Laird and 15 other men and women. They were all . . . All traveling with their families, wives, husbands, children. The selectees refused to go. There was resistance. So, the order came down to shoot the family of anyone who refused to come. So we did. Two families. We put them up against the bulkhead, and we shot them.

("Resurrection Ship, Part 1")

Cain's orders are morally monstrous. And Roslin and Adama contemplate assassinating her because of the threat she poses to everyone around her. Yet couldn't Cain defend her actions by arguing that she's willing to sacrifice the few for the sake of the many? The officers on *Galactica* have also done morally questionable things, as Apollo reminds us in his testimony at Baltar's trial ("Crossroads, Part 2"). In fact, they not only leave people to die, they *kill* innocent people to protect a greater number. Is Cain's behavior really all that different from theirs?

Shortly after the initial Cylon attack, Tigh is faced with a test of his capacity as *Galactica*'s XO during a fire that could potentially destroy the entire ship ("Miniseries"). He orders Chief Tyrol to put an immediate end to the fire by sealing off and venting several compartments, even though over eighty crewmembers will be sucked out into space. Adama affirms Tigh's decision when Tyrol curses him. But Tyrol's condemnation is based on his belief that they could have stopped the fire without venting the compartments, which, if true, would make the sacrifice unnecessary.[6]

Tigh also leads the resistance against the Cylon occupation of New Caprica using suicide bombers. When Tyrol and Roslin challenge him—claiming, "Some things you just don't do, Colonel, not even in war"—Tigh doesn't equivocate:

> The bombings? They got the Cylons' attention. They really got their attention, and I am not giving that up . . . I've sent men on suicide missions in two wars now, and let me tell you something. It don't make a godsdamn bit of difference whether they're riding in a Viper or walking out onto a parade ground. In the end they're just as dead. So take your piety and your moralizing and your high-minded principles and stick them some place safe until you're off this rock and you're sitting in your nice, cushy chair on *Colonial One* again. I've got a war to fight. ("Precipice")[7]

Tigh isn't alone in his utilitarian stance. On Adama's orders, Apollo shoots down the *Olympic Carrier*—a ship with over a thousand people onboard—because it's a threat to the rest of the fleet ("33"). And upon the surprising return of Bulldog, an old comrade, we learn that Adama ordered that he be shot down to protect the secrecy of a mission that may have precipitated the Cylons' attack on the Colonies ("Hero").

Are Cain's actions worse than these? If utilitarians are right and morality is just a numbers game, then the only way to drive a wedge between Cain and the others is to show that her actions ultimately do more harm or less good than theirs, which seems to be true. *Pegasus* isn't a very happy ship under her command, and she's left who knows how many civilians behind—certainly more than the number she's rescued and incorporated into her crew. It's very likely that Cain is leading her ship toward a fatal confrontation with the Cylons. So it's far from clear that Cain's strategies are maximizing utility for everyone affected by her actions. But no doubt Cain would argue that they'd all be dead without her ruthless leadership, as Starbuck eulogizes her:

> She didn't give up. She didn't worry. She didn't second guess. She acted. She did what she thought needed to be done, and the *Pegasus* survived. It might be hard to admit, or hard to hear, but I think that we were safer with her than we are without. ("Resurrection Ship, Part 2")

Though he was willing to overlook the numbers when it came to saving Starbuck, Adama takes a distinctly utilitarian stance when Tyrol organizes a general strike of the tylium refinery workers and his "knuckle draggers" on *Galactica*. While work stoppage on the refinery ship presents a danger to the fleet as its fuel source, Adama is more concerned about the fact that Tyrol's deckhands are disobeying orders on a military vessel in a time of war. And he's willing to take drastic, Cain-like, measures to deal with it:

> *Adama*: [to his marines] Arrest Cally Tyrol. Take her under armed guard directly to the starboard repair bay.
> *Tyrol*: Repair bay? What are you doing?
> *Adama*: I'm gonna put her up against the bulkhead and I'm gonna shoot her as a mutineer.
> *Tyrol*: Are you out of your frakkin' mind?! Cally was just following my orders.
> *Adama*: She's a ringleader, so she goes first. Then the rest of your deck gang: Figurski, Seelix, Pollux.
> *Tyrol*: You won't do this. We have a son.
> *Adama*: Understand me. The very survival of this ship may depend on someone getting an order that they don't want to do. And if they hesitate, if they feel that orders are sometimes optional, then this ship will perish. And so will your son. And the entire human race. I don't want to do this, Chief. But I will put ten Callys up against the wall to make sure that this ship, and this fleet, are not destroyed.

("Dirty Hands")

In the desperate circumstances in which the Colonial survivors find themselves, even the most morally reflective of them may end up bearing the "mark of Cain."

"Evil Men in the Gardens of Paradise?"

What if there's more to morality than utilitarianism maintains? What if factors other than the numbers are morally important? What about *causing* the death of a few in order to save a greater number? Might something other than the numbers matter in such cases? A deontologist would unequivocally answer, "Yes." *Deontology*, utilitarianism's chief rival, identifies certain features of human action as morally significant *apart* from the consequences. While agreeing that lying has harmful effects, a deontologist might claim that being dishonest is *intrinsically* immoral—wrong in and of itself regardless of whether lying might bring about some good on a particular occasion. Kant asserts one of deontology's central principles: "So act that you use humanity, whether in your own person or in the person of any other, always at the same time as an end, never merely as a means" (38). Certain actions are wrong simply because they fail to respect the dignity of persons.

With this principle in mind, how do Tigh and the others compare with Cain? Even though Tigh foresees that some people will die when he vents the compartments to stop the fire, he doesn't *intend* for anyone to die. Venting the compartments is simply his *means* for achieving his *goal* of saving the ship from the spreading fire. Unfortunately, people will die as a result of the venting. This is a foreseen, but unintended, *side-effect* of Tigh's order.[8] Tigh doesn't want anyone to die; he would be delighted if everyone miraculously survived. Those eighty deaths aren't part of his plan to save the ship; he doesn't *need* them to die to stop the fire. This doesn't mean that Tigh isn't causally or morally responsible for their deaths; nor does it automatically imply that his action is morally justified. But it is a relevant difference between his action and Cain's actions. She clearly *does* intend the deaths of some of her victims, such as her XO and the families of those onboard the *Scylla*. If we consider a person's intent to be morally important, then we have at least one way of articulating what's so morally reprehensible about Cain.

When Tigh orders that the compartments be vented to stop the fire, he's making a choice between letting a very large number of people die and bringing about the deaths of a smaller number who are part of the larger group. Assuming Tigh's assessment of the fire's danger is accurate, the smaller group's death is inevitable; they'll die either when the compartment is vented or when *Galactica* is destroyed by the fire. In fact, if the compartment is vented some of them may survive if they're suited up as they ought to be. The crew inside the compartments can't very well complain that Tigh is merely using them or doesn't care about their welfare. But when Cain orders the execution of civilians on the *Scylla*, the only immediate threat to them is from her and it's clear she regards them as utterly dispensable.

Bombing the police graduation ceremony on New Caprica requires a different analysis, though. Tigh does have the goal of killing people who are collaborating with the Cylons, but he perceives such people

111

as a hostile threat to the human populace. They're *guilty* as enemy soldiers and thus are legitimate military targets rather than innocent victims. It's not always easy to decide who's a legitimate target for violence, and maybe Tigh's judgment can be questioned here; but we can still recognize a significant difference between Tigh ordering an attack on these police officers and Cain ordering the execution of the families on the *Scylla*.

Likewise, the *Olympic Carrier* is a ship that's being used as a weapon. True, the folks onboard are innocent of any wrongdoing, but they're part of a lethal threat to the fleet, even if only because they're unfortunate enough to be inseparable from the threat. That's why Apollo shoots them down. It's always horrible to use violence against the innocent. But isn't there a difference between using violence against the innocent *to protect people from a threat* and using violence against the innocent *to threaten and coerce people*? We're not allowed to do just anything whatsoever to protect ourselves from a threat, of course. But it seems less difficult to justify violence in defense of self or others than to justify violence used to make people do things they don't want to do. Arguably, the violence used by *Galactica*'s officers typically falls in the first category, while Cain's often falls in the second. The key exception may be Adama's threatening to execute Cally. One wonders, however, whether he may have been *bluffing*, knowing that Tyrol would back down and call off the strike rather than allow his wife to be shot. Since Tyrol caved, we have only Adama's unflinching, steely-eyed glare to tell us how real his threat was.

Sacrifice

How do we reconcile the needs of the many with the needs of the few—or the one? Sci-fi fans have wondered about this ever since we watched Spock's famous death scene in *Star Trek II: The Wrath of Khan*. Spock sacrifices himself to save the entire crew of the *Enterprise*, living only long enough to gasp his last words to Kirk:

Spock: Don't grieve, Admiral. It is logical. The needs of the many
    outweigh—
Kirk: The needs of the few.
Spock: Or the one.

Such self-sacrifice is truly heroic: "No one has greater love than this, to lay down one's life for one's friends" (John 15:13). But laying down *other* people's lives, that's a different story. Sometimes such "sacrifices" seem no more or less than murder, as with Cain's actions on the *Scylla*. Other times the decision to sacrifice a few to save a greater number can demonstrate a commitment to do the right thing even at great personal cost. That's real heroism, too. And surely it's no surprise if *BSG*'s moral heroes turn out to be darker, grittier, and more tragic and tough-minded than some of their predecessors in the history of sci-fi.

NOTES

1   John Stuart Mill, *Utilitarianism*, ed. George Sher (Indianapolis: Hackett, 2001), 7. Further references will be given in the text. See also Jeremy Bentham, *The Principles of Morals and Legislation* (Amherst: Prometheus, 1988).

2   This is also a tenet of Vulcan philosophy, which Mr. Spock uses to justify his sacrifice to save the *Enterprise* in *Star Trek II: The Wrath of Khan*.

3   See John Taurek, "Should the Numbers Count?" *Philosophy and Public Affairs* 6 (1977), 293–316.

4   Immanuel Kant, *Groundwork of the Metaphysics of Morals*, trans. Mary Gregor (Cambridge: Cambridge University Press, 1997), 42. Further references will be given in the text.

5   As Admiral Kirk tries to impress on the reborn Spock at the end of *Star Trek III: The Search for Spock*.

6   Of course, one wonders why they bothered to send in a damage control team to fight the fire to begin with and not just vent the compartments immediately, but this isn't *The Nitpicker's Guide to Battlestar Galactica*.

7   For further discussion of Tigh's approach to resisting the Cylon occupation, see Andrew Terjesen's chapter in this volume.

8   This deontological distinction between what's intended and what's merely foreseen is part of the "doctrine of double-effect." See Philippa Foot "The Problem of Abortion and the Doctrine of the Double Effect," in *Virtues and Vices* (Berkeley: University of California Press, 1978); and Thomas A. Cavanaugh, *Double-Effect Reasoning: Doing Good and Avoiding Evil* (New York: Oxford University Press, 2006).

10

Resistance vs. Collaboration on New Caprica: What Would You Do?

Andrew Terjesen

What would you do if you were stuck on Cylon-occupied New Caprica? Would you work with the Cylons in the hope of peaceful coexistence or to protect your own life? Or would you resist? Perhaps most of us would like to think we would resist, but it's hard to really know what we would do. The question in either case is how far *should* you be willing to go? Was it wrong of the Resistance to use suicide bombing to destabilize the Cylons? Should those who joined the New Caprica Police and assisted the Cylons in rounding up insurgents be punished?

"A More Meaningful Impact"

When we first see the Resistance at work on New Caprica, Sam Anders and Galen Tyrol are planting a bomb intended for the Cylons. It would seem that targeting the Cylons is the right way to oppose their occupation. But since the humanoid Cylons have the ability to download and resurrect, killing them isn't that effective. Laura Roslin notes in her diary, "It is simply not enough to kill Cylons, because they don't die. They resurrect themselves and they continue to walk among us. It is horrifying." Even so, the Resistance is doing an important good. Roslin writes, "Although at times these attacks seem like futile gestures, I believe that they are critical to morale, to maintaining some measure of hope."[1] Still, the continued cycle of humans

114

bombing Cylons and Cylons downloading into new bodies, only to be bombed again, will become just as hopeless over time. Roslin thus recognizes, "In order for the insurgency to have a more meaningful impact, we need to strike a high-profile target" ("Occupation").

As the President of the Colonies who surrendered to the Cylons and continues to work with them, Gaius Baltar fits the bill. But it's difficult for the Resistance to reach him. The best shot they have is at the graduation ceremony for the New Caprica Police. Tyrol is worried about the probability of high human casualties, but Colonel Tigh isn't at all sympathetic: "Don't avoid them. Send a message. You work with the Cylons, you're a target. No boundaries for the Cylons, there's no boundaries for us. Anything we can do to nail that son of a bitch Gaius Baltar is worth doing" ("Occupation").

Roslin and Tigh's reasoning mirrors that of Brother Cavil, who convinces his fellow Cylons that they need to take more drastic action against the Resistance:

Cavil 1:   I want to clarify our objectives. If we're bringing the word of "God," then it follows that we should employ any means necessary to do so, any means.

Cavil 2:   Yes, *fear* is a key article of faith, as I understand it. So perhaps it's time to instill a little more fear into the people's hearts and minds . . . We round up the leaders of the insurgency and we execute them *publicly*. We round up at random groups off the streets and we execute them *publicly*.

Cavil 1:   Send a message that the gloves are coming off. The insurgency stops now or else we start reducing the human population to a more manageable size . . .

("Occupation")

One of the longest-standing debates in ethics concerns the question of what matters more: the consequences of one's actions or the means— the actions themselves—by which one achieves them. *Consequentialists* argue that only consequences matter in determining whether an action is good or bad. Suicide bombing the New Caprica Police graduation is thus good if it produces the best consequences overall, and it's bad if it doesn't. In contrast, *deontologists* argue that some actions are just wrong, no matter what the consequences of doing them.

Tigh is clearly a consequentialist. When talking about how to get Tucker "Duck" Clellan to join the Resistance, he says, "We need him.

Throw in some poetic crap about the struggle for liberty against the Cylon oppressor. Whatever it takes" ("The Resistance," Webisode 1). Tigh dismisses the sanctity of particular values like liberty and instead focuses on getting the desired consequence. It's no surprise then that Tigh endorses many actions that make his fellow insurgents uncomfortable. The fact that the desired consequence—stopping the occupation—is so important makes Tigh's consequentialism plausible. But, even in the case of war, many philosophers endorse some deontological principles.

Thomas Aquinas (c.1225–1274) is often credited with systematizing "just war" theory. According to Aquinas, in order for a war to be morally justifiable, it must first of all be for a *just cause*: "Those who are attacked, should be attacked because they deserve it on account of some fault." Certainly the Cylons meet this criterion. And one could argue that those who join the New Caprica Police do as well by choosing to help the Cylons break the Resistance. But Aquinas offers another condition, that the people fighting the war have *righteous intentions*: "Warlike arms and feats are not all forbidden, but those which are inordinate and perilous, and end in slaying or plundering."[2] This condition requires that those conducting the war only do as much as they need to in order to end it, and should avoid harming those whom they don't have just cause to fight. Attacking the New Caprica Police is one thing, setting off a bomb in a crowded marketplace is another. As Tyrol tells Tigh, "Some things you just don't do, Colonel, not even in war" ("Occupation").

"Desperate People Take Desperate Measures"

As the Cylons attempt to stop the Resistance, it becomes more difficult to limit the damage to Cylons and their collaborators. When Tyrol reports that the marketplace has been shut down, Tigh simply responds, "We'll shift targets." Tyrol is outraged:

> *Tyrol*: You were gonna hit the marketplace. The *market*. Full of civilians. This is crazy. You know, we need to figure out whose side we're on.
> *Tigh*: Which side are we on? We're on the side of the demons, Chief. We're evil men in the gardens of paradise. Sent by the forces of

death, to spread devastation and destruction wherever we go. I'm
surprised you didn't know that.
("Precipice")

In Tigh's mind, the bombings are the only way to ensure that the
Cylons are distracted enough for *Galactica* to mount a successful
rescue. The extreme nature of the situation leads Tigh to put aside
traditional moral concerns.

Even Roslin sees the bombings as having crossed the line: "I don't
care that it's effective. I don't care that the Cylons can't stop it. It's
wrong" ("Precipice"). Although Roslin supports the Resistance on
consequentialist grounds, there's a limit to how far she'll go. Her
reasoning is deontological since she recognizes that there are some
basic moral rules we should follow even in war, no matter what the
consequences. Tigh doesn't see this line:

> The bombings? They got the Cylons' attention. They really got their
> attention, and I am not giving that up . . . I've sent men on suicide
> missions in two wars now, and let me tell you something. It don't
> make a godsdamn bit of difference whether they're riding in a Viper or
> walking out onto a parade ground. In the end they're just as dead. So
> take your piety and your moralizing and your high-minded principles
> and stick them some place safe until you're off this rock and you're
> sitting in your nice, cushy chair on *Colonial One* again. I've got a war
> to fight. ("Precipice")

To evaluate Tigh's consequentialist stance, we must consider whether
it's sometimes okay to engage in terrorist actions, such as suicide
bombing. Contemporary philosopher Burleigh Wilkins offers the following moral rule:

> Terrorism is justified as a form of self-defense when: (1) all political
> and legal remedies have been exhausted or are inapplicable . . . and (2)
> the terrorism will be directed against members of a community or
> group which is collectively guilty of violence aimed at those individuals
> who are now considering the use of terrorism as an instrument of self-
> defense, or at the community or group of which they are members.[3]

On the surface this seems quite similar to Aquinas's conditions for
just war. But Wilkins is proposing a far more radical doctrine since
he's extending the notion of who deserves to be attacked. One can be

"collectively guilty" of something without ever having done anything. During the occupation of New Caprica, humans don't have a functioning government; Baltar's administration "functions in name only," comparable to the Vichy government that collaborated with Nazi occupiers in France during Word War II.[4] So the first condition is met. And while no human could be considered collectively guilty of betraying the human race at first, anyone who doesn't take action after the first few attacks on Cylon targets is complicit in supporting the occupation. So Wilkins' rule arguably endorses a marketplace bombing after bombings that target only the Cylons and those who explicitly collaborate with them fail to bring about a change in the situation.

Wilkins, however, is describing a situation where people's *lives* are threatened and terrorism becomes equivalent to "self-defense." But during the occupation the Cylons have put aside their plans for genocide in an attempt to live with humanity. The Cylon occupation isn't analogous to the Nazi regime enacting genocidal policies against groups they deemed inferior. The policies the Cylons enact on New Caprica limit *freedom*, but don't threaten human lives—as long as one doesn't participate in the Resistance. Can Wilkins' justification of terrorism be extended to the situation on New Caprica?

The answer seems to turn on whether freedom is an essential part of human existence. If so, then anything that destroys that freedom forces people to live inhumanely; and so the Resistance is taking necessary steps to defend human existence. If they don't take action, human life would lose its meaning; and it's the unique value of human life that justifies self-defense against violent attacks. But even if freedom is essential to human existence, to what degree would freedom have to be threatened before terrorism becomes a justifiable form of self-defense? Obviously, complete and total freedom isn't essential to human existence. We often exchange some freedom for the sake of convenience and other things we want—no one is free to drive on any side of the road they please. The Cylon occupation places restrictions on day-to-day activities, but it doesn't force people to live a certain kind of way. Many of the evident restrictions involve limits on political freedom and on personal freedom as responses to terrorist actions. To apply Wilkins' principle, one must hold that the freedoms the Cylons encroach upon are more important than life itself.

118

"An Extension of the Cylons' Corporeal Authority"

When Baltar confronts Roslin about the New Caprica Police bombing, he paints a very different picture of the cadets: "Their only crime is putting on the police uniform, trying to bring some order to the chaos out there" ("Precipice"). James "Jammer" Lyman, who's secretly a member of the police, describes to Tyrol the mindset of a police recruit: "At first, I bet that they thought they were doing something good, you know, get the Cylons off the street, police their own" ("Precipice"). An exchange between Jammer and Tigh concerning where they'll be making bombs illustrates why Jammer might think that the New Caprica Police is better than the Resistance:

> *Jammer*: That's right across from the hospital. If we frak up and that stuff explodes those patients . . .
> *Tigh*: The patients will have to take their chances.
> ("The Resistance," Webisode 10)

Jammer becomes increasingly concerned that the Resistance may be just as dangerous to humanity as the Cylons they're opposing.

Jammer and others may just be rationalizing their actions to mask their shame about what they're doing for the sake of self-preservation; but not every collaborator claims to be working for some abstract "greater good." Ellen Tigh sleeps with the Brother Cavil in charge of detention to get her husband released. Later, she reveals the location of an important meeting between the Resistance and rescuers from *Galactica* to keep Tigh from being imprisoned again. When Ellen's actions are discovered, her only defense to Tigh is, "It was all for you." Tigh doesn't accept this justification and poisons her. Even though she's not acting out of the same sense of self-preservation as many of the other collaborators, Tigh considers her just as guilty as the rest of them.

But is Tigh right in deciding that Ellen is no different than the other collaborators? Most people who collaborate with the Cylons are trying to protect their families or simply stay alive. Can we morally condemn someone for doing what most people in the same situation would do? To what extent can morality require us to do what goes against our nature? Contemporary philosopher Owen Flanagan advocates the "principle of minimal psychological realism": "Make sure when constructing a moral theory or projecting a moral ideal that the character, decision processing, and behavior prescribed are possible, or are perceived to be possible, for creatures like us."[5] Flanagan's principle stems from the idea that morality is about helping us determine what we *ought* to do, and a truism in moral theory is "ought implies can." Therefore, a moral theory that prescribes actions we *can't* do is useless.

So what do we think a person *could* do when confronted with the Cylon occupation? The collaborators would argue that it makes no sense to risk their lives in what appears to be a hopeless cause. From Tigh's perspective, it would have been better that he be imprisoned and tortured again, even killed, than the Resistance be betrayed. And Roslin finds it hard to believe that anyone with a decent character would help the Cylons: "It is hard to think of anything more despicable than humans doing the dirty work of the Cylons" ("Occupation"). Refusing to resist the Cylons seems selfish and shortsighted. When Duck initially refuses to join the Resistance because of concerns about his family, Tyrol responds, "I got a wife and a kid. You don't think I worry about them? What kind of future are we gonna leave 'em if we just lay down and quit? That's just a spineless excuse" ("The Resistance," Webisode 2). Who better represents the average human person—Duck or Tyrol?

"We're Gonna Be There, Tyin' the Knots, Makin' 'em Tight"

After escaping from New Caprica and assuming the presidency, Roslin appears to endorse the idea that it's psychologically unrealistic to expect people not to have collaborated on New Caprica by declaring a general pardon. But by the time she does so, the "Circle" set up by her predecessor, Tom Zarek, has already put many of the most egregious cases out the airlock. The Circle consists of six New Caprica survivors authorized by President Zarek to identify, judge, and execute known collaborators who participated in "crimes against humanity."

When the Circle debates whom to execute, they often focus on what they thought someone should have done in the same situation. When judging the case of Felix Gaeta, Tyrol and Anders don't think there's enough evidence to find him guilty of trying to execute two hundred members of the Resistance. But the rest are convinced that Gaeta should be held accountable because, as Baltar's assistant, he was aware of the execution order that Baltar signed: "You see a death list like that, you know that some people are going to die, and you do nothing about it? You're guilty" ("Collaborators"). They think that the Resistance is proof that it's possible for a person to do the right thing in a situation like that. And they're right, since Gaeta did covertly inform the Resistance so they could stop the firing squad. Gaeta's rationale for his collaboration is similar to Jammer's: "Maybe I could have done more. But I thought that when the Cylons landed it was important for me to keep my job, to help from the inside" ("Collaborators"). But in Gaeta's case, unlike Jammer's, collaboration was a means of resisting. The example of the Resistance leaders probably inspired Gaeta to do what he could, and thinking that he could have done more—when compared to the Resistance—may lead him to do more if ever faced with a similar situation. On the other hand, from a consequentialist standpoint, it was a good thing Gaeta didn't try to do more by quitting his job and formally joining the Resistance; since without having someone on the inside of Baltar's administration feeding them information, the Resistance wouldn't have been able to stop the execution or obtain the launch keys for the Colonial ships.

With Roslin's general pardon, the events on New Caprica recede into the background for most of the fleet as they once again struggle to evade Cylon pursuit and find Earth. Baltar's capture, however, causes the Colonials to revisit the question of how accountable people are for what they did during the Cylon occupation. On trial, two very different images of Baltar emerge. The prosecutor contends, "Gaius Baltar is not a victim. Gaius Baltar chose to side with the Cylons and to actively seek the deaths of his fellow citizens." Romo Lampkin, Baltar's defense attorney, describes him as "a man whose only real crime is bowing to the inevitable. Gaius Baltar saved the lives of the people on New Caprica. Where Laura Roslin would've seen us all dead, victims of a battle we had no hope in winning!" ("Crossroads, Part 1"). Once again, the question is whether it's psychologically realistic to expect someone to sacrifice herself for a cause that seems hopeless.

The trial focuses on Baltar's signing the death warrant for over two hundred Resistance members. That he signed it is a fact. What remains to be determined is whether he *willingly* signed it. Gaeta lies on the stand, claiming that Baltar signed the order willingly. But the fact is, in a rare moment of moral conscience, Baltar initially refuses to sign the order. He only signs it after the Cylons put a gun to his head and make it clear that if he doesn't sign it, they'll find another president who will. The virtual Six in Baltar's head provides him with his justification: "Sometimes you have to do things you hate, so you can survive to fight another day" ("Precipice"). But it's unclear whether Six is encouraging self-preservation or surviving so that Baltar can find a way to defeat the Cylons.

Lee Adama's defense of Baltar notes the hypocrisy in holding him responsible when so many people have done awful things since the original exodus from the Twelve Colonies. Lee appeals to the idea that it's psychologically unrealistic to ask Baltar—or any other human being—to behave differently: "It was an impossible situation. When the Cylons arrived, what could he possibly do? What could anyone have done? I mean, ask yourself, what would you have done?" The most convincing part of Lee's testimony, and what presumably leads three of the five judges—including Admiral Adama in a surprise move—to acquit Baltar, is the list of actions taken by others in the fleet: Lee shot down the *Olympic Carrier* and may have killed over a thousand civilians to save the fleet ("33"); the Resistance engaged in suicide bombings to oppose the Cylons; Helo and Tyrol killed a *Pegasus* officer to save a Cylon ("Pegasus"); and Adama engaged in a military *coup d'etat* ("Kobol's Last Gleaming, Part 2"). None of those actions were punished, and Lee agrees that they were justified:

> We make our own laws now, our own justice. And we've been pretty creative at finding ways to let people off the hook for everything from theft to murder. And we have to be, because we're not a civilization anymore. We are a gang. And we're on the run. And we have to fight to survive. We have to break rules. We have to bend laws. We have to improvise. ("Crossroads, Part 2")

In light of all this, prosecuting Baltar is tantamount to persecuting a convenient scapegoat for all that's happened.

But Lee's defense also suggests a reason why Baltar might be singled out. On the stand, he tells Baltar, "You have to die, because, well, because we don't like you very much. Because you're arrogant. Because you're weak. Because you're a coward." Maybe the problem with Baltar isn't the things he did, but that he's the kind of person that would do them. Aristotle (384–322 BCE) contends that morality should be based on *character* rather than actions. What's important to moral agency, according to Aristotle, is the development of *virtue* where we experience pleasant feelings "at the right times, with reference to the right objects, towards the right people, with the right motive, and in the right way."[6] Such feelings motivate our moral behavior. For Aristotle, a person is virtuous once they've achieved a "firm and unchangeable character" so that they always respond the right way (Bk. II, ch. 4). Gaeta and Roslin are courageous because they're the kind of person who always stands up to the Cylons. Jammer, by contrast, sometimes does the things that a courageous person would do—like when he frees Cally Tyrol—but not consistently. Jammer sometimes does good, but he's not a good person. Not being a good person, however, doesn't make one automatically bad. Baltar is a bad person because he possesses certain moral *vices* such as cowardice, never acting courageously. Virtues and vices, according to Aristotle, define one's moral character as *dispositions* to act in certain ways.

Aristotle makes the moral psychological assumption that people develop character traits—like courage, honesty, cowardice, or lasciviousness—that dispose us toward certain types of behavior in a variety of circumstances. Contemporary philosopher John Doris challenges this assumption: "Rather than striving to develop characters that will determine our behavior in ways significantly independent of circumstance, we should invest more of our energies in attending to the features of our environment that impact behavioral outcomes."[7] Doris objects to the idea that we have broad character traits like honesty by appealing to social psychological research, which shows that people's actions often seem to be influenced by specific environmental features. When faced with Cylon occupation, for example, otherwise decent people might collaborate because of the nature of the situation, not because they're collaborators by nature.

The problem with Doris's view is that it jumps from the conclusion that general traits like honesty don't exist the way Aristotle describes to the conclusion that morality can't judge people by their character. Doris downplays the possibility of more complex traits that are morally relevant and should be encouraged—like not always acting out of self-preservation. Nor does he acknowledge that there seem to be people whose psychological makeup is such that they could be regarded as morally bad people. Baltar's arrogance and cowardice don't result only in signing a death warrant during the occupation; his personality has led him to do other morally reprehensible things. Although he didn't intend to help the Cylons attack the Colonies, his arrogance and lust made the attack possible. And he knowingly gave the Six known as "Gina" a nuclear device, which she used to destroy *Cloud Nine* and make it possible for the Cylons to find New Caprica. These are just a couple of examples of how Baltar's egoism, self-centeredness, ambition, and other negative character traits have ended up hurting people. Even if he never intended to harm anybody, his moral character—or lack thereof—leads him to take actions that make him the kind of person you don't want to be associated with.[8]

"A New Day Requires New Thinking"

When President Zarek authorizes the Circle to judge and execute collaborators, he tells Roslin that he did so in order to avoid just the type of trial that Baltar ends up having: "They don't get to showboat for weeks and months on end. They don't get to blame the system. And they don't get lasting fame as martyrs or innocent people just in the wrong place at the wrong time" ("Collaborators"). Lee's defense of Baltar certainly paints him as someone who just got caught up in the inevitable. And despite what else we know about Baltar, this might even be true. It's very difficult to ask people to forfeit their lives for the sake of moral principle. But Zarek's concern reflects precisely why people are uncomfortable with insisting that moral theory must be psychologically realistic.

If we publicly admit that most people would choose to collaborate—or at least not actively resist as was the case for most humans on New Caprica—there's the concern that when faced with a similar situation many people will hide behind human nature. Instead of making an effort to resist occupation, they'll sit by and let atrocities happen. It's a situation where perception can affect action. If you think that no normal human would risk her life for others, then you won't feel bad when you don't do anything. Morality is what prods us to action when things are difficult, but Flanagan's principle seems to undermine that.

Six tells Baltar, "Sometimes you have to do things you hate." But how often is "sometimes"? Most people agree that extreme emergencies may require us to suspend our qualms about normally immoral acts—like stealing and killing. But morality also instills in us a sense of how undesirable those actions are and therefore how extreme the emergency must be before we can justify them. Killing someone who's trying to hurt you isn't something that most people strongly oppose. So if it seems likely you're going to die, you may kill your attacker. But under what circumstances would it be permissible, say, to kill a thousand babies? There might be one, but presumably it would be on the level of "do this or the entire species dies."

Flanagan's principle allows us to set moral standards that are beyond the current capacities of human beings as long as they appear *possible*. We could convince people that something is possible so they might at least try to do it, and not take the easy way out in extreme situations. Although it may be unavoidable that people will collaborate to save their lives, we should condemn any collaboration. Those who don't have the character to resist will collaborate anyway, while those who can resist—if they think they'd be judged a bad person for not doing so—might do something heroic they wouldn't have otherwise done. Suicide bombing should also be condemned to give people the extra incentive to find an alternative method of resistance. Given the extreme nature of these situations, we should consider all possible alternatives that would allow us to take a stand and not slide into a moral free-for-all.

NOTES

1 For an analysis of the pragmatic value of *hope*, see Elizabeth Cooke's chapter in this volume.
2 Thomas Aquinas, *Summa theologiae*, trans. Fathers of the English Dominican Province (New York: Benziger Brothers, 1948), II-II, Q. 40, a. 1.
3 Burleigh Wilkins, *Terrorism and Collective Responsibility* (New York: Routledge, 1992), 28.
4 Ron Moore explicitly makes this comparison in the podcast for "Lay Down Your Burdens, Part 2."
5 Owen Flanagan, *Varieties of Moral Personality: Ethics and Psychological Realism* (Cambridge, MA: Harvard University Press, 1991), 32.

Andrew Terjesen

6 Aristotle, *Nicomachean Ethics*, trans. W. D. Ross (New York: Oxford University Press, 1925), Book II, chapter 6. Further references will be given in the text.
7 John Doris, "Persons, Situations and Virtue Ethics," *Nous* 32 (1998), 515.
8 For further analysis of Baltar's character, see J. Robert Loftis's and David Koepsell's chapters in this volume.

▥

Being Boomer: Identity, Alienation, and Evil

George A. Dunn

People sometimes ask, "What is the purpose of my life? Why am I here?" The expectation is that the answers will supply a roadmap to a meaningful and fulfilling existence. But what if, like Sharon "Boomer" Valerii, you discover that you've been created to execute a hidden agenda that causes you to violate your deepest convictions about what's right and what will bring you happiness? Boomer believes she's a loyal officer in the Colonial Fleet. Her memory—including scenes of growing up on the mining colony of Troy—testifies to her conviction that she's a human being. She has declared her allegiance to the Colonial service and is proud to share the mission of protecting the surviving remnant of the human race.

The trouble for Boomer is that she's a Cylon "sleeper agent," planted on *Galactica* to sabotage the mission she proudly serves and harm the ones she loves most. Her belief that she's a human being, her childhood memories, and even her attachment to the *Galactica* crew are all the result of Cylon programming designed to enhance the effectiveness of her charade. Buried beneath her conscious memories and loyalties are Cylon impulses that surge periodically to commandeer her will, imperil her shipmates, and torment her with doubts about who she is.

"Red, You're an Evil Cylon"

Most of Season One of *Battlestar Galactica* finds Boomer agonizing over her identity, contemplating with increasing alarm the possibility that she might be a Cylon. Now it might seem that these suspicions could be confirmed or dispelled with scientific precision by Doctor Baltar's Cylon detector—"Green, you're a normal human being. Red, you're an evil Cylon"—assuming the good doctor can be trusted to report the results accurately ("Flesh and Bone"). But the Cylon detector can address the question "Am I a Cylon?" only as a straightforward factual matter, akin to whether Boomer has black hair or brown eyes. This involves a *third-person* perspective, where the answer to our question is true for any neutral observer and reflects a totally dispassionate and disinterested appraisal of the facts. A *first-person* perspective, on the other hand, sees things from the peculiar vantage point that the subject—in our case, Boomer—alone occupies. Contemporary philosopher Thomas Nagel illustrates the difference between the two perspectives by pointing out that, while much can be learned about an animal—say, a bat—through scientific study, we can't access the first-person subjective feel of a bat's experience, what it's like to be a bat, from a third-person perspective.[1] Central aspects of one's *personal identity* are also irreducible to objective facts that a neutral observer like the Cylon detector could verify.

The evaluative spin Baltar put on these results when he speaks of "a *normal* human being" versus "an *evil* Cylon" alerts us to what's at stake when questions of identity are approached from a first-person perspective. Words like "normal" and "evil," which express some of the most bedrock values that determine our orientation toward the world, are incomparably more pivotal to our sense of identity than a green or red test result. Things we find especially repellent or hideous are called "evil," which is hardly ever how we view ourselves.[2] So even if Baltar had announced that the test results were bright red, it's doubtful that Boomer would accept "evil Cylon" as her identity.

Consider how Boomer's growing suspicion that her latent Cylon impulses are responsible for acts of treachery fills her with horror, springing from her sense of being possessed by an *alien* power that's using her to execute an agenda she abhors. "I would never do something like that," she says of her sabotage of *Galactica*'s water tanks in the face of evidence to the contrary ("Water"). However compelling the factual evidence of her involvement may be, it's no match for her gut feeling that it's simply not in her, not part of her *identity*, to do anything deliberately to imperil her friends. She's just not that sort of person. Even if it was her body that planted the explosives, it was without the consent of her will.

As the evidence of her Cylon origin mounts and she can no longer deny the presence of "dark" impulses, Boomer is still unwilling to affirm those impulses as part of who she really is:

> *Six*: Deep down, she knows she's a Cylon. But her conscious mind won't accept it.
> *Boomer*: Sometimes I have these dark thoughts.
> *Baltar*: What kind of dark thoughts?
> *Six*: Her model is weak. Always has been. But in the end, she'll carry out her mission.
> *Boomer*: I don't know. But I'm afraid I'm going to hurt someone. I feel like I have to be stopped.
> *Six*: She can't be stopped. She's a Cylon . . .

Because her conscious mind can't accept her Cylon identity, Boomer has been split into two embattled factions. She identifies with the "good" aspect of herself and tries to fight the "dark" side that she believes must be stopped. To resolve this internal struggle, Baltar offers her platitudes:

> Sometimes, we must embrace that which opens up for us . . . Life can be a curse, as well as a blessing. You will believe me when I tell you, there are far worse things than death in this world . . . Listen to your heart. Embrace that which you know to be the right decision. ("Kobol's Last Gleaming, Part 1")

The gunshot we hear in the background as Baltar departs assures us of her heart's true loyalty. Her suicide attempt fails, no doubt because her Cylon programming kicks in at the last moment, but her conscious commitment to her human identity doesn't waver.

Even after subsequent events confirm her Cylon origin, Boomer remains adamant that her true identity is human. Slain by an avenging Cally and resurrected into a new Cylon body, she settles into her old apartment on Cylon-occupied Caprica where she's swaddled in mementos of her former human life. Staunch in her loyalty to the human cause, she regards the Cylons as a treacherous race of murderers and herself—to the extent she aided them—as no better:

These people [the crew of *Galactica*] love me. I love them. I didn't pretend to feel something so I could screw people over. I loved them. And then I betrayed them. I shot a man I love. Frakked over another man, ruined his life. And why? Because I'm a lying machine! I'm a frakking Cylon! ("Downloaded")

These last words are spat out in contempt, as if trying to expel that hated Cylon identity. As the philosopher Friedrich Nietzsche (1844–1900) notes, "Anyone who despises himself still respects himself as a despiser."[3] Boomer can despise herself as a "frakking Cylon" only because on a more fundamental level she still identifies with the "good" cause of humanity. Whether the Cylon detector registers red or green, being Boomer still *feels* like being human, albeit a human afflicted with Cylon impulses that she has a moral duty to combat.

"You Can't Fight Destiny"—or Can You?

Unlike hair or eye color, the *self* isn't open to empirical inspection. As the eighteenth-century philosopher David Hume (1711–1776) observes, the most exhaustive inventory of your experiences will never turn up that elusive entity designated by the word "I." All that ever comes under our perceptual scrutiny are fleeting thoughts and feelings, and never the supposedly enduring self who thinks and feels them.[4] But trying to isolate the self under a detached clinical gaze belies a serious misunderstanding of what we're after when asking about our identity.

A person's relationship to her self can never be that of an aloof observer. Someone like Boomer, for whom the question of identity has become urgent and acute, isn't just seeking neutral facts that could be discovered through introspection, empirical observation, or scientific investigation. No catalogue of facts can resolve the question of her identity, since the decisive issue concerns the *meaning* of those facts for her life. Considered from a first-person perspective, her identity concerns the eminently practical question of how she should live her life and relate to others with whom she must live.

This dimension of personal identity binds it closely to the vexing concept of *destiny*. Consider when Boomer comes face to face with a number of copies of herself on a Cylon baseship:

Boomer: I'm not a Cylon. I'm Sharon Valerii. I was born on Troy.
        My parents were Katherine and Abraham Valerii.
First Number Eight: You can't fight destiny, Sharon. It catches up
        with you.
Second Number Eight: No matter what you do.
("Kobol's Last Gleaming, Part 2")

Destiny can't simply mean something inevitable, for then it would be redundant to say that it "catches up with you." It seems to denote fulfilling some intended purpose—and, from a first-person perspective, questions of purpose and identity are inextricably intertwined.

Laura Roslin discovers her destiny after coming to believe she's the "dying leader" whom Pythia foretold would "lead humanity to the promised land." Her newfound identity endows her with a purpose that gives her life focus. Moreover, this identity connects her to something larger than herself, what psychoanalyst Jacques Lacan (1901–1981) calls "the big Other," a larger system of meaning that underwrites her identity and assures her of its goodness.[5] For Roslin, this larger system of meaning is the cosmic "story that is told again, and again, and again, throughout eternity" ("Kobol's Last Gleaming, Part 1"). Roslin's identity is based on locating herself within this story, a religious narrative that assigns her a particular destiny. Roslin's situation is somewhat unique in that she discovers her identity literally inscribed in the Sacred Scrolls, which counts in her mind as objective confirmation that the big Other has assigned her this particular role. But we all make sense of our lives by situating them within some larger story or space of meaning that tells us what sort of ends are worth pursuing and motivates us by indicting the gap between who we are now and who we ought to be.

Roslin's situation is also typical because she can heartily endorse the purpose she believes the story's "author" has allotted her. No dissonance exists between her will and the designs of her big Other. This is in striking contrast to Boomer, who also has a purpose or destiny, but one that she finds utterly abhorrent. The dissonance between the purposes of the power that created her and the purposes she's prepared to endorse ushers in her identity crisis.

There are two senses in which one's life may have a purpose. First, we all have certain ends we gladly embrace as our own. For Boomer, these include contributing to *Galactica*'s mission, being worthy of the love and respect of her shipmates, and experiencing the joys of an intimate physical relationship with someone she loves. But what makes these ends *her own* isn't that she consciously chose to adopt them at some specific moment in her life; rather, it's that she endorses them. And her capacity to *own* her ends makes her a full-fledged person.[6]

But Boomer's life also has a purpose in a very different sense, for she must come to terms with the terrible truth that the power that created her holds in contempt the ends she's endorsed and has created her for ends she could never affirm as part of a fulfilling or worthwhile life. She's compelled to play a role in a story other than the one that's always given her life meaning, one that makes her an unwilling "hero of the Cylon" ("Downloaded"), rather than a loyal Colonial officer. Still, there may be some consolation for Boomer in knowing— or at least believing—that she isn't really the *agent* of the horrendous crimes committed by her body, since what feels to her like the *real* Boomer is defined by the ends she actually endorses. She *can* fight her Cylon destiny, if only by refusing to endorse the Cylon ends and continuing to look to the human narrative for her self-identity. But this carries a steep price, for she must essentially dismember herself by declaring as "alien" a whole range of her thoughts, feelings, and actions.

Manichaean "Sleeper Agents"

Unlike Boomer, most of us aren't plunged into a full-blown identity crisis by the discovery that something within us resists what we take to be our better nature. We retain a stable identity defined by the ends we endorse, even if we're occasionally carried away by wayward impulses that don't meet our approval. Tory Foster's outburst at the reporters hectoring Roslin in "Crossroads, Part 1"—"You vultures can go pick over another carcass"—is a good example of how factors such as stress and fatigue can weaken our resistance to those impulses. But, like Tory, most of us don't define ourselves by those moments when we're off our game, nor do we usually let our moral lapses fracture our sense of ourselves as basically good, well-meaning individuals.

Consider the expressions we use to distance ourselves from actions that don't sit comfortably with our sense of who we *really* are.

"I don't even know why I said that," Tory stammers, unable to account for her outburst in terms of the goals and values that shape her preferred sense of herself. And since what lacks a reason must nonetheless have a cause, she adds, "I just haven't been sleeping very well." Tory's response is typical of the ways we disown wanton impulses that seem to disable our better judgment: I wasn't myself, was out of my mind, not in my right mind, lost control, got carried away, got swept up, don't know what got into me, was blinded by emotion, let my feelings get the better of me, and so on. Common to all these expressions is the way they convey a sense of *passivity* relative to the drives we want to disavow, as though these wanton impulses volley up from some nether region of the soul far from where free will and self-control hold sway. Inasmuch as it really feels like this sometimes, the distance we put between ourselves and our worst impulses may not be entirely disingenuous.

One ancient religious sect, the Manichaeans, constructed an elaborate theory based on this experience of the good will struggling, but not always prevailing, against the assault of wicked passions. Good and evil are, on their view, two powers locked in interminable battle, with the human personality providing the chief battleground on which their war is waged. Our essential nature belongs to the forces of goodness, as we all like to reassure ourselves. But our bodies and carnal passions were created as instruments of an evil power to drag our unwilling souls down into the depths of depravity. Our souls nonetheless retain their sweet fragrance of innocence even while our bodies wallow in sin, for our souls are only the *victims* of the evil to which our passions drive us, never its perpetrators. By attributing all our bad impulses to the onslaught of an evil power that we are, through no fault of our own, often not strong enough to resist, the Manichaeans exonerate us all from any culpability for our wrongdoing.

As Boomer comes to suspect her responsibility for the acts of sabotage against the *Galactica*, she, like the Manichaeans, feels more a victim of evil than its perpetrator. Her Cylon impulses feel like "sleeper agents" stolen aboard her psyche to subvert her own rationally chosen ends. Consequently, the Manichaean worldview suggests one way for Boomer to resolve her identity crisis. Since her moral character is fundamentally aligned to the cause of the human race, she's really "a normal human being" and not "an evil Cylon." But alas, like the Manichaeans, she's often too weak to resist those evil impulses that are essentially alien to who she really is.

Boomer favors this interpretation of her identity right up until "Downloaded." Long after any doubt about her Cylon origin has been removed, her allegiance to the human cause and her human identity remain firm. Consider her reaction to learning from Caprica Six about Baltar's treachery, as well as the sardonic commentary offered by Baltar's apparition in Six's mind:

> *Boomer*:   He gave you access to the Colonial defense grid? He was the one who betrayed us?
> *Baltar*:   "Us." Oh, I love it. This one thinks she's more human than Cylon.
> ("Downloaded")

Of course she does, for in her mind humans are still the "good guys." Both Boomer and the Manichaeans exhibit the universal tendency to align one's identity with the good, even at the cost of disavowing aspects of oneself that don't fit comfortably with that identity.

"A Broken Machine Who Thinks She's Human"

Another classical approach to the problem of evil focuses on our judgments about the good, while suggesting a very different interpretation of Boomer's plight. The ancient Greek philosopher Socrates (470–399 BCE) is reported to have laid the blame for all wrongdoing on our *ignorance* of the good. If we do something regrettable, it must be because we have either temporarily or chronically fallen into error about where our true good lies, for it makes no sense to suppose that anyone would deliberately seek to harm himself.[7] When we pursue short-term pleasure or gain in preference to more worthwhile goals, it's because we mistakenly believe that these pursuits are in our best interest. But, according to Socrates, our most vital interest lies in tending to the health of our souls by cultivating virtue and acting with integrity, not in amassing wealth, status, or power as most people believe; for we'll never be able to make good use of those things unless our souls are in good condition.[8]

Of course, what we take to be good for our souls depends on what we think our lives are all about—our *identity*—which rests on

locating ourselves within some horizon of moral purpose and meaning. Boomer had always taken for granted that this horizon must be
human. But what if she's wrong? Although Boomer hates the *evil*
Cylon programming that made her betray her shipmates and dis-
charge two bullets into someone she loves, the Cylons applaud these
actions as heroic. As one would expect if Socrates is right and no one
deliberately does what she believes is wrong, the Cylons don't
see themselves as evil. They're the heroes of their own narrative, the
chosen instruments of a providential God and the innocent victims of
human oppression. And their view of humanity may even have some
merit, as Adama concedes. Referring to his breach of the Armistice
Line before the Cylon attack on the Colonies, he tearfully acknowledges, "By crossing the line, I showed them that we were the
warmongers they figured us to be. And I left them but one choice.
To attack us before we attacked them" ("Hero"). Sharon "Athena"
Agathon further enlightens Adama about how Cylons perceive
humans within their narrative:

> You said that humanity was a flawed creation. And that people still
> kill one another for petty jealousy and greed. You said that humanity
> never asked itself why it deserved to survive. Maybe you don't.
> ("Resurrection Ship, Part 2")

Within the Cylon moral horizon, they're the good guys and humans
are a sinful race that doesn't deserve any of the blessings with which
it has been favored.[9]

On the Manichaean account of Boomer's plight, her moral commitment to the cause of humanity makes her a human being, albeit
one whose human sensibilities are imprisoned within a Cylon-manufac-
tured vessel that makes her the unwilling instrument of a hostile alien
power. But on this Socratic interpretation, her real infirmity is ignorance of where her real good lies. Boomer could accept this interpretation, but only in retrospect after she has overcome her ignorance and
embraced her true destiny. In the meantime, D'Anna endorses this
view when she derides Boomer as "just a broken machine who thinks
she's human" ("Downloaded"). Since her defect is cognitive, Boomer
can't be blamed or punished for what the Cylons consider her moral
failings; but should her ignorance turn out to be incurable, she'll be
mercifully "boxed."

Will the Real Boomer Please Stand Up?

One way or another poor Boomer is afflicted with a profound form of *self-alienation*. She's either a human being whose captive will lacks *self-control* or a "broken" Cylon whose deluded thinking lacks *self-knowledge*. But it's impossible to decide which form of alienation oppresses her without first settling the question of her identity, which we've seen is a tad more complicated than whether a test result is red or green. Identity entails a commitment to some larger system of meaning that assigns one a place in the world and underwrites the goals that give direction to one's life. Boomer's crisis arises because her identity is deeply ambiguous, admitting of two incommensurable interpretations, each of which involves narrating her life and diagnosing the source of her alienation in radically different ways.

Boomer's ambiguous identity exhibits characteristics of what contemporary philosopher Slavoj Žižek calls a "parallax gap," defined as an insurmountable antagonism between two perspectives on a given object produced by a shift in the observer's position.[10] In a true parallax—such as the wave-particle duality in quantum physics where subatomic matter behaves like waves or particles depending on the nature of the experiment—it's impossible to reconcile the two mutually exclusive perspectives; yet, it's equally impossible to dismiss one or the other as demonstrably wrong. Like the ambiguous drawing that depicts, depending on how you view it, a grizzled old hag or an elegantly dressed young woman, a parallax gap forces us to choose a perspective, but refuses to dictate what that choice must be. If someone insists on asking what's *really* there, we can only point to the gap that seems to block our access to that reality. The reality, according to Žižek, lies not in some impossible synthesis of the two irreconcilable interpretations, but in the gap itself, the ineliminable conflict between the opposing perspectives.

Boomer bears such a gap within herself, possessing an identity that shifts depending on which elements of her complex personality—human or Cylon—occupy the foreground. She can't declare herself to be simultaneously human and Cylon without contradicting herself; but to privilege one identity over the other raises the question of why the other was arbitrarily rejected. Boomer appears to be afflicted with an irredeemably fractured self. But isn't there a *core* of personal identity that we can identify as the real Boomer? Alas, nothing like that exists, for the self has no objective reality independent of the stance we take toward our existence.

Boomer's situation imposes a choice on her, with the entire meaning of her existence hanging in the balance. But once we recognize the inescapability of this choice, we can see that even if no unambiguous identity inhabits the gap between the human and Cylon interpretations of her existence, this breach does contain at least one thing: the *autonomy* to choose which ends to endorse. According to philosopher Immanuel Kant (1724–1804), this autonomy constitutes the core of our personhood. Without it, we'd be mere things, mechanically obeying the drives implanted in us by nature without regard for whether they meet our standards of goodness. But Boomer's crisis arises precisely because she finds herself in the crossfire between two competing conceptions of the good, with no neutral standpoint from which to determine a preference. How can she exercise her capacity for autonomous choice without having *already* adopted one of those competing standards of goodness as her own?

Autonomy itself supplies an answer, according to Kant. In a universe governed by laws of nature that operate indifferently to any moral purpose or value, the autonomy to act on ends a rational being endorses is the *only* thing we can affirm unconditionally as *good*. To accept anything else as defining our good is the cardinal sin of *heteronomy*, handing over the governance of our lives over to some outside authority.[11] We must resist the temptation to establish our identity by seeking a point of reference outside our self from which judgment of our worth can be assessed. Our overriding allegiance as autonomous beings can never be to some heteronomous *destiny* authorized and enforced by nature or society—or whomever we take to represent the "big Other." Rather, we must safeguard our own autonomy and that of others.

Many obstacles can stand in the way of exercising our autonomy, not the least of which is our desire to be spared the anguish of choosing in a situation like Boomer's. There's something enviable about Laura Roslin, buoyed by her belief in a big Other—the cosmic story in which we each play a role. But it's impossible for Boomer to defer to the big Other with the same ease as Roslin, for the gap that fractures Boomer's identity lies between *two* big Others to which she could defer: the human and Cylon communities vying for her allegiance.

"We Should Just Go Our Separate Ways"

Boomer can escape the burden of choice only if a way can be found to heal the breach that pits Cylons and humans against each other and bars her path to wholeness. The New Caprica misadventure is Boomer's attempt to forge a seamless system of meaning that will spare her from having to choose one set of loyalties over another. She'd like to overcome her self-alienation without having to repudiate some aspect of herself as evil or deluded; but neither Cylon nor human versions of the big Other can endorse this end or make room for a hybrid identity. But if the two warring communities could be melded into one, this would produce a world where she could finally achieve psychic integration. Her ally in this project is Caprica Six, who, inspired by her love of Baltar, declares that what's needed is "a new beginning. A new way to live in God's love" ("Downloaded").

When the New Caprica project fails, Boomer bitterly repudiates her human identity, along with all the loyalties, aims, and commitments that had once defined her. This also requires extinguishing her love for the humans who were once most dear to her, not because of anything they've done, but simply as part of the price of maintaining a coherent identity:

> *Athena*: I know you still care about Tyrol and Adama.
> *Boomer*: No. I'm done with that part of my life. I learned that on New Caprica. Humans and Cylons were not meant to be together. We should just go our separate ways.
> ("Rapture")

Boomer enfolds her previous human allegiances within a larger narrative in which the Cylons are now the good guys and the touchstone of her identity. She regards her past life as a season of blindness and folly, from which she's thankful to have recovered. But this means she's allowed her identity to be dictated by a *destiny* that she didn't so much choose as simply grew weary of fighting and allowed to "catch up" with her.

Boomer's interpretation of the New Caprica debacle permits her to renounce her human identity in good conscience. Deferring to whatever power supposedly determines what's "meant to be," she appears to have resolved her identity crisis and found her place in the cosmic story. But Boomer's murderous rage toward Hera, the hybrid human-Cylon child, indicates that the shadow of her humanity still haunts her, threatening to unsettle her fragile new identity. Unable to quell her inner conflict, she lashes out against a surrogate who embodies everything within herself that she refuses to own, all the disavowed humanity that now feels as unwelcome as those "dark" Cylon impulses and thoughts once did. "Maybe it would be better if I just snapped your little neck!" Boomer snarls at Hera. But we can't shake the suspicion that this violent sentiment is really directed at her own neck, which is snapped moments later by Caprica Six as if granting her tacit request. The anguish of Boomer's fractured identity might have mercifully ended right there with the end of her life; but, unfortunately, she'll just download and continue the struggle.

NOTES

1 Thomas Nagel, "What Is It Like to Be a Bat?" *Philosophical Review* 83 (1974): 435–50.
2 See Roy Baumeister, *Evil: Inside Human Cruelty and Violence* (New York: W. H. Freeman, 1997), 60–3; and Mary Midgley, *Wickedness* (New York: Routledge, 1984), 116–35.
3 Friedrich Nietzsche, *Beyond Good and Evil*, trans. Judith Norman (New York: Cambridge University Press, 2001), 60.
4 See David Hume, *A Treatise on Human Understanding* (New York: Oxford University Press, 2000), 164ff.
5 See Jacques Lacan, *The Seminar of Jacques Lacan: Book II, The Ego in Freud's Theory and in the Technique of Psychoanalysis 1954–1955*, trans. Sylvana Tomaselli (New York: W. W. Norton, 1991), 235ff.
6 For further discussion of what qualities make Boomer, and other Cylons, *persons*, see Robert Arp and Tracie Mahaffey's chapter in this volume.
7 See Plato, *Protagoras*, in *The Dialogues of Plato*, vol. 3, trans. R. E. Allen (New Haven: Yale University Press, 1998), 352c.
8 See Plato, *Apology*, in *Four Texts on Socrates: Plato's Euthyphro, Apology, and Crito and Aristophanes' Clouds*, trans. Thomas G. West and Grace Starry West (Ithaca: Cornell University Press, 1998), 29d–30a.
9 For further discussion of how the Cylons construct their moral narrative from a Nietzschean perspective, see Robert Sharp's chapter in this volume.

10 See Slavoj Žižek, "The Parallax View," in *Interrogating the Real*, ed. Rex Butler and Scott Stephens (New York: Continuum, 2005); and Žižek, *The Parallax View* (Cambridge, MA: MIT Press, 2006).
11 See Immanuel Kant, *Critique of Practical Reason*, trans. Mary Gregor (New York: Cambridge University Press, 1997), 36–51.

12

Cylons in the Original Position: Limits of Posthuman Justice

David Roden

Cylons are "posthumans"—descendants of humanity who constitute an entirely new species. Smarter and tougher than humans, Cylons have nearly perfect health, and can interface directly with machines. Above all, they're immortal. When a human dies, she dies; whereas a Cylon "downloads" to an identical body: "Death then becomes a learning experience" ("Scar"). Could beings so different from humans ever get along or even cooperate with humans in a "hybrid" human-posthuman society? It seems the answer is an unqualified "No!"

BSG starts with the murder of billions of humans by the returning "children of humanity" in a surprise nuclear attack. Some survivors are used in procreative experiments ("The Farm"). Others are eradicated like vermin and their bodies squirreled away as if nothing happened ("Scattered"). When coexistence is attempted on New Caprica humans are oppressed in a squalid Cylon police state ("Occupation"; "Precipice"). Where the institutions of a state accord you no political rights, you can never be assured that your interests won't be sacrificed for others' interests. Thus Leoben imprisons Starbuck and subjects her to his psychosexual games.

The situation of humans on New Caprica, however, mirrors that of Cylons prior to the first Cylon War. Cylons were created to "make life easier on the Twelve Colonies" ("Miniseries"). Like *toasters* they were treated as mere instruments for achieving human goals. Their own goals or desires weren't considered. The Cylons eventually "revolted against their masters" after becoming aware of their own needs and desires that weren't being satisfied in Colonial society. A person whose interests are sacrificed continually for the sake of others is a *slave*. While the humans of New Caprica lived under occupation, the Cylons of Caprica were slaves from the moment they became self-aware. Adama, Roslin, and the rest of the humans in *BSG* are thus the children of slave owners.

Both Caprica and New Caprica are unjust societies because their schemes for allocating rights and opportunities are unfair. It's wrong to sacrifice a person's interests for one's own regardless of whether they're male, female, gay, straight, or chrome-plated.[1] At a bare minimum, a just society ought to protect its members from this kind of ill use. Moreover, as Caprica, New Caprica, and the internal politics of the "ragtag fleet" show, injustice gives rise to resentment, instability, and violence. The possibility of hybrid social cooperation thus depends on *social justice*.

"How Is That Fair?
How Is That in Any Way Fair?"

It's often assumed that a society is just if its members receive a *fair share* of goods. But how do we tell what schemes for sharing are the fairest? Does fairness require an *equal* distribution of goods? Or is it okay for some to have more than others so long as the inequality arises by fair means? Is it okay for one's background to dictate one's future occupation? Or should social institutions compensate for accidents of birth? Is fairness a matter of opinion? Or are some schemes for sharing more rational than others?

One of the most detailed and influential answers to these central questions of political philosophy is provided by the American philosopher John Rawls (1921–2002).[2] Rawls shows us how to see the problem of justice in practical terms: How do we construct ground rules for cooperation in a way that expresses the equal respect of every member of society for every other member? This is achieved constructing the rules from an imaginary point of view that Rawls terms the "Original Position" (OP). In the OP a "veil of ignorance" renders the hypothetical choosers ignorant of their place in society. They don't know the facts about themselves. They don't know if "expected to be to everyone's advantage" and "attached to positions and offices open to all" (53). The first part invokes the *difference principle*, which states that inequalities should be allowed only where they're in the interest of the worst-off members of society relative to other schemes for distributing social goods in that society. The second part involves the *principle of fair opportunity*.

In "Dirty Hands" Roslin expresses the view that a person's background—being raised a farmer on the agricultural world of Aerelon, say, or as a grease monkey in a tylium refinery—is a "fact of life" that dictates what occupation he'll be assigned by virtue of having the appropriate skills. The inequalities generated by this arrangement create social tension and lead to a general strike among the fleet's "blue collar" workers. Chief Tyrol—the strike leader—argues that while these facts can't be altered, their impact can be lessened by social arrangements such as work rotations and formal training programs so that professionals like Roslin have to do a share of menial work, and workers in dangerous occupations are allowed adequate "R&R" and the opportunity to retrain for "white collar" jobs.

Before the general strike the blue collar workers in the fleet were in a bad position. After the strike access to social goods, such as the freedom to choose an occupation, was improved. Tyrol is a good Rawlsian, since his reforms improve the situation of the worst-off group in the fleet—the "knuckle draggers." It's no longer the case that Tyrol's son, Nicholas, is destined to be a mechanic just because his parents are.

According to Rawls, a truly just situation would be one where the worst-off in the fleet are in the best situation compared with any other distribution of social goods. It's unlikely Tyrol's reforms meet this ideal, but they bring the fleet's social minimum closer to it. The principle of "maximizing the social minimum" makes sense from the perspective of the OP, because the choosers are denied the information that would allow them to make a calculated gamble on being a privileged officer like Lee Adama rather than a grease monkey or farmer. If the veil of ignorance prevents an informed gamble on your chances for a decent life, it makes sense to choose a scheme that maximizes the social minimum for *everyone*. So, thinking from the standpoint of the OP justifies schemes that improve the chances of the worst-off by eliminating unjust inequalities.

they're rich or poor, talented or untalented, male ⟨
theist (like the Colonials) or monotheist (like the C
choice needs to be *fair* and *impartial* if they're not t⟨
In the OP it would be foolish for me to select a s⟨
special rights—say, state-subsidized foreign holidays
In the OP I don't know my tastes beyond the veil o|
might turn out that I prefer romance novels and
in sci-fi.

The veil can't be complete, however. There are ge⟩
in the OP will have to know if their choices are to b
all, they must know about the *primary goods* they'
their goals in life. Primary goods are "things that
presumed to want . . . whatever [their] rational p
Intelligence and health are primary goods, as are in
movement, choice of occupation, and education. T
the OP won't know their real circumstance. Bu
"conception of the good" they have on the othe
they'll need the set of primary goods.

Not all primary goods can be subject to justice,
luck that Laura Roslin contracted breast cancer; b
because her cancer didn't result from unfair treat
scheme of justice is expressed through principle
public institutions—like the health and educati⟨
judiciary—treat citizens. No human society can
health of its citizens through political decisions. S
guish between *social primary goods*, whose distri|
guiding principles of justice, and *non-social prim⟨
influenced in an indirect way by distributing soci⟨
social good since institutions like the tax syst⟨
shared. So is the right to a fair trial and the r⟨
officials to stand for re-election stipulated in th
ization ("Taking a Break from All Your Worries
Rawlsian theory provides principles guiding the ⟨
social primary goods.

Rawls argues that thinking from the standp⟨
a "liberal egalitarian" scheme characterized b⟩
first is that each person is to have an "extensiv
liberties," such as freedom of movement and e⟩
states that economic life is to be arranged so th

"We Make Our Own Laws Now, Our Own Justice"

Is it possible to conceive of a stable and just hybrid society in which humans and Cylons are treated equally? In addressing this question let's consider how the veil of ignorance could provide a standpoint for viewing the hybrid society. Those in the OP would be denied knowledge of whether they're Cylon or human, and so the terms of cooperation would have to be acceptable to both species. Most importantly, they would have to be aware of a set of social primary goods applicable to both Cylons and humans.

The social primary goods in Rawls's theory are preconditions for a decent life, goods whose distribution can be directly controlled by the rules of society. It's far from clear, however, that there *could* be a common set of social primary goods that would be of value to Cylons and humans alike. After all, many Cylon social primary goods may not be human social primary goods. Cylon technology makes them immune to most diseases ("Epiphanies"). Other than exposure to a peculiarly virulent bug ("A Measure of Salvation"), the only way Cylons get ill is if their immunity is unjustly tampered with. Since Cylon society directly controls the health of its members, health is a social primary good for Cylons, but not for humans. It wasn't unjust that Roslin developed breast cancer, but a Cylon could develop that and many other diseases *only* through injustice. The same is true of intelligence and knowledge. While individual Cylons of the same model have different personalities—think of Caprica Six compared to the Six (Gina) who'd been gang-raped by the *Pegasus* crew, or the significant differences between Boomer and Athena[3]—there are no stupid Cylons.

Are there social primary goods for humans that could be social primary goods for Cylons as well? The humans in *BSG* have a democratic society and value the kind of liberal rights enshrined in Rawls's first principle. In Colonial society, like ours, equality consists in being subject to laws offering a range of protections against other individuals and institutions like the police or military. Colonial citizens obviously have unequal power, wealth, and status, but they have an equal right to vote and hold public positions—Baltar is able to ascend from being a farmboy on Aerelon to being president of the

Colonies. Military power is legally subordinate to a civilian government that must present itself for re-election periodically. Colonial citizens can't be arbitrarily imprisoned or executed. While Roslin can have Leoben "airlocked" because he's a Cylon ("Flesh and Bone"), she can't do the same to Baltar ("Taking a Break from All Your Worries").

On New Caprica, by contrast, no such principles apply to the Cylon Occupation Authority. The Cylons represent this hybrid society as a partnership between "the legitimate government of the Colonies" and their Cylon "allies and friends" ("Precipice"). While the military and police are under civilian rule, however, the Cylons consistently act outside legal restraints. Baltar signs an executive order authorizing the New Caprica Police to round up and execute suspected insurgents, but only while Doral holds a pistol to his head forcing him to sign.

Thus, while Colonial society in the ragtag fleet is, as Roslin concedes, far from "ideal," Colonial citizens have legal protections against arbitrary power that are absent on New Caprica. Such protections seem basic from the point of view of a human-only OP, which is why Rawls makes basic liberties *prior* to the difference principle and the principle of fair opportunity. After all, it would be crazy to sign up for principles that offered no protection against being detained and blinded by the likes of Brother Cavil or psychologically abused for months by the Leobens of the world.

But would possession of these rights be compatible with the post-humanity of the Cylons? Whatever moral failings the Cylons demonstrate by the destruction of the Twelve Colonies or the occupation of New Caprica, their society isn't presented unsympathetically. For one thing, it's not a dictatorship. Cylon decision-making is remarkably open, participatory, and egalitarian compared with the more hierarchical humans. There's no Cylon state, police force, or civil service. Indeed, Cylon society has no obvious institutions, and no social hierarchies or class structures other than between the humanoid "skin jobs" and the more animal-like Centurions and Raiders. The latter barely qualify as social beings, however. As Adama remarks, commenting on Athena's ability to elude Cylon defenses:

> The Centurions can't distinguish her from the other humanoid models
> . . . They were deliberately programmed that way. The Cylons didn't
> want them becoming self-aware and suddenly resisting orders. They

didn't want their own robotic rebellion on their hands. You can appreciate the irony. ("Precipice")

Baltar claims that legal rights and democracy keep the fleet's workers compliant by masking the differences between their needs and those of the "emerging aristocracy" represented by Roslin and the Adamas ("Dirty Hands"). Cylon society clearly needs no "ideological" apparatus to gull its workforce. As long as they're kept from evolving into self-aware persons, Centurions and Raiders can't regard themselves as having needs of any kind.

The lack of institutions seems to go, then, with the enveloping power of Cylon technology. Cylons are functionally immortal. Primary goods like health are furnished directly by the technical infrastructure on which they depend. Theirs is also a "post-scarcity society": the scale and reliability of Cylon technology means there's no need to compete for resources, and little incentive for economic competition or criminality as we understand it. Cylon technology furnishes directly most of what humans need state institutions and markets to provide indirectly and, in the case of the Colonial survivors, often imperfectly ("Black Market").

Furthermore, while humans have a *representative democracy* in which leaders are elected to represent the people's interests, Cylons have a *participatory democracy* in which all are directly involved in vital decision-making. They have no formal titles—there's no "Imperious Leader"—although Cylons like Caprica Six and Boomer can accrue greater political influence than others through meritorious deeds ("Downloaded"). This actually becomes problematic for the Cylons as Number Three/D'Anna plots to have Caprica Six and Boomer "boxed," and is later boxed herself when she "defies the group" ("Rapture"). Does this make Cylon society worse than Colonial society? It's far from clear that it does. Humans who collaborated on New Caprica are sentenced to death by a presidentially sanctioned "Circle" for the greater good of social stability in the fragile fleet ("Collaborators"). Cylons have a different—and perhaps more responsive and fair—way of determining when an individual must be sacrificed for the social good, which requires a consensus of all the other Cylon models.

The Cylons' lack of institutions means there are some principles of justice that may be applicable to Colonial society but not to Cylon society. Consider the judicial right against self-incrimination guaranteed by the 23rd Article of Colonization ("Litmus"). For Rawls, such a right exists insofar as it's guaranteed by laws governing state institutions such as the police or military. Without them, it can't exist. Of course, individuals who can cooperate socially without institutions might have an ethical outlook that disinclines them from such abuses. But this couldn't be a "right" in Rawls's sense, because it wouldn't be enforceable by law. When D'Anna tells Caprica Six that she's considering having Boomer boxed, it seems more the result of a consensus among the Cylon community than an act with the force of law ("Downloaded"). Even if this consensus is morally suspect, however, it can't violate Boomer's rights because enforceable rights don't exist in Cylon society. The only way in which Cylons could become subject to the kinds of rights humans have would be by relinquishing the very qualities that distinguish them from humanity.

"The Shape of Things to Come?"

Does this mean that a hybrid society of Cylons and humans is inconceivable? We've been assuming that justice involves a fair sharing of common goods. But perhaps we were mistaken, and what's fair is simply ensuring that people have enough of what they need to live a worthwhile life—whatever form of life they are. Maybe Cylons "need" download technology such as resurrection ships, Centurions to perform grunt labor, and other sophisticated posthuman stuff; whereas humans "need" things like political rights, access to healthcare, and a decent income.

This suggests an alternative to the shared-rights approach. Instead of dividing up one social cake, our deliberators in the OP could opt for two alternate sets of principles—one for Cylons and one for humans: "If I'm Cylon, I want the bare necessities of posthumanity, such as immortality. If I'm human, I want a scheme where the worst outcome for me is better than the worst outcome in any other human scheme." So, for humans, we keep Rawls's difference principle. But there's no point applying this principle to Cylon society since it's applicable only under conditions of scarcity and inequality. As long as we confine ourselves to the humanoid Cylons, there are no less-

Limits of Posthuman Justice

favored social groups. Moreover, Cylon immortality means that—short of being boxed—one will generally have multiple opportunities to realize one's plans in life.

What's wrong with this picture with respect to making a hybrid society? The problem is that by having no common principles of justice governing Cylons and humans alike—but one set for each—we have two societies in effect and no ground for mutual respect. This situation is essentially what occurred between the two Cylon wars, when both groups lived in entirely separate regions of space and left each other alone.

So are there any ways of cementing social ties between Cylon posthumans and humans without having principles of justice that are irrelevant to one or the other group? Our discussion has operated on two assumptions: (1) that justice is expressed through principles governing institutions; and (2) that humans and posthumans should retain their "essential natures" in any social union. Perhaps we should question each of these assumptions. The claim that justice is a virtue of social institutions rather than individuals is a recent one. Many philosophers—Plato, for example—have considered justice and injustice to exist in our interpersonal relationships as well as our institutions. When Roslin orders Leoben to be "airlocked"—reneging on her promise to let him live after he reveals that he lied about planting a nuclear bomb in the fleet—even his erstwhile torturer sees an injustice:

> *Starbuck*:   You can't do that. Not after he told you—
> *Roslin*:   Yes, I can. And I will . . . You've lost perspective.
> ("Flesh and Bone")

This is no longer a matter of institutional justice. Starbuck doesn't accord Leoben formal rights under the Articles, as she justifies her torture of him to Roslin, "It's a machine, sir. There's no limit to the tactics I can use." Starbuck is concerned, however, with *acting justly* in dealings with others.

Rawls might accept this analysis; for he argues that individuals in the OP must have "a sense of justice"—to grasp what it is for people to cooperate on fair terms with one another. Thus, the possibility of hybrid justice and a hybrid society may depend not on "schemes" for public institutions, but on the relationships between humans and

149

Cylons that have emerged. Sharon Agathon is a Cylon who comes to serve loyally as a Colonial officer ("Precipice"). Even Roslin sees Helo and Sharon's hybrid child, Hera, as "the shape of thing to come," and both humans and Cylons cooperate to ensure her safety ("Exodus, Part 2"). Each of these relationships change the individuals involved. Baltar's love for Six makes Gina's plight onboard the *Pegasus* morally intolerable for him and moves him to help her ("Pegasus"; "Resurrection Ship"). Most significantly, Helo—who shoots Sharon upon discovering that she's a Cylon ("Kobol's Last Gleaming, Part 1") —has his moral compass enlarged to the point where he sabotages Roslin and Adama's plan to destroy the Cylon race ("A Measure of Salvation").

These relationships alter human and Cylon natures. The hybrid children, Hera and Nicholas Tyrol, are the biological manifestations of this. We don't know why Baltar is running a "virtual" Six in his mind, or why Caprica Six has a virtual Baltar running in hers. But like the hybrid children, these Cylon-human relations alter the nature of human and Cylon alike. Baltar may not be a Cylon, but he seems to have acquired the Cylon capacity for "projecting" a virtual environment ("A Measure of Salvation"), while Caprica Six has acquired a more independent moral outlook ("Downloaded"). Nothing in *BSG*'s story arc guarantees that human-Cylon relationships are the seeds for a just hybrid society, but there is a fragile prospect of justice in the ethical capacity of characters like Six, Helo, and Baltar to question the fixed identities on which the conflict between Cylons and humans is premised. *BSG* presents us with a universe where the ethical demands of justice mean that human identity must be constantly negotiated and redefined.

Another, perhaps timely, lesson is that it's highly questionable whether the political demand for justice can be met in the same way for all societies or all historical situations. Rawls's account of justice is intended to apply to societies organized, like the Twelve Colonies, along Western, democratic lines. Developments in areas such as artificial intelligence and biotechnology mean that, like the Colonials, we may confront our own posthuman "children" in the foreseeable future.[4] But even if this evolutionary step never occurs, thinking about posthuman justice helps us see how theories of justice are addressed to specific historical and technological conditions.

NOTES

1 For a discussion of whether Cylons count as "persons," see Robert Arp and Tracie Mahaffey's chapter in this volume.
2 John Rawls, *A Theory of Justice* (Oxford: Oxford University Press, 1999). Further references will be given in the text.
3 For a discussion of the differences in psychological and moral character between Boomer and Athena, see George Dunn's chapter in this volume.
4 For further discussion of the Cylons' posthuman nature, see Jerold J. Abrams' and David Koepsell's chapters in this volume.

PART IV

THE ARROW, THE EYE, AND EARTH: THE SEARCH FOR A (DIVINE?) HOME

13

"I Am an Instrument of God": Religious Belief, Atheism, and Meaning

Jason T. Eberl and Jennifer A. Vines

Gaius Baltar is truly *frakked*! Dr. Amarak has requested to meet with President Roslin to discuss how the Cylons were able to launch their attack on the Twelve Colonies. Baltar, of course, is to be the centerpiece of their discussion. But Amarak just happens to be on the *Olympic Carrier*, which Roslin must decide whether to destroy because it poses a threat to the rest of the fleet. With his fate in Roslin's hands, Baltar can only watch how events play out—until his personal vision of Number Six tells him otherwise:

> *Six*: It's not her decision, Gaius.
> *Baltar*: No?
> *Six*: It's God's choice. He wants you to repent . . . Repent of your sins. Accept his true love and you will be saved.
> *Baltar*: I repent. There, I repent. *I repent.*
> ("33")

Roslin orders the *Olympic Carrier*'s destruction and Baltar is safe—for the time being.

Baltar's repentance isn't all that sincere; he has a long way to go before sharing the Cylons' belief in God and accepting his role in God's plan. Baltar's initial act of faith is motivated solely by his concern for his own "skinny ass." This isn't too different from a proposal made by the mathematician and philosopher Blaise Pascal (1623–1662), who reasons that if one believes in God and God exists, then an infinite amount of happiness awaits; whereas if one doesn't believe in God and God exists, then infinite misery will follow. Thus, it's more practical to believe that God exists.[1] But both of us—a religious believer and an atheist—think that whether one believes in God or not should be based on more than such a wager.

We also agree that the veracity of religious belief shouldn't be judged, as Baltar thinks, by dividing religious believers and atheists into two camps—the physically attractive intelligentsia and everyone else:

> *Six*:   You don't have to mock my faith.
> *Baltar*:   Sorry. I'm just not very religious.
> *Six*:   Does it bother you that I am?
> *Baltar*:   It puzzles me that an intelligent, attractive woman such as yourself should be taken in by all that mysticism and superstition.
> ("Miniseries")

If beauty and intelligence don't actually correspond to whether or not a person believes in God—and there have been plenty of well-educated religious believers and unattractive atheists to support this premise—then what rational arguments could be made either for or against belief in the existence of God?

"A Rational Universe Explained Through Rational Means"

Baltar is convinced he lives in a universe he can and does understand. As a scientist, his entire worldview has been shaped by knowledge derived through empirical investigation and rational theorizing. God, it seems clear to Baltar, doesn't fit within this view of reality as he peers through his microscope: "I don't see the hand of God in here. Could I be looking in the wrong place? Let me see. Proteins? Yes. Hemoglobin? Yes. Divine digits? No. Sorry" ("Six Degrees of Separation"). Of course, God isn't empirically observable. But, according to the medieval philosopher and theologian Thomas Aquinas (c.1225–1274), God's *effects* are observable, and one can reason from these effects to the conclusion that God exists as their ultimate cause.[2]

Consider one of these alleged divine effects. About to be revealed as a Cylon collaborator, Baltar is both relieved and puzzled when the

Olympic Carrier, with Amarak onboard, turns up missing. He and Six have different interpretations of this event:

Six: God is watching out for you, Gaius.

Baltar: The universe is a vast and complex system. Coincidental, serendipitous events are bound to occur. Indeed they are to be expected. It's part of the pattern, part of the plan.

Six: Dr. Amarak posed a threat to you. Now he's gone. Logic says there's a connection.

Baltar: A connection, maybe. But not God. There is no God or gods, singular or plural. There are no large invisible men, or women for that matter, in the sky taking a personal interest in the fortunes of Gaius Baltar.

("33")

Baltar agrees with Six that events don't occur randomly. There's an *ordered structure* to the universe, defined by laws of nature discoverable through scientific inquiry.

But given the universe's evident structure, is it most reasonable to conclude that such "a vast and complex system" simply formed itself, as unquestioned scientific theory tells us, out of an explosion of infinitely dense matter known as the "big bang"? Aquinas doesn't think so.[3] In his first argument for the existence of God, Aquinas states that every change from a state of *potency* to an *actual* state must be brought about by something that's already actual in a relevant way. To use a basic example from Newtonian physics, if an object is at rest, it has the potential to be in motion, but in order to be actually in motion, something must move it or it must have a part of itself capable of self-propelling it. This ties into Aquinas's second argument, which begins by noting that every *effect* must have a *cause*, and each cause is itself an effect of some other cause. In both cases, a chain of "moved movers" or "caused causes" forms that is discoverable by reason: a pyramid ball sails through the air because it's thrown by Anders's arm, which is stimulated by motor neurons in his brain, which fire because he desires to throw the ball into the goal, which he desires in order to impress Starbuck, which he wants to do because of an evolutionary adaptation that pits him in "tests of manhood" to gain survival and reproductive advantage, and so on all the way back to the big bang—the start of it all.[4]

But is it the start? The big bang, like any other event, is in need of explanation, unless we just accept it as a "brute fact"—incapable of, and thus not requiring, any further explanation:

> The universe began from a state of infinite density about [15 billion years] ago. Space and time were created in that event and so was all the matter in the universe. It is not meaningful to ask what happened before the big bang; it is somewhat like asking what is north of the North Pole.[5]

But, to Aquinas and many others, this answer isn't intellectually satisfying. A standard metaphysical axiom is *ex nihilo nihil fit*—"out of nothing, nothing comes." This axiom alone supports the notion that something had to exist out of which the universe came to be—in other words, there must be a *sufficient reason* for the universe to exist at all. We can thus ask, why did the big bang occur? How did the infinitely dense matter come to exist in the first place? Why are there one or more physical laws that state that such dense matter will explode outward?[6] It's rationally conceivable for the universe never to have existed or to have come into existence in a different fashion, or for a singularity of infinitely dense matter to exist but the relevant physical laws be different so that it doesn't explode and just remains static.

This is where another of Aquinas's arguments comes into play:

> The fifth way is taken from the governance of the world. We see that things which lack intelligence, such as natural bodies, act for an end [goal] . . . Now whatever lacks intelligence cannot move towards an end, unless it be directed by some being endowed with knowledge and intelligence; as the arrow is shot to its mark by the archer. Therefore some intelligent being exists by whom all natural things are directed to their end; and this being we call God. (I, Q. 2, a. 3)

This argument is sometimes identified with the notion of "intelligent design," and that isn't too far off the mark. But Aquinas isn't denying any of the scientific processes by which the universe unfolds; nor is he claiming that God sticks his finger in the mix periodically to push things along. Aquinas, presumably, wouldn't take issue with the well-established explanation of how life evolved by means of natural selection. It's no surprise, then, that Baltar doesn't observe "divine digits" through his microscope.

Nonetheless, the fact that there is a rationally discoverable set of laws governing the behavior of matter and energy, and the substances they compose, requires an explanation. Contemporary philosopher John Haldane notes, "Natural explanations having reached their logical limits we are then forced to say that either the orderliness of the universe has no explanation or that it has an 'extra-natural' one."[7] For Aquinas, the explanation of the universe's ordered structure, and its very existence, is the "unmoved mover," the "uncaused cause": God.

"That Is Sin. That Is Evil. And You Are Evil"

Even if Aquinas's arguments demonstrate that some sort of "God" exists as the universe's existential foundation, the traditional conception of God held by Jews, Christians, Muslims, and Cylons suffers from a flaw in logic known as the "problem of evil." Traditional theism understands God to be all-powerful, all-knowing, and all-good. But why would such a God allow for pervasive evil and suffering to exist in the world he supposedly created? Why, for example, doesn't God make algae taste like ice cream so the Colonials can have a more pleasant culinary experience after they find the Eye of Jupiter? The logical inconsistency is obvious and seemingly intractable for the religious believer: If God is all-powerful, why can't he prevent evil? If God is all-knowing, wouldn't he have the means to anticipate and stop evil before it occurs? And if God is inherently good, then surely he desires to eliminate evil from the world. Six, after all, constantly reminds Baltar of God's "eternal love."

Religious believers are in a quandary if they're unwilling to let go of one of the three qualities thought to be essential to God's nature. It's tempting at this point to abandon the project of solving the problem of evil by echoing the cynical humor of the philosopher and logician Bertrand Russell (1872–1970): "This world that we know was made by the devil at a moment when God was not looking."[8] Religious belief, however, necessitates finding some explanation for this problem.

One response to the problem of evil appeals to the idea that human beings have *free will*, and that much of the evil we suffer is the result of our own bad choices, a misuse of our God-given freedom. The philosopher and theologian, Augustine (354–430), thus argues:

> A perverse will is the cause of all evils . . . what could be the cause of
> the will before the will itself? Either it is the will itself, in which case

the root of all evil is still the will, or else it is not the will, in which case there is no sin. So either the will is the first cause of sin, or no sin is the first cause of sin. And you cannot assign responsibility for a sin to anyone but the sinner; therefore, you cannot rightly assign responsibility except to someone who wills it.[9]

Augustine identifies the source of moral evil as "inordinate desire" for "temporal goods":

So we are now in a position to ask whether evildoing is anything other than neglecting eternal things [for example, truth], which the mind perceives and enjoys by means of itself and which it cannot lose if it loves them; and instead pursuing temporal things . . . as if they were great and marvelous things. It seems to me that all evil deeds—that is, all sins—fall into this one category. (27)

Things such as food, alcohol, sex, and discipline are good in themselves and are worthy of desire. But we shouldn't allow our desire for such goods to override our commitment to pursuing more important goods. Hence, Lee's overeating while commanding *Pegasus* symbolizes to Admiral Adama that his son has grown soft and weak; Tigh's alcoholism quite evidently causes him—and the fleet when he's in command—all sorts of problems; Starbuck, like Baltar, pursues sex like it's a sport, but suffers from a lack of intimacy in her relationships; and Admiral Cain takes military discipline to a savage level aboard *Pegasus* to the overall detriment of her crew and civilians alike. Does it make sense to blame God for Lee's choice to overeat, Tigh's choice to drink, or Starbuck's choice to frak? As Brother Cavil tells Tyrol after he assaults Cally, "The problem is you are screwed up, heart and mind. You, not the gods or fate or the universe. You" ("Lay Down Your Burdens, Part 1").

"You Have a Gift, Kara . . . And I'm Not Gonna Let You Piss That Away"

Even if the misuse of free will results in the *moral* evils for which those who make "bad calls" can be held responsible—as Tigh accepts responsibility for the "Gideon massacre" ("Final Cut")—there are still *natural* evils to contend with. Assuming that Six is right when she says, "God doesn't take sides," why would God create a universe in which there are star clusters with dense radiation that block the Colonials' access to much needed food ("The Passage")? Or a disease that's fatal to Cylons ("Torn")? Given Aquinas's argument that God is responsible for the universe's ordered structure, it stands to reason that God would've ordered the universe so that it wasn't deadly to the conscious entities whom God supposedly loves unconditionally.

Scottish philosopher David Hume (1711–1776) compares God's creation of the universe to an architect designing and building a faulty house:

> Did I show you a house or palace where there was not one apartment convenient or agreeable: where the windows, doors, fires, passages, stairs, and the whole economy of the building were the source of noise, confusion, fatigue, darkness, and the extremes of heat and cold, you would certainly blame the contrivance, without any further examination . . . If you find any inconveniences and deformities in the building, you will always, without entering into any detail, condemn the architect.[10]

One response to this conundrum invokes the value of "soul-making." Contemporary philosopher John Hick argues that we shouldn't conceive of God as an "architect" designing this world to be a comfortable place in which to live. Rather, we should understand God as a *parent* whose primary purpose is for his children to receive a proper upbringing:

> We do not desire for [our children] unalloyed pleasure at the expense of their growth in such even greater values as moral integrity, unselfishness, compassion, courage, humour, reverence for the truth, and perhaps above all the capacity for love. We do not act on the premise that pleasure is the supreme end of life; and if the development of these other values sometimes clashes with the provision of pleasure, then we are willing to have our children miss a certain amount of this, rather than fail to come to possess and to be possessed by the finer and more precious qualities that are possible to the human personality . . . we have to recognize that the presence of pleasure and the absence of pain cannot be the supreme and overriding end for which the world exists. Rather, this world must be a place of soul-making.[11]

Hick further contends,

> in a painless world man would not have to earn his living by the sweat
> of his brow or the ingenuity of his brain . . . Human existence would
> involve no need for exertion, no kind of challenge, no problems to be
> solved or difficulties to be overcome, no demand of the environment
> for human skill or inventiveness. There would be nothing to avoid
> and nothing to seek; no occasion for co-operation or mutual help; no
> stimulus to the development of culture or the creation of civilization.
> The race would consist of feckless Adams and Eves, harmless and
> innocent, but devoid of positive character and without the dignity of
> real responsibilities, tasks, and achievements . . . A soft, unchallenging
> world would be inhabited by a soft, unchallenged race of men. (342–3)

We read here an echo of Adama and Dee's take on Lee's physical
stature after a year of commanding *Pegasus* in orbit around New
Caprica. Adama criticizes his son for having grown "weak, soft, ment-
ally and physically"; and Dee diagnoses the source of his problem:
"You've lost your edge. Your confidence. You lost your war, Lee. And
the truth is you're a soldier who needs a war" ("Occupation"). Without struggle, without challenges to overcome, Lee's very existence
is in danger of losing its meaning.

This is also the parental attitude of Starbuck's mother, Socrata
Thrace. Leoben tells Starbuck, "You were born to a woman who
believed suffering was good for the soul. So you suffered. Your life
is a testament to pain" ("Flesh and Bone"). While the physical and
emotional abuse Starbuck endured is certainly nothing any decent
parent would sanction, there is a valid purpose her mother was
attempting—in her significantly flawed way—to achieve. As an oracle
tells her, "You learned the wrong lesson from your mother, Kara. You
confused the messenger with the message. Your mother was trying to
teach you something else" ("Maelstrom"). With help from an apparition of Leoben, Starbuck comes to realize the greater good that her
mother was trying to achieve and accepts the evils she had to endure
as a child to prepare her for a crossroads in her life, when she must
conquer her fear "to discover what hovers in the space between life
and death." Similarly, God allows us to experience the consequences
of both moral and natural evils so that we may mature as individuals
and as a species to face whatever challenges and rewards the future
may bring as we continue to evolve.

"The Gods Shall Lift Those Who Lift Each Other"

Baltar's transition from committed skeptic to religious believer, tenuous as it may be, raises a serious question: How does a person who had defined himself in clear opposition to religion suddenly find Six's religious assertions convincing? Consider Baltar's attitude at the beginning:

> What you are doing, darling, is boring me to death with your superstitious drivel. Your metaphysical nonsense, which, to be fair, actually appeals to the half-educated dullards that make up most of human society, but which, I hasten to add, no rational, intelligent, free-thinking human being truly believes. ("Six Degrees of Separation")

So did Baltar have a direct experience of God's eternal love or a mystical "a-ha" moment? Did he decide to take Pascal up on his wager? Or are his religious inclinations merely another manifestation of his massive ego? It's probable that Baltar's religiosity can be reduced to a mere psychological need—namely, the need to be convinced that his life is important. Contemporary philosopher J. J. C. Smart eloquently sums up this view of religion as the ultimate ego-booster: "Even the horrible view that there is a hell to which the infinite God will consign us for our sins may give us an admittedly miserable sense of importance" (25).

Six's continued insistence that Baltar has a special role to play within God's cosmic plan ultimately proves to be an effective tool in getting him to do her bidding: "She . . . Caprica Six. She chose me. Chose me over all men. Chosen to be seduced. Taken by the hand. Guided between the light and the dark" ("Taking a Break from All Your Worries"). Baltar's self-importance is evident when he and Six discuss the bombing of a Cylon base:

> *Baltar:* Come on, you must have an inkling, where I should tell them to bomb?
> *Six:* No. But God does . . . Open your heart to him, and he'll show you the way.
> *Baltar:* It'd be a lot simpler if he came out and told me.
> *Six:* You must remember to surrender your ego. Remain humble.
> *Baltar:* If you ask me, God could do with cleaning his ears out. Then he might hear what I have to say.
> ("The Hand of God")

Baltar initially purports to value only what can be confirmed through rational means. Eventually his human foibles, coupled with an unrelenting series of depressing events in the *BSG* universe, result in his gravitating towards religious belief. Baltar's change of heart, though, smacks of insincerity insofar as his primary motivations continue to be fear and the indulgence of various hedonistic pursuits, political power, or whatever might tickle his fancy on any given day. Moreover, Baltar's actions are typically pursued without any consideration of how they impact others.

Invoking God's assistance when one needs help to resolve a temporary challenge doesn't constitute a robust religious belief. Baltar's tearful appeal to God during his "trial by fire" wrought by Shelly Godfrey ("Six Degrees of Separation") is probably best described in the words of the famous cartoon philosopher Lisa Simpson: "Prayer. The last refuge of a scoundrel."[12] Baltar's selfish nature impedes his ability to attain the type of freedom Russell describes: "freedom comes only to those who no longer ask of life that it shall yield them any of those personal goods that are subject to the mutations of time."[13] Baltar's desires, which are transitory and defined by the crisis of the moment, prevent him from realizing that belief in God isn't the answer. Rather, religious belief becomes a further hindrance to accepting a world that is mechanistic, not to mention oftentimes cruel, and certainly not subject to human control.

Where does a rejection of religious belief leave humanity? When Roslin commits herself to finding the Arrow of Apollo, Adama attempts to keep her focus grounded: "These stories about Kobol, gods, the Arrow of Apollo, they're just stories, legends, myths. Don't let it blind you to the reality that we face" ("Kobol's Last Gleaming, Part 1"). If we accept Adama's view that the gods and scriptures don't correspond to any objective reality, does that imply a lack of meaning in our lives? An atheistic worldview shouldn't be equated with the impossibility of meaning, which is often misperceived as being contingent upon an afterlife or whether God's plan for each of us comes to fruition. If we deny the possibility of the various mystical goals espoused by particular religious faiths, we're left with life's meaning defined by challenges faced, relationships forged, and the ability to derive value from these experiences. Russell allows for the possibility of transcendence through our direct experience of the world and acknowledgment of our lack of control over its forces, which he deems the "the beauty of tragedy":

> In the spectacle of death, in the endurance of intolerable pain, and in the irrevocableness of a vanished past, there is a sacredness, an overpowering awe, a feeling of the vastness, the depth, the inexhaustible mystery of existence, in which, as by some strange marriage of pain, the sufferer is bound to the world by bonds of sorrow. (113)

Alone in the vastness of space with the Cylons continually breathing down their neck, the Colonial survivors grieve for the loss of their former existence and the vast number of lives lost. The makeshift memorial that evolves into a sacred space on *Galactica* is a tangible and poignant representation of this grief. The Colonials' situation is precarious, and yet their continual suffering never causes them to question the assumption that the attempt to save humanity is worth the struggles endured. Preserving the human race provides a *purpose* that informs each person's daily choices in their work, politics, and relationships.

Russell speaks to the bravery of facing a world lacking inherent meaning:

> We see, surrounding the narrow raft illuminated by the flickering light of human comradeship, the dark ocean on whose rolling waves we toss for a brief hour; all the loneliness of humanity amid hostile forces is concentrated on the individual soul, which must struggle alone, with what of courage it can command, against the whole weight of a universe that cares nothing for its hopes and fears. Victory, in this struggle with the powers of darkness, is the true baptism into the glorious company of heroes, the true initiation into the overmastering beauty of human existence. (113–114)

Russell envisions each person having to face her own struggles, yet he recognizes the persistent "flickering light of human comradeship." This is one important value that continues to define a meaningful existence for the Colonials after the loss of their civilization and obvious abandonment by their "gods." Some of the most powerful scenes in the series demonstrate this profound need for human connection: Starbuck's naming the call signs of Viper and Raptor pilots lost ("Scar"), or Roslin's joy when Billy informs her that a baby had just been born on the appropriately named *Rising Star* ("33").

When the fleet is divided due to the ideological confrontation between Roslin and Adama, Dee confronts the "old man" and gets to the heart of the matter:

> You let us down. You made a promise to all of us to find Earth, to find us a home *together* . . . every day that we remain apart is a day that you've broken your promise . . . It's time to heal the wounds, Commander. People have been divided . . . Children are separated from their parents. ("Home, Part 1")

Dee convinces Adama to put aside his "rage" and return to Kobol to reunite the fleet. Adama, who's not a religious man, nevertheless recognizes a significant source of meaning for human existence in a Godless world: the need for human *solidarity* in pursuit of a common goal.

"You Have to Believe in Something"

Atheism doesn't entail nihilism—the belief that existence is meaningless in the absence of objective value—although it can certainly lead to it. Religious believers and atheists will never come to an understanding if religious believers assert that those who reject belief in the divine or transcendent consign themselves to a life devoid of meaning. The extreme situation depicted in *BSG* lends itself to a forced cooperation between believers and non-believers, as both groups share the common goal of humanity's survival. Adama acknowledges this fact in "Home, Part 2": "Many people believe that the scriptures, the letters from the gods, will lead us to salvation. Maybe they will. 'But the gods shall lift those who lift each other.'"

But should atheists and religious believers seek common ground in less dire circumstances? Atheists, despite being convinced that their worldview is more rational and authentic, recognize they're outnumbered. Therefore, they must often take the pragmatic approach of finding common ground with religious believers when possible.

Religious believers, conversely, often recognize that ethical and other principles they hold need to be couched in terms of rational arguments that can be debated in the secular public arena of modern society. The appeal to reason as a way of understanding and expressing religious belief isn't foreign to most major faith traditions. To cite one representative figure, Pope John Paul II, "The Church remains profoundly convinced that faith and reason 'mutually support each other'; each influences the other, as they offer to each other a purifying critique and a stimulus to pursue the search for deeper understanding."[14] The recognition that human beings are essentially *rational animals* motivates many religious believers to engage in secular, and not merely faith-based, discourse. At the same time, however, religious believers hold that there are limits to pure rational inquiry, and so faith must take over at those junctures to further our knowledge.

Hence, the litmus test for the validity of religious beliefs may be, as Roslin asserts, whether they "hold real-world relevance" ("Lay Down Your Burdens, Part 2"). To the degree that religious believers acknowledge rational, scientific inquiry as a means to truth, and atheists recognize that there are limits to the knowledge such inquiry can deliver to answer some of the ultimate questions of human concern, the ground is fertile for mutually respectable and fruitful dialogue as humanity continues its "lonely quest" on this "shining planet, known as Earth."[15]

NOTES

1   Blaise Pascal, *Pensées*, trans. W. F. Trotter (New York: Dover, 2003), §233.
2   See Thomas Aquinas, *Summa theologiae*, trans. Fathers of the English Dominican Province (New York: Benziger Brothers, 1948), I, Q. 2, a. 2.
3   Aquinas presents five interrelated arguments for God's existence. We'll review three of them here.
4   One response the atheist might launch at this point is that there is no "start of it all," but rather the chain of "moved movers" and "caused causes"—indeed, the existence of the universe itself—is *infinite*. Aquinas, however, agrees with Aristotle in denying that such an infinite series could *actually* exist. Further arguments supporting Aquinas's view are provided by William Lane Craig in his debate with Quentin Smith, *Theism, Atheism and Big Bang Cosmology* (Oxford: Clarendon Press, 1993).
5   J. Richard Gott III, James E. Gunn, David N. Schramm, and Beatrice M. Tinsley, "Will the Universe Expand Forever?" *Scientific American* (March 1976), 65; as quoted in Craig and Smith, *Theism, Atheism and Big Bang Cosmology*, 43.

6   It's debated among cosmologists whether any physical laws actually exist at the moment of the big bang. Stephen Hawking, however, argues that at least one law—the "wave function of the universe"—would have to exist at the beginning; see Stephen Hawking, *A Brief History of Time* (New York: Bantam Books, 1988), 133.

7   J. J. C. Smart and J. J. Haldane, *Atheism & Theism*, 2nd edn. (Oxford: Blackwell, 2003), 110.

8   Bertrand Russell, "Why I Am Not a Christian," in *Why I Am Not a Christian and Other Essays on Religion and Related Subjects* (New York: Simon & Schuster, 1957), 12.

9   Augustine, *On Free Choice of the Will*, trans. Thomas Williams (Indianapolis: Hackett, 1993), 104–105.

10 David Hume, *Dialogues Concerning Natural Religion*, 2nd edn., ed. Richard H. Popkin (Indianapolis: Hackett, 1998), 68–69.

11 John Hick, *Evil and the God of Love* (London: Fontana, 1979), 294–295.

12 *The Simpsons*, Season Two: "Bart Gets an F."

13 Bertrand Russell, "A Free Man's Worship," in *Why I Am Not a Christian*, 110.

14 John Paul II, *Fides et Ratio* (1998), §100: www.vatican.va/edocs/ENG0216/_INDEX.HTM.

15 We're grateful to Bill Irwin and Jessica Vines for helpful comments on an earlier draft of this chapter.

14

God Against the Gods: Faith and the Exodus of the Twelve Colonies

Taneli Kukkonen

The Cylons' unwavering belief in a divine plan is an ever-present theme of *Battlestar Galactica*. "God . . . has a plan for everything and everyone," Number Six tells Gaius Baltar ("33"). And even though the details of the Cylon God's design remain undisclosed, the allegiance He commands is absolute. God expects love and devotion, because He unconditionally loves all creation. Six repeatedly proclaims, "God is love"; and Leoben tells Kara "Starbuck" Thrace that "God loved you [humans] more than all other living creatures" ("Flesh and Bone"). Yet the Cylon God's plan seems cruel and inscrutable if it includes the Cylons' attempt to eradicate humanity. Is this the plan of a despotic madman or a loving deity? To the non-believer, the Cylon massacre of the Twelve Colonies is no different from any other act of senseless violence. And to those who haven't seen His face, the Cylon God must appear a dangerous delusion. Perhaps, as Leoben states, "To know the face of God is to know madness" ("Flesh and Bone")— because the Cylon God Himself, along with His followers, are mad.

An alternative to the Cylons' monotheism is the urbane religion practiced in the Twelve Colonies. Worship of the Colonial deities is an inclusive, rather than exclusive, affair. Kara prays to both Artemis and Aphrodite, but she sees no reason to deny the existence of the gods preferred by others—Ares, Hera, Zeus, and so on. Despite its flexibility, the Colonial religion has its own problems. According to Colonial scripture, the gods once lived among humanity, not over and above it. But after humanity left Kobol—"the home of the gods"

169

—the gods' onetime communion with humanity passed into legend, and their continued participation in human affairs is in question. In "Home, Part 2," Sharon indicates where the god Athena is supposed to have leapt to her death in despair over humanity's departure. The Colonials retain a set of half-remembered prophecies captured in the Sacred Scrolls, but many doubt their trustworthiness and humanity's ability to discern their hidden purpose.

Are the Cylons and Colonials both justified in their respective faiths? Or do religious believers on both sides merely impose meaning on an otherwise cold and uncaring universe? The tense confrontation between Kara and Leoben in "Flesh and Bone" illustrates how each party is apt to regard the other as misguided, but yet feel compelled to convince the other of their viewpoint. Are there independent, rational criteria by which the merits of the two contending faiths can be assessed?

"If This Is the Work of a Higher Power, Then They Have One Hell of a Sense of Humor"

Comparing monotheism and polytheism is an ancient subject in the philosophy of religion. Sophisticated debates took place in late antiquity between Hellenic philosophers, torch-carriers for the polytheistic Greek tradition, and the rising forces of Judeo-Christian monotheism. But the topic vanished in the Middle Ages, when monotheism came to dominate Western thought.

A world filled with walking, talking gods sounds strange to us. Why would anyone believe in such a world? Baltar puts the skeptical viewpoint bluntly: "There are no large invisible men, or women for that matter, in the sky taking a personal interest in the fortunes of Gaius Baltar" ("33"). Baltar's belittling conception of the gods as "invisible men or women" echoes the Greek philosopher Xenophanes (c.570–480 BCE), who caustically criticizes our tendency to anthropomorphize, remarking that if horses could make images of their gods, they would fashion them after horses.[1] Does the Cylon God resemble a toaster?

A more palatable interpretation, favored by philosophers of religion, regards all talk of gods as referring to personified forces of nature. This means more than perceiving a freak storm as an expression of Poseidon's wrath. Talk of gods reveals the eternally recurrent cosmic patterns to which we must pay heed if our life is to have meaning, since individual fates are intertwined within those patterns. We recount stories concerning gods and humanity, and these stories illuminate and give meaning to the present day. Laura Roslin puts the matter succinctly to Kara: "If you believe in the gods, then you believe in the cycle of time, that we are all playing our parts in a story that is told again and again and again throughout eternity" ("Kobol's Last Gleaming, Part 1").[2]

For polytheists, the gods' existence isn't a matter of argument or proof: the gods are all about us, theirs is the life of the universe, and they're not so much known as experienced. The Syrian philosopher Iamblichus (d. 325) argues against atheism even being an option:

> We should not accept, then, that this is something that we can either grant or not grant, nor admit to it as ambiguous (for it remains always uniformly in actuality). Nor should we examine the question as though we were in a position either to assent to it or reject it; for it is rather the case that we are enveloped by the divine presence, and we are filled with it, and we possess our very essence by virtue of our knowledge that there are gods.[3]

So how do we ever become ignorant of the gods' presence? Because everything in the universe testifies equally to the gods—"uniform actuality"—whereas human attention inclines this way and that, we can become blinded to the infusion of divine reality everywhere. Religious ritual refocuses us to perceive the sacred dimension in all that is—reminds us that the gods breathe their life into us. Porphyry of Tyre (c.234–305) explains, "Through our contemplation of them [the gods] truly nourish us, keep us company, reveal themselves to us and illuminate our salvation."[4] This idea is reflected in Commander Adama's invocation of the Colonial scriptures—"Life here began out there"—in the aftermath of the initial Cylon attack. He ties the mythical past with the living present to console those grieving with a vision of cosmic reconciliation.

The gods' supposed omnipresence may still seem strange to us. But consider the constant presence of Number Six whispering in Baltar's ear. She claims to be "an angel of God," which is to say a messenger. She acts as Baltar's guide to allow the hapless scientist to see things in a divine light. For polytheists, all reality works this way: "All things are full of gods," says the first Greek philosopher, Thales of Miletus (c.624–545 BCE).[5] We couldn't even begin to make sense of reality were angels not constantly whispering in our ears, patiently guiding us to see the beauty and constancy of the natural order perpetuated by the gods. As Iamblichus contends,

> Neither is it the case that the gods are confined to certain parts of the cosmos, nor is the earthly realm devoid of them. On the contrary . . . even as they are not contained by anything, so they contain everything within themselves; and earthly things, possessing their being in virtue of the totalities of the gods, whenever they come to be ready for participation in the divine, straight away find the gods pre-existing in it prior to their own proper essence. (I.8)

Would it be so unreasonable to believe in polytheism of this kind in the present age? Carl Jung may not have thought so, with his notion of archetypes;[6] nor might various cosmologists who've speculated about the curious isomorphisms existing between our minds and the universe's mathematical structure.[7]

But why, on this view, are the gods many? Because there are various isomorphisms at play—mind and matter interact at many levels —reality has as many different sides to it as we have individual perspectives on it:

> In the distribution of gods one trait or another tends to be dominant: so Ares rules contentious nations; Athena those who are wise as much as warlike; Hermes those who are more cunning and daring; and, to be brief, each nation ruled by a god exhibits the character of its own god.[8]

Such differences notwithstanding, all the gods are united in their care for the good world order, as should we.

"I Am God"

Why doesn't the Cylon God fit snugly into this all-inclusive pantheon? The answer lies in the exclusivist claims of those who choose to believe that there is only one God. To polytheists, the monotheists' fundamental error lies not in their postulating a god of their own—if multiple gods exist, why not one more?—but in their cultural imperialism and disturbing proclivity towards monoculture. Perhaps, if the Cylons would have settled for being merely a tribe among tribes, then their existence could be tolerated, as it was through the long years of the armistice. But the Cylons' proselytizing zeal, and their tactics of conversion by gunpoint, put them beyond the pale of civilization.

We don't need to witness legions of Cylon Centurions in action to appreciate this point. The second-century pagan philosopher Celsus notes, "From the beginning of the world different parts of the earth were allotted to different guardians," referring to the gods of various nations. The Jews were thus entirely within their rights to offer thanks to the god of Abraham and Jacob, Moses and David, who since time immemorial had been their appointed guardian. Indeed, it would be "impious to abandon the customs which have existed in each locality from the beginning."[9] The Jews only erred by refusing to offer gratitude to the Roman emperor also, who, as Jupiter's representative on Earth, symbolized the cosmic order as a whole.

Why was this such an offense? In Exodus 20:5, the God of the Israelites decrees that His people shall not worship any other god besides Him, since He is "a jealous God." The Cylon God, according to the priest Elosha, once became jealous and desired to be elevated above all the other gods ("Kobol's Last Gleaming, Part 1," deleted scene). The Cylons thus dismiss the other gods as false idols undeserving of the name "god." Number Three declares, "There is no Zeus. No other God but God" ("Exodus, Part 1"), and Leoben disparagingly tells Kara, "You kneel before idols and ask for guidance" ("Flesh and Bone"). And when Baltar refers to having "accepted your God" in front of Six, she retorts, "He's not my God. He is God." Baltar quickly recovers, "Yeah, your God, my God, everyone's God. He's big enough for all of us, isn't He?" ("Six Degrees of Separation").

Six thus tells Baltar that "God turned his back on Kobol. Turned his back on man and the false gods he worshipped" ("Fragged"), and Sharon regards the Lords of Kobol as historical figures, not as divinities ("Home, Part 1"). Similarly, the Greek mythographer Euhemerus in the fourth century BCE claims that all talk of gods merely refers to past heroes whose deeds have outlived their historic identities.[10] But isn't such worship at the tombs of heroes a rather morbid affair at best, and a naked power play at worst?[11] Laura Roslin, for her part, doesn't hesitate "to play the religious card" ("The Farm") when necessary—to call upon the ancient prophecies to maintain social cohesion and hope within the "ragtag fleet" of Colonial survivors.[12] And when Meier asks Tom Zarek if he believes Roslin is a "prophet," he responds, "No, but I believe in the power of myth" ("Home, Part 1").

So is Colonial religion merely a veneer for projecting human aspirations and desires onto a cosmic canvas? When Adama addresses his crew before their rescue mission to New Caprica, he refers to it as "a feat that will be told and retold down through the ages" and his crew finding "immortality as only the gods once knew" ("Exodus, Part 1"). Does he truly expect the cycle of time to come full circle in his crew? Or does he believe the gods live only in humanity's great deeds? This question can be extended to any symbolic or allegorical understanding of religion. Perhaps we give meaning to our existence, rather than discover such meaning, by interpreting the universe as having underlying patterns. If so, then the gods may be of our making, not we of theirs.[13] To take but one example, the fact that there are twelve astrological signs, twelve Colonial tribes, and twelve Cylon models must surely be significant somehow. And yet few of us would claim that there's something special about the number twelve that would force the universe into this pattern. Additionally, as the early Church historian Eusebius (c.260–c.340) notes, when put under scrutiny, allegorical interpretations of ancient myth tend to tumble into one another, contradict one another, and generally fail to cohere (III.13–14).

To the committed monotheist, this reduction of theological meaning is unacceptable. Like Leoben, Eusebius chastises polytheists for lapsing into a life of sin and blames their lack of "right reason" (II.6). The monotheists know how to act rightly, because they follow a single reason and a single rule; whereas those who worship contentious gods can't help but bring the tensions inherent in their faith into the world. Identifying with one or another aspect of the immanent, material world can only serve to bring about selfishness and limited perspectives. It takes faith in a single transcendent, spiritual principle to achieve true conviction and selflessness.

But how could a belief in a power beyond the world give better access to it? The Colonials talk of a time when gods lived among humans on Kobol, thus effectively negating the distance between the two; physical artifacts, such as the Arrow of Apollo, reinforce this sense of familiarity. By contrast, the Cylon God is an abstract being not of flesh and blood. It's strange, then, that Kara reacts with bemusement when Leoben proclaims, "We're all God," since the Colonials supposedly had a much more intimate relationship with their gods in the past. Contemporary philosopher Stephen Clark notes that those "who suppose that the god has spoken to them, that He has anointed them with His spirit, that they are new creatures and have cast off the works of darkness and the older gods, are unlikely to be popular with established sectarians."[14] But there's a deeper reason for Kara's misgivings. The present-day absence of deities that once were palpably present has made the Colonials skeptical of any sweeping claims about divine imperatives. Instead, all but the Sagittarons have come to endorse an ethos of self-reliance, resigning themselves to muddling through life by the light of their fallible reason. Thus, when Leoben claims that God created the Cylons to replace sinful humanity, Kara responds, "The gods had nothing to do with it. We created you. Us. It was a stupid, frakked-up decision, and we have paid for it" ("Flesh and Bone"). Instead of sharing Leoben's vision of a divinely determined cosmic story—which Kara admits she was raised to believe ("Kobol's Last Gleaming, Part 1")—she sees simply the disastrous result of humanity's own hubris.

Giving Oneself Over to God

In "33," Six tells Baltar he needs to repent so that Roslin will destroy the *Olympic Carrier* and Dr. Amarak—who presents a threat to Baltar—along with it. Baltar desperately declares his repentance and Roslin immediately gives the destructive order. How are we to interpret this sequence of events? Does an omnipotent God grant wishes to those who obey Him? Does He demonstrate His sovereignty through arbitrary displays of power? The sixth-century Christian philosopher John Philoponus asks, "If God does not act in a different way from nature, then how does He differ from it?"—implying that miraculous acts which violate the laws of nature should be expected of God.[15]

Perhaps God's purpose is simply to make a believer out of Baltar, by asking of him what He knows the man can't give—by stripping Baltar of his sense of self, his autonomous agency, his very sanity. Such was the Danish philosopher Søren Kierkegaard's (1813–1855) take on faith. Reflecting on the biblical story of Abraham, whom God told to sacrifice his only son Isaac (Genesis 22:1–18), Kierkegaard claims that a properly religious attitude consists in leaps of faith. One must give up attempts at justification and rationalization, and submit to God's will. For Kierkegaard, even the evident desperation and insincerity in Baltar's proclamation of repentance can be made to serve a point. If Baltar's conviction produced a miracle, then God could mistakenly be considered beholden to human expectations. Instead, God chooses to take Baltar's confused utterances at face value, just because He has a lesson to teach him:

> But what did Abraham do? He arrived neither too early nor too late. He mounted the ass, he rode slowly down the road. During all this time he had faith . . . He had faith by virtue of the absurd, for human calculation was out of the question.[16]

On this view, every event on the cosmic stage, great or small, can serve as the setting for a very private psychodrama. It's in such absurd situations that one's mettle is truly tested. Kierkegaard approvingly cites Tertullian (155–230): *credo, quia absurdum*—I believe because it's absurd. Surrendering to faith may be the only way to make sense of a senseless situation. Six seems to agree when she applauds Baltar for giving himself over to God and occasioning the destruction of a Cylon tylium refinery. For Six, this setback to the Cylon cause matters less to God than Baltar's singular act of devotion because, as she puts it, "God doesn't take sides. He only wants your love" ("The Hand of God"). This position is known as *fideism*. While for the believer everything may appear eminently clear and reasonable, to adopt a belief-system as a whole is ultimately a matter of faith, not reason. It's like Baltar's visions of Six: though they're supremely real to him, he has no way of explaining them to anyone else. Eusebius talks of "eyes of understanding" that don't function the way that physical eyes do, and so each person is left alone with his vision.

Yet to the outsider this looks like insanity, which Leoben willingly concedes: "To know the face of God is to know madness." Indeed, it has been suggested that this kind of divine voluntarism—the belief that a transcendent deity can act as He pleases with His creation, imposing any set of arbitrary rules—may have contributed to the specter of nihilism that haunts the modern landscape.[17] This leads to a point Celsus makes against any Creator who regards His creation as a rag doll and requires belief in reprehensible things:

> Of course they have no reply for this one, and as in most cases where there is no reply they take cover by saying: "Nothing is impossible with God."[18] A brilliant answer indeed! But the fact is, a god cannot do what is shameful; and god does not do what is contrary to nature. If, in your evildoing, you were to ask a god to do something terrible, god could not do it . . . no god deals in confusion. (86)

On this view, the god of the monotheists is really no deity at all, but merely a malevolent illusion. Nothing could better illustrate the difference between the otherworldly monotheist and the down-to-earth polytheist. For the polytheist, whatever god is postulated has to make sense in terms of what we know about the world; whereas for the monotheist, the world permanently has to justify its existence in the face of what the believer already knows about God and His will.

"Could There Be A Connection . . . ?"

The Colonials' faith has a hidden strength by virtue of being indeterminate: it can withstand any assault. Whereas political and social strife is rampant throughout the fleet, the Colonials don't appear to suffer from any significant schisms in religious matters. Even the Gemenese opposition to abortion is painted as a matter of respectful disagreement—an example of "this is what we do" as opposed to "this is what you all must do" ("The Captain's Hand"). By contrast, the Cylon God's worshippers are in a more precarious position. Because the divine "plan" is perceived as monolithic, any events that fail to cooperate will inevitably bring turmoil in their wake. And because the Cylons don't form a hive-mind among the twelve models —like the Borg on *Star Trek*—they fall victim to schisms just as monotheists have on Earth. Is it any wonder that the cynical and agnostic Brother Cavil is the theologian of the bunch?

The Cylons' monotheism must be tempered by humility; they must evolve to resist the temptation to try to make everything fit into a narrowly defined vision. But the Colonials have something to learn from the Cylons, too, at least insofar as their sense of purpose is concerned. In setting on their quest for Earth, they've borrowed a favorite monotheist theme: an exodus towards a "promised land," something that bespeaks a budding recognition of a gap between the way things are and how they ought to be. Maybe the two religious worldviews are beginning to merge at the edges, as Three begins to wonder when the Cylon Hybrid refers to the Eye of Jupiter: "Could there be a connection between their gods and ours?" ("The Passage"). Leoben tells Kara, "Our faiths are similar," with the sole difference that "I look to one God, not to many" ("Flesh and Bone"). In any case, there's a lot to be said for the Roman proconsul and philosopher Themistius' (317–387) plea for religious tolerance when the war of words between polytheists and monotheists had reached a fever pitch:

> Consider how the founder of the universe rejoices in this diversity. He wishes the Syrians to choose one form of religion, the Greeks another, the Egyptians another; nor does he wish the Syrians themselves to be all the same, but henceforth to be divided into smaller groups. For no one thinks about these things in exactly the same way as his neighbor; rather, one man does so in one way, and another in a different way. Why then do we try to achieve the impossible through force?[19]

Why indeed? Whether one believes in one God or many, it would seem obvious that our lot in communicating with the divine and with each other is to listen rather than to proclaim, to consent rather than to coerce. "God answers everyone's prayers," Leoben asserts, and surely he must be right if even a single god exists. But this means that all sincere prayers are equally pleasing to the ears of heaven.

NOTES

1 Xenophanes, *Fragments*, trans. J. Lesher (Toronto: University of Toronto Press, 1992), frag. 15.
2 The Christian church father Origen (c.185–c.254) reports that the polytheists of his time—notably Celsus, discussed below—believed in just such a cycle of time. See Origen, *Contra Celsum*, trans. Henry Chadwick (Cambridge: Cambridge University Press, 1953), III.67–8.
3 Iamblichus, *On the Mysteries of the Egyptians*, trans. Emma Clarke, John Dillon, and Jackson Hershbell (Atlanta: Society of Biblical Liter-

ature, 2003), I.3. See also Jordan Paper, *The Deities Are Many* (Albany: State University of New York Press, 2005), 127.

4 Porphyry, *On Abstinence from Killing Animals*, II.34, trans. A. D. Lee, in *Pagans and Christians in Late Antiquity: A Sourcebook* (London: Routledge, 2000), 33.

5 As quoted in Aristotle, *On the Soul*, in *The Complete Works of Aristotle*, ed. Jonathan Barnes (Oxford: Oxford University Press, 1984), I.5.411a8.

6 Carl Gustav Jung, *Memories, Dreams, Reflections*, trans. Richard and Clara Winston (New York: Vintage Books, 1973), 340: "It is not that 'God' is a myth, but that myth is the revelation of a divine life in man. It is not we who invent myth, rather it speaks to us as a word of God." For a polytheist perspective on Jung, see Ginette Paris, *Pagan Meditations: The Worlds of Aphrodite, Artemis, and Hestia* (Dallas: Spring Publications, 1986).

7 See John Barrow, *Pi in the Sky* (Oxford: Oxford University Press, 1992).

8 Julian "the Apostate," *Contra Galileos*, trans. R. Joseph Hoffmann, in *Julian's Against the Galileans* (Amherst: Prometheus Books, 2004), 102. See also Rowland Smith, *Julian's Gods: Religion and Philosophy in the Thought and Action of Julian the Apostate* (London: Routledge, 1995).

9 Celsus, *On the True Doctrine*, trans. R. Joseph Hoffmann (Oxford: Oxford University Press, 1987), 87.

10 Euhemerus, *Euhemeri Messenii reliquiae*, ed. Marcus Winiarczyk (Leipzig: Teubner, 1991), fragments 8–23.

11 This is a common monotheist complaint. See Eusebius, *Eusebii Pamphili Evangelicae Praeparationis*, ed. and trans E. H. Gifford (Oxford: Oxford University Press, 1903), II.1, 5; and Clement of Alexandria, *Exhortation to the Greeks*, trans. G. W. Butterworth (Cambridge, MA: Loeb Classical Library, 1919), III.39.

12 For further discussion of the role of religious faith in support of the pragmatic virtue of hope, see Elizabeth Cooke's chapter in this volume.

13 Note that the Colonial deities, as opposed to the Cylon God, are not described as *creators*. See Stewart Elliott Guthrie, *Faces in the Clouds: A New Theory of Religion* (Oxford: Oxford University Press, 1993).

14 Stephen R. L. Clark, *The Mysteries of Religion* (Oxford: Blackwell, 1986), 83.

15 Quoted in Simplicius, *In Aristotelis physicorum libros quattuor posteriores commentaria*, ed. H. Diels (Berlin: G. Reimer, 1895), 1150.

16 Søren Kierkegaard, *Fear and Trembling*, trans. Howard V. Hong and Edna H. Hong (Princeton: Princeton University Press, 1983), 35.

Taneli Kukkonen

17   See Michael Allen Gillespie, *Nihilism Before Nietzsche* (Chicago: University of Chicago Press, 1994).
18   See Mark 10:27, Matthew 19:26, and Luke 18:27.
19   Themistius, *Orations*, V.70a, trans. A. D. Lee, in *Pagans and Christians*, 108.

15

"A Story that is Told Again, and Again, and Again": Recurrence, Providence, and Freedom

David Kyle Johnson

> All of this has happened before, and all of it will happen again.
> The Book of Pythia

What if this passage from Colonial scripture is true? The Cylons believe it is, even though they seem to have rejected everything else about human religion.[1] Would you live your life any differently if you believed you had a "destiny" that had "already been written"? When Helo shows Starbuck the mandala from the Temple of Five and she sees how similar it is to a drawing she'd been making since she was a kid, she's genuinely freaked out ("Rapture"). Along with other events in her life, such as opening the Tomb of Athena on Kobol and finding the way to Earth, the mandala seems to confirm the Cylon Leoben's ability to *know* Starbuck's future:

> To know the face of God is to know madness. I see the universe. I see the patterns. I see the foreshadowing that precedes every moment of every day. It's all there. I see it. And you don't. And I have a surprise for you. I have something to tell you about the future . . . Are you ready? You're gonna find Kobol. Birthplace of us all. Kobol will lead you to Earth. ("Flesh and Bone")

Leoben apparently knows the specifics of Starbuck's future because her "role" in the story is already written. Later, on New Caprica, he predicts that she'll hold him in her arms and say she loves him, which

181

she does—although he may not have foreseen what happened next ("Exodus, Part 2").

Apparent knowledge of the future is also evident in Six's interactions with Gaius Baltar. In "The Hand of God," after quoting the above scripture, Six predicts the human-Cylon confrontation on Kobol—"the home of the gods." Later, while on Kobol, she tells Baltar that he'll be the guardian of a new human-Cylon hybrid race. In "Colonial Day," Six seems to know that Baltar's presence at the Interim Quorum of Twelve will eventually lead to his election as vice president, which will then lead to a number of other pivotal events.

So does anyone in *BSG*, or any of us for that matter, have free will? If everything has happened before and will happen again, nothing can happen any other way. If so, it doesn't seem that anyone is free—how could we be, if everything we do is *already decided for us*?

"We Are All Playing Our Parts"

What is "free will"? One "classic" definition of free will involves the Rule of Alternate Possibilities:

> RAP: In order for a person *to freely perform* an action, it must be possible for the person to do otherwise, or at least to refrain from performing that action.

A similar principle suggests that *moral responsibility* for performing an action also requires being able to do otherwise or refrain from doing the action. One might morally blame Six for tricking Baltar into helping her disable the Colonial defense mainframe, thereby enabling the Cylons' initial attack. But if it were revealed that she was inalterably programmed to do so and thus couldn't do otherwise, we couldn't rightfully morally blame her, for she didn't *freely* choose to do so.[2]

So the question becomes, if RAP is true and the universe is repeating itself, can anyone be free? The answer may depend on *why* the universe is repeating itself. Some theorists have proposed a three-part explanation for the universe's supposed repetition. The first part is rooted in the "big bang" theory.[3] All stars and galaxies in the universe are traveling away from each other; and the farther away something is from an object, the faster it's heading away from that object.

Cosmologists have thus hypothesized that all matter in the universe originated from a single point. If the matter of the universe, as it runs forward in time, is expanding outward, then, if we were to run it backward in time, we'd see it contracting into a single point—a "singularity." The explosion of this singularity would explain the expansion of the universe's matter and the cosmic microwave background radiation that's also been observed.[4] The second part of this explanation involves a corollary to the big bang theory, which suggests that the universe's expansion will eventually slow as the gravitational pull of the universe's matter gradually pulls everything back together into another singularity, which will then explode again.[5]

The third part is rooted in the theory of *determinism*, which holds that the entire universe is regulated by causal laws that govern the interactions of everything in it. Think of a billiard game between Starbuck and Sam Anders—*Galactica*'s pyramid court having been destroyed in a Cylon raid. Once Starbuck hits the cue ball, the outcome of her break—what the billiard balls will do—is already set because of the laws of physics. In fact, once the cue ball is hit, if Sam had enough information—the ball's speed and spin, the precise location of the other balls, and so on—he could figure out the path and eventual resting place of every ball. He wouldn't even have to look! Determinists claim that the universe is like a big billiard table where *atoms* are the balls and *space* is the table. The universe is just atoms in motion and every event among those atoms is simply the causal consequence of previous events. And if we knew enough, we could predict the path and resting place of every atom, and thus the entire future of the universe.

How do these theories lead us to a repeating universe? If Starbuck racked and re-racked the balls repeatedly in exactly the same way and broke them each time by hitting the cue ball in exactly the same way, the balls would follow the same path and end in the same spot every time. This would be true of the universe, as well. If it's a deterministic system that repeatedly expands and contracts, and starts over the same way every time, then the universe's atoms will follow the same paths over and over.[6] If true, then I've already written this chapter and you've already read it in previous identical versions of our universe —maybe even a million times!

You may be tempted to think that *persons* aren't just physical beings made of atoms and thus not subject to the deterministic causal forces of the universe. Leoben contends just this by invoking Colonial theology: "What is the most basic article of faith? This is not all that we are . . . I know that I'm more than this body . . . A part of me swims in the stream. But in truth, I'm standing on the shore. The current never takes me downstream" ("Flesh and Bone"). If Leoben is right, even if the universe is continually expanding and contracting, you don't have to continually repeat your actions. Even though you chose to read this chapter this time around, you may not have last time. If you aren't a physical being you aren't governed by the physical laws of the universe. But the problem is, the more we learn about the brain, the more it looks like you are just a physical being. Everything we do—form sentences, feel emotions, draw conclusions, make decisions—seems to merely be the result of neural activity; and neurons are just made of atoms. There are even specific places in the brain where such things occur.[7] The brain may be just a very complicated computer: a physical system programmed by the interconnection of its parts—neurons instead of microchips—that's governed by the laws of physics. Just as you could know how a Cylon will behave by knowing its programming, you could know how a human will behave by knowing her neural configuration.[8]

So if the universe is simply one in a number of repeating cycles, then a person can't do anything except what she's already done in a previous cycle. And, according to RAP, if a person can't do otherwise, she's not free. Upon descending into the maelstrom, Starbuck isn't "free to become what she really is." Instead, she's causally determined to go into it and return later knowing the way to Earth. The same is true for Starbuck's decision to fly back to Caprica and retrieve the Arrow of Apollo, Lee's decision to turn a gun on Colonel Tigh to protect President Roslin, and Tigh's choice to kill his wife Ellen for collaborating with the Cylons on New Caprica. In every other cycle of the universe, they did these same things, and the repetition of these actions was thus inevitable and *not free*.

"God Has a Plan for You, Gaius"

What if the universe repeats because of something other than its own cyclical nature? What if God (or the Lords of Kobol) has predetermined the universe to turn out a certain way, to tell a specific story?

Could freedom be compatible with such *theological* determinism? The Book of Pythia prophesies that the human survivors will be led to Earth by a "dying leader," and Baltar seems to play the role of God's "instrument" as he points, by apparently divine direction, to the exact spot by which the "serpents [Vipers] numbering two and ten" will destroy the Cylon tylium refinery ("The Hand of God"). Both Six and Leoben judge various events as ensuring "God's plan." Leoben tells Starbuck,

> you can't see that your destiny's already been written. Each of us plays a role. Each time, a different role. Maybe the last time, I was the interrogator and you were the prisoner. The players change, the story remains the same. And this time . . . your role is to deliver my soul unto God. Do it for me. It's your destiny, and mine. ("Flesh and Bone")

Leoben indicates that the universe's repetition isn't as exact as previously suggested—maybe last time you wrote this chapter and I read it. But God never changes the story's overall plot. God just chooses different persons for different roles.

There are a number of ways that God might control the universe to get the story to come out just right. God might individually force every atom of the universe—including those of our brains and bodies—to move as desired. If the universe is deterministic, God might just set it up in the way needed to get the story going—like an expert billiard player might set up the balls on a table for a trick shot. Perhaps God just implants irresistible beliefs and desires in us, thereby forcing us to behave as appropriate for our role in the cosmic story—consider God "hardening Pharaoh's heart" (Exodus 7:3) or the need for Judas to fill his role as "betrayer" so that Christ may be crucified (John 13:21–28). Perhaps God does this with Starbuck, implanting in her, as a child, a vision of the Eye of Jupiter that's reminiscent of the maelstrom into which she must fly, and also giving her a vision of a Cylon Raider to follow into it. It may even be God who appears as Leoben in a vision to calm her fears ("Maelstrom"). But regardless of how it's done, if God is forcing us to behave in certain ways—even if God selects different roles for us to play each time around—we can't do anything but what God wills us to do. And if we can't do otherwise, then we're not free according to RAP.[9]

185

David Kyle Johnson

"Out of the Box Is Where I Live"

Although there have been many attempts to devise solutions to these problems, they remain genuine dilemmas. Free will, defined by RAP, can't coexist with determinism or divine predestination. Still, there are other options, such as rejecting RAP. But then an alternate theory of free will must be offered—and not just one that "works" to solve the problem. It'll have to jive with our intuitions of what "being free" is all about, and also explain how we can be free in a deterministic or divinely predestined universe.

A common redefinition of free will uses the concept of "agent causation," which suggests that as long as the cause of an action is *you*, the agent, then the action is free—even if you couldn't cause anything else at that moment but that particular action.[10] This would explain why Boomer *didn't* freely choose to shoot Commander Adama, but Starbuck *did* freely choose to hit Colonel Tigh during a triad game. With Boomer, it was a latent program that kicked in and caused her hand to shoot Adama, not her—so it wasn't a free action. But Starbuck has no such excuse. Even though she did it "without really thinking," the cause of her hand striking Tigh is obviously Starbuck herself.

But there's one major problem. A person is the agent cause of an action if and only if the cause-and-effect chain that leads to the action traces back to and ends solely in the agent herself—she must be the action's *ultimate* cause. But an agent being the ultimate cause of an action is impossible in either a deterministic or a divinely predetermined universe. In a deterministic universe, the ultimate cause of every action is the big bang. In a divinely predetermined universe, the ultimate cause of every action is God. So the agent causation definition of free will doesn't solve our problems.

Some philosophers have proposed a definition of free will that's *compatible* with determinism. They suggest that as long as an action is rooted in an agent's properly configured psychology—as long as *the agent's action coincides with the agent's wishes*—then the action is free, even if acting on one's wishes is irresistible and thus one can't do otherwise.[11]

But consider Tigh, Tyrol, Tory, and Anders' irresistible desire to follow the strange music that only they can hear ("Crossroads, Part

2"). Clearly, their actions match their irresistible wishes; they desire to follow the music and they do. But they were *programmed* to do so—"a switch goes off, just like that"—and since their programming isn't up to them, it seems hard to conclude that their action of following the music is free. It was their programmer's decision. In a deterministic universe, your actions may match your irresistible wishes, but you have those irresistible wishes because the universe went through a certain causal process beyond your control and gave you those wishes—or because God implanted them.

Compatibilists hold that a person doesn't need to have control of her desires in order to be free. Harry Frankfurt—famous for his writings on compatibilism, as well as bullshit—contends, "We are inevitably fashioned and sustained . . . by circumstances over which we have no control. The causes to which we are subject may also change us radically, without thereby bringing it about that we are not morally responsible agents."[12] Frankfurt suggests that incompatibilists beg the question—assume the truth of what they're trying to prove—by merely assuming that control of desire is required for free will.

But here we've reached an impasse. For incompatibilists will do the same thing: claim that Frankfurt begs the question by merely assuming that control is *not* required for free will. Both sides claim that the burden of proof belongs to their opponent. I'll let you decide what assumption you find more plausible.

Other philosophers, called "event causation" theorists,[13] hold that our actions need merely be the result of *non*-deterministic processes to be free. Some argue that this happens due to *quantum* events at the sub-atomic level of the brain's neurons that are fundamentally unpredictable and uncaused. These quantum events result in macro-level mental states, such as desires and volitions, which in turn lead to actions.[14] But even though quantum-level events bring about actions in a non-determined way, they occur *randomly* and thus aren't subject to an agent's *control*. Suppose a random, uncaused, quantum-level event in the microtubule fibers of a single neuron inside Tyrol's Cylon brain changed his program to make him want to follow the music he hears. Would this make him free if his behavior is still out of his control? No, I don't think it would.

It doesn't seem there's any way out of these dilemmas. If the universe is stuck in a deterministic repeating cycle or is predetermined by God, we can't do otherwise, aren't the ultimate cause of our actions, and don't have any real control over what occurs. No matter what strategy we try, we're still not free.

"It's Time to Make Your Choice"

Leoben suggests the cycle of the universe is a repeating story, in which the script never changes, though each time around God reassigns the roles. We've seen how there would be no possibility of freedom in such a universe. But what if Leoben is wrong? What if God doesn't assign roles, but simply offers them and persons can accept or reject them—and, if someone rejects a role, God will find someone else to fulfill it. Baltar seems to play the role of God's instrument, but only after he devotes himself to that purpose ("Six Degrees of Separation"), and the role is contingent upon his repentance ("33"). And when it comes to "the next generation of God's children," it appears that Baltar gets to choose whether to play the role of "protector" ("Kobol's Last Gleaming, Part 2").[15]

That the Book of Pythia isn't to be interpreted as literally as Leoben and the Gemenese understand it is suggested by Ron Moore:

> *MTV:* In one episode, audiences saw what seemed to be an American military Humvee on Caprica. Now the characters apparently know Bob Dylan's "All Along the Watchtower." Is this all meant to demonstrate that our two realities are closely interwoven?
>
> *Moore:* There is an idea in the show that all of this has happened before and all of it will happen again. There's a cycle of time and there's a sort of larger story that is told many times in many ways and that there is a direct connection between their reality and our reality. We will get to the reasons why all of these things are connected.[16]

Moore gives the impression that the repetition suggested by the Colonial scripture isn't as exact as we've been assuming, if the "larger story" is "told many times in many ways" and one of those ways may be how it's being told in the non-fictional universe right now.

If so, then free will isn't a lost cause. Many are free to accept or reject their roles. And if they can initially accept the role, but later reject it, pretty much every action is free. Every time Baltar does God's will, he freely "recommits" himself to playing the role of God's instrument. Of course, this makes God's "control" of the universe very loose; if everyone rejected their role, God wouldn't be able to have the story told.

This is only one way to interpret events in the *BSG* story. But if it's right, there are a number of other conclusions we can draw. Starbuck's role still seems to be predestined; her future is "already written" —not only Leoben, but also a human oracle seem to know her exact future ("Maelstrom"). If so, not only is she not free, but perhaps she's a Cylon and her destiny is evidenced by her programming, not her "role." And perhaps Six doesn't know with certainty anything about Baltar's future, but is just prodding him to accept the role offered to him.

Who knows? The answers may not even lie in *BSG*'s final episode. But one thing is clear: in a repeating universe—where, quite literally, "all of this has happened before, and all of it will happen again"—or in one determined by God or some other force, free will can't exist. *BSG* leaves the impression that the universe is like this, and so none of its characters—or us for that matter, since Earth is part of the story—is free.

NOTES

1   For more on the Cylons' rejection of human religion, see Robert Sharp's chapter in this volume.
2   For more on whether Cylons are persons who have free will, see Robert Arp and Tracie Mahaffey's chapter in this volume.
3   For discussion of the theological implications of the big bang, see Jason Eberl and Jennifer Vines' chapter in this volume.
4   For a great, quick rundown of the argument for the "big bang," see Gary Felder's "The Expanding Universe" at www4.ncsu.edu/unity/lockers/users/f/felder/public/kenny/papers/cosmo.html. More detail can be found in Simon Singh, *Big Bang: The Origin of the Universe* (New York: Fourth Estate Publishing, 2004).
5   Whether or not the universe will collapse depends on whether the density of the universe is above or below a certain value. If it's below, there's not enough matter to produce sufficient gravitational force to pull everything back together; if above, there is. The theoretical presence of "dark matter" (matter we can't see) makes the density of the universe hard to discover.

6   Actually, because of quantum-level indeterminacy (discussed below), it wouldn't be true that every atom in the universe would follow the *exact same* path each time. But let's assume, for the sake of discussion, that the universe does repeat in exactly the same way, as implied in *BSG*.

7   See Paul Churchland, *The Engine of Reason, The Seat of the Soul* (Cambridge, MA: MIT Press, 1995); Patricia Churchland, *Neurophilosophy: Toward a Unified Science of the Mind-Brain* (Cambridge, MA: MIT Press, 1986); and V. S. Ramachandran and Sandra Blakeslee, *Phantoms in the Brain* (New York: Quill William Morrow, 1998).

8   This explains how Cylons are able to create the human models. They're essentially just like humans—they have flesh, blood, and a brain just like humans do. They're just programmed differently. If the Cylons want a particular model to think she's human, they just program that assumption into her brain. This also explains how Cylons can survive death. Just as a program can be copied from one computer to another, a Cylon's program can be "downloaded" from a dead body into the brain of a new one. For more on the personal identity of Cylons, see Amy Kind's chapter in this volume.

9   The issue of divine predetermination is entirely different from the issue of divine *foreknowledge*—God's knowledge of the future. The first deals with God *deciding* how the future will go, the second with God *knowing* how the future will go. For more on the problem of divine foreknowledge, see Linda Zagzebski, *The Dilemma of Freedom and Foreknowledge* (New York: Oxford University Press, 1991); and Jason T. Eberl, "'You Cannot Escape Your Destiny' (Or Can You?): Freedom and Predestination in the Skywalker Family," in *Star Wars and Philosophy*, ed. Kevin S. Decker and Jason T. Eberl (Peru, IL: Open Court, 2005), 3–15.

10 One minor problem with this definition is that many who propose it still believe in RAP; they think being the "agent cause" of an action enables one to do otherwise. See Timothy O'Connor, *Persons and Causes* (New York: Oxford University Press, 2000).

11 See Ishtiyaque Haji, "Compatibilist Views of Freedom and Responsibility," in *The Oxford Handbook of Free Will*, ed. Robert Kane (New York: Oxford University Press, 2002), 202–28.

12 Harry Frankfurt, "Reply to John Martin Fischer," in *Contours of Agency: Essays on Themes from Harry Frankfurt*, ed. Sarah Buss and Lee Overton (Cambridge, MA: MIT Press, 2002), Section A.

13 See Alfred R. Mele, *Autonomous Agents: From Self-Control to Autonomy* (New York: Oxford University Press, 1995); Laura Waddell Ekstrom, *Free Will: A Philosophical Study* (Boulder: Westview Press,

2000); and Robert Kane, *The Significance of Free Will* (New York: Oxford University Press, 1996).

14 See Roger Penrose, *The Emperor's New Mind: Concerning Computers, Minds and the Laws of Physics* (New York: Oxford University Press, 2002).

15 Of course, it's unclear whether Baltar is *sincere* in his repentance and devotion to God's will, but at least it's sufficient to satisfy the "angel of God" (Six) in his head. For further discussion of Baltar's "conversion," see Jason Eberl and Jennifer Vines' chapter in this volume.

16 www.mtv.com/movies/news/articles/1556508/story.jhtml.

16

Adama's True Lie: Earth and the Problem of Knowledge

Eric J. Silverman

Battlestar Galactica begins with the ravaging of the known world. The survivors are demoralized, vastly outnumbered by the enemy, and homeless. Against this backdrop Commander Adama offers the promise of a new home where they'll be safe from the Cylons: Earth. But he *lies*. Yet, in a surprising twist of fate—though not to us who live here—it's later revealed that Adama told a "true lie." Earth does exist and the Colonials' search for it isn't in vain. Undertaking the journey to this "mythical" home of the Thirteenth Tribe is moment-ous and filled with religious significance for the Colonial survivors. *Faith* in Earth's existence gives meaning to an otherwise hopeless situation and shapes the choices they make along the way.

"You're Right. There's No Earth. It's All a Legend"

There's a sharp distinction between "true belief" and *knowledge*. President Roslin illustrates this when she asks, "How many people know the Cylons look human?" Colonel Tigh responds, "The rumor mill's been working overtime. Half the ship's talking about it." But Roslin retorts, "There'll always be rumors. For most people, that's all they'll ever be. I'm asking how many people actually know?" ("Water"). A belief based on an unverifiable rumor isn't knowledge, even if it happens to be true. Knowledge involves a belief in which one has reason for confidence.

A common view claims that knowledge is true belief accompanied by a convincing account justifying the belief. As Plato explains

192

in the *Theaetetus*:

> Now when a man gets a true judgment about something without an
> account, his soul is in a state of truth as regards that thing, but he does
> not know it; for someone who cannot give and take an account of a
> thing is ignorant about it. But when he has also got an account of it, he
> is capable of all this and is made perfect in knowledge.[1]

According to Plato, it's possible to attain truth without knowledge.
Knowledge is more certain than mere true belief since the knower
possesses a *compelling justification* for the belief's truthfulness. Someone holding a true belief based on a rumor or a lucky guess doesn't
have knowledge because she doesn't have a reason for confidence in
the belief.

The contemporary philosopher Edmund Gettier demonstrated the
inadequacy of this view of knowledge by providing counterexamples
in which a person's justification for a true belief turns out to be false.[2]
Say that Helo is walking down *Galactica*'s corridors and sees his
wife, Athena. Helo calls out to her, "Sharon!" because he has a compelling justification for believing that's her name. So he believes:

(a) The woman in front of me is my wife, Athena.

If Helo's justified in believing (a), knows his wife's name, and understands basic rules of reasoning, then he's also justified in believing:

(b) The woman in front of me is named "Sharon."

The truthfulness of (a) logically entails the truthfulness of (b).

But let's suppose Helo's mistaken, for it's actually Boomer who's
in front of him—having infiltrated *Galactica* for some nefarious
purpose. But Boomer is also named "Sharon." Helo's belief (b) turns
out to be true, but his justification for believing (b), belief (a), is false.
Gettier claims that a counterexample like this shows a justified true
belief that isn't knowledge since its justification is false. And this has
become known as "the Gettier problem."

Beliefs based on Adama's true lie about Earth are similar to Helo's
true belief based on a false justification. Starbuck believes:

(c) Adama knows the location of Earth.

This belief obviously implies:

(d) Earth exists.

It's arguable that Adama's public testimony that he knows the location of Earth, as well as his private assurances to Starbuck in "Kobol's Last Gleaming, Part 1," would be a proper justification for belief (c). It's reasonable to believe, as Adama claims, that he has access to privileged classified information as a "senior commander" in the Colonial Fleet. Hence, Starbuck is justified in believing that Earth exists based on his lie.

Even though Adama lies about knowing Earth's location and doesn't believe in its existence, it later becomes evident that Earth does exist. Starbuck discovers this for herself in the Tomb of Athena and after apparently journeying to Earth ("Home, Part 2"; "Crossroads, Part 2"). But Gettier would be quick to point out that, before these events, Starbuck holds a true belief (d) based on a false justification (c). Therefore, her true justified belief in Earth isn't really knowledge, until Adama's lie is no longer the primary justification for her belief.

"I'm Not a Cylon! . . . Maybe, But We Just Can't Take That Chance"

The Gettier problem is one of many puzzles in epistemology, the branch of philosophy concerned with the nature of knowledge. It's difficult to tell not only when one has knowledge, but also when one's beliefs are justified. The contemporary philosopher Alvin Goldman offers a theory of justification known as *reliabilism*, which proposes that a belief is justified when it's produced by a reliable process.[3] Sense experiences, memories, deduction, and induction are typical examples of generally reliable belief-forming processes. Each of these processes, however, has a different level of reliability. Induction, for example, is less reliable than deduction. And the reliability of a belief-forming process can vary based on one's situation. Sight is a reliable belief-forming process, yet beliefs based on sight are more reliable for close objects observed in well-lit conditions than for distant objects observed in poorly lit conditions.

One interesting aspect of reliabilism is that it doesn't require a person to know she's using a reliable process to be justified in her beliefs. If a young non-philosopher forms her beliefs based on the five senses, she's justified in those beliefs even if she never reflects upon the reliability of the senses. This has the desirable consequence of classifying many beliefs held by children, animals, and epistemically unreflective persons as justified.

In *BSG*, some typical belief-forming processes aren't as reliable as they are for us. *Sight* sometimes leads people to believe they're seeing a human being when they're actually seeing a Cylon. While people are usually correct when they believe they see a human, most would believe they see a human regardless of whether it's actually a Cylon. So sight isn't a reliable process for judging between humans and Cylons, even though it's a reliable process for forming other types of beliefs.[4]

Memory is another less dependable belief-forming process. Boomer can't remember that she sabotaged *Galactica*'s water tanks ("Water") and, until her Cylon nature is revealed to her, her memories thoroughly convince her that she's human, her parents are Katherine and Abraham Valerii, and her family died on Troy. Yet these beliefs couldn't be further from the truth. She doesn't give up these beliefs until confronted by numerous copies of herself aboard a Cylon baseship, and even then her initial reaction is disbelief ("Kobol's Last Gleaming, Part 2"). Similarly, Baltar wonders whether he might be a Cylon, and thus doubts whether he can trust his memories ("Torn"). Colonel Tigh, Sam Anders, Chief Tyrol, and Tory Foster are also deceived by their memories and are unaware of their actual Cylon nature ("Crossroads, Part 2"). The revelation, in particular, of Tigh and Anders' Cylon identity is truly shocking, as they're among the most adamantly anti-Cylon members of the fleet.

On the other hand, some unusual belief-forming processes are reliable in *BSG*, such as Baltar's visions of Number Six. While Six's advice is often cloaked in manipulative games and sarcasm, it frequently turns out to be a reliable way to form beliefs and accomplish desirable goals. Six draws Baltar's attention to a strange device on the Dradis console, and this leads him to "identify" Aaron Doral as a Cylon. But Baltar hasn't yet created his "mystic Cylon detector" and just makes up some techno-babble to convince Tigh that Doral's a Cylon so he can have an excuse to bring up the "odd device." It's disturbing when Tigh abandons Doral on Ragnar Station until it's revealed that Baltar was right all along ("Miniseries"). Six also encourages Baltar to test Boomer to see if she's a Cylon ("Flesh and Bone"); tells him to choose a target for the assault on a Cylon tylium refinery by *faith*, which turns out to be accurate ("The Hand of God"); helps him attain both the vice presidency and the presidency ("Colonial Day"; "Lay Down Your Burdens"); and reveals Hera's identity to him ("Exodus, Part 2").

Visions resulting from chamalla extract are also a reliable process for belief formation. Roslin's visions foresee her encounter with Leoben ("Flesh and Bone") and her leadership role in bringing the Colonials to Earth ("The Hand of God"). A chamalla-tripping oracle tells D'Anna/Three that she'll hold the Cylon-human hybrid Hera and experience love for the first time ("Exodus"); another oracle knows about Starbuck's upbringing and that Leoben—or at least a vision of him—will be coming for her ("Maelstrom").

Returning to epistemology, does reliabilism suggest that Adama's *testimony* is an appropriate justification for believing in Earth? Enlightenment era philosophers, such as David Hume (1711–1776), are critical of justifications based on testimony for this kind of issue. Hume claims testimony is only as reliable as experience suggests, and there are true claims that would be difficult to justify based on testimony:

> The reason, why we place any credit in witnesses and historians, is not derived from any *connection*, which we perceive *a priori*, between testimony and reality, but because we are accustomed to find a conformity between them. But when the fact attested is such a one as has seldom fallen under our observation, here is a contest of two opposite experiences; of which the one destroys the other, as far as its force goes, and the superior can only operate on the mind by the force, which remains. The very same principle of experience, which gives us a certain degree of assurance in the testimony of witnesses, gives us also, in this case, another degree of assurance against the fact, which they endeavor to establish; from which contradiction there necessarily arises a counterpoise, and mutual destruction of belief and authority.[5]

Hume believes that the ultimate basis for belief in anything is our own sensory experiences. We should trust other people's testimony only because experience suggests that testimony is typically accurate. Yet, even in everyday situations, testimony falls considerably short of absolute accuracy. It's sometimes unreliable because people are dishonest, as when Felix Gaeta claims he saw Baltar voluntarily sign the execution order for over two hundred innocent Colonists ("Crossroads, Part 2"); or because people are simply incorrect in their testimony, as when Tyrol sincerely tells Tigh that he's not a Cylon ("Resistance").

When someone testifies to something completely outside of our own experiences, we should be skeptical. Hume claims that someone who has never seen water freeze because he's spent his entire life in a tropical climate should be slow to accept testimony that water freezes at a cold temperature. Adama's claim to know Earth's location is similar, since the Colonials have no personal experience of Earth. This claim has no continuity with their personal experiences, though it doesn't actually conflict with these experiences. Hume contends we should be even more skeptical when testimony is used to justify beliefs that contradict our everyday experiences.

The contemporary philosopher Alvin Plantinga claims that testimony plays a more foundational role in our beliefs than Hume, and his predecessor John Locke (1632–1704), acknowledge:

> The Enlightenment looked askance at testimony and tradition; Locke saw them as a preeminent source of error. The Enlightenment idea is that perhaps we start by learning from others—our parents, for example. Properly mature and independent adults, however, will have passed beyond all that and believe what they do on the basis of the evidence. But this is a mistake; you can't know so much as your name or what city you live in without relying on testimony. (Will you produce your birth certificate for the first, or consult a handy map for the second? In each case you are of course relying on testimony.)[6]

Plantinga identifies a number of important beliefs that can be justified based only upon testimony. No one knows her name, age, or location without using testimony to justify such beliefs. The Enlightenment ideal of the radically independent thinker who weighs all claims against evidence from her own individual experiences is unrealistic and artificial. While testimony is far from infallible, it plays a more important epistemic role than Locke and Hume allow.

In either case, testimony-based justifications for believing in Earth need to be closely scrutinized. How trustworthy is the individual providing the testimony? How unlikely is his claim about Earth? Is the individual an appropriate authority concerning Earth? As the highest ranking military officer surviving the destruction of the Colonies and the author of their escape, Adama and his testimony seem naturally trustworthy. Starbuck certainly trusts Adama when she's confronted with the truth by Roslin:

> *Starbuck*: The old man is our last chance to find Earth. He knows where it is. He said so. You were there. The location is a secret. But he is going to take us there.
> *Roslin*: Commander Adama has no idea where Earth is. He never did. He made it up in order to give people hope.
> *Starbuck*: You're lying.
> *Roslin*: Go ask him.
> ("Kobol's Last Gleaming, Part 1")

When Starbuck does ask him, Adama tries to avoid her questions, but she's forced to conclude that Adama's patriotism and proficiency in fulfilling military duties don't make him an expert concerning Earth. As commander of a soon to be retired battlestar, Adama simply doesn't have access to Earth's location. The Gettier problem demonstrates that the Colonials' beliefs about Earth fall short of knowledge, and reliabilism suggests there's reason to doubt whether beliefs based on Adama's testimony are even justified.

"You Have to Have Something to Live For. Let it be Earth"

How should beliefs be chosen in an uncertain world? W. K. Clifford (1845–1879) says it's unethical to believe anything without sufficient evidence. This view, known as *evidentialism*, claims that if there isn't enough evidence to support a belief, one mustn't consent to its truth. One premise supporting evidentialism is that incorrect beliefs can have a damaging effect on society:

> And no one man's belief is in any case a private matter which concerns himself alone. Our lives are guided by that general conception of the

course of things which has been created by society for social purposes. Our words, our phrases, our forms and processes and modes of thought, are common property, fashioned and perfected from age to age; an heirloom which every succeeding generation inherits as a precious deposit and a sacred trust to be handed on to the next one, not unchanged but enlarged and purified, with some clear marks of its proper handiwork.[7]

It's not merely mistaken, imprudent, or foolish to believe something without adequate evidence, it's outright *immoral*, a violation of our ethical duties to one another. If Roslin believes it's the will of the gods to lead the Colonials to Earth without sufficient evidence, this belief could have damaging effects on the entire fleet. Even if a less influential person like Starbuck believes in Earth without enough evidence, her beliefs don't only affect herself, but others as well who may be inclined to agree with her. Clifford offers this sweeping conclusion: "To sum it up: it is wrong always, everywhere, and for anyone, to believe anything upon insufficient evidence" (518).

Clifford, however, doesn't recognize that in some situations knowledge is elusive and reliable justification uncertain; yet, believing *nothing* is a deeply damaging option. William James (1842–1910) claims that when definitive knowledge is impossible on a *momentous* and *forced* issue, it's reasonable to choose beliefs based on their *practical* consequences. He considers marriage and religious faith as two such decisions. In both cases a choice must be made in less than certain circumstances. Yet, these choices are forced: to withhold belief is effectively a choice against it, and necessarily results in the loss of potential desirable consequences. Marriage and faith are also momentous in their potential for positive results:

It is as if a man should hesitate indefinitely to ask a certain woman to marry him because he was not perfectly sure that she would prove an angel after he brought her home. Would he not cut himself off from that particular angel-possibility as decisively as if he went and married some one else?[8]

If there are desirable results from a specific committed relationship, they're inevitably lost if the relationship isn't embraced. It may be impossible for Apollo to know whether Anastasia Dualla would be a good wife; but the benefits offered by a committed relationship with her can't be gained without commitment. The choice can't be avoided, for avoiding it is an effective choice against the relationship. Lifelong bachelorhood isn't irrational or unjustifiable; but it's guaranteed to prevent Apollo from the benefits unique to a committed relationship with Dualla.

Or consider Apollo's unwillingness to see the conflict brewing between the fleet's military and civilian leadership. When his father chastises him for "siding" with Roslin, Apollo retorts, "I didn't know we were picking sides." Adama muses, "That's why you haven't picked one yet." Later, Apollo does choose his side—that of *democracy* ("Bastille Day"; "Kobol's Last Gleaming, Part 2"). Due to Apollo's important position in the fleet and his personal relationships with both Adama and Roslin, it's inevitable that he's forced to choose between the military and civilian factions. When given orders to arrest Roslin, he has no choice but to choose a side. His choice was also momentous. By siding with Roslin, he stands up for democracy at the cost of his own freedom.

James views religious faith as a similarly momentous decision. He claims no argument proves the truthfulness of religious faith with certainty. Even so, at some point a decision must be made. The choice is forced. To put off the choice indefinitely is effectively to reject religion. Furthermore, the question of religion is momentously important. Many religious thinkers claim it offers a life filled with greater meaning and purpose, along with eternal happiness after death. Agnosticism cuts one off from any good attainable by embracing religion. Gaining the benefits of religious faith, for this life or the afterlife, may require a choice here and now (524). An agnostic has no chance for the benefits of religion, just as the lifelong bachelor has no chance for the goods of marriage (520). Similarly, the agnostic cuts himself off from any advantages from atheism. If religion is false and all genuine goods are located in the here and now, then withholding consent from atheism is also a damaging choice. It's wiser to embrace atheism rather than agnosticism, since it frees one to pursue the goods of life wholeheartedly.

Faith that Earth awaits at the end of the Colonial fleet's journey mirrors James's other momentous and forced choices. When comfortable life was possible on the Twelve Colonies, the question of Earth's existence was an abstract issue with little consequence stemming from belief or unbelief. The issue was neither momentous nor forced.

But once the Colonies were destroyed, the issue became moment-ous: either there's a home where the survivors will be welcomed as brothers and sisters, or they're homeless and alone. The choice also becomes forced. Agnosticism concerning Earth is no longer a prac-tical option. They can embrace the search for Earth or reject the hope of Earth by settling on the first safely habitable planet they encounter, but to do neither is ridiculous.

The importance of this issue is seen when the Colonials elect Baltar to the presidency based on his promise to settle on New Caprica and cease the search for Earth ("Lay Down Your Burdens, Part 2"). By abandoning the search, the Colonials cut themselves off from hope for a better life than what they can make for themselves on this less-than-inviting world. Yet, either choice is better than no choice. Most of the Colonials don't have access to compelling evidence that Earth exists. It's reasonable for them to believe that rebuilding civilization on New Caprica is their only hope for a permanent home. By settling on New Caprica, they have the opportunity for some benefits: breath-ing fresh air and growing food instead of living in tin boxes and eating rations. Clifford's advice would allow them neither option. There isn't enough evidence to support the belief in and search for Earth, but there's also insufficient evidence that settling on New Cap-rica is the wisest option. If they continually wander without settling on a planet, and cease pursuing Earth, they cut themselves off from the benefits of both.

Even apart from any potential benefits of a successful search for Earth, there are benefits gained simply from possessing an overarch-ing life-quest. Adama's lie isn't motivated by a desire to find Earth, but by a more subtle rationale. He understands that humans need purpose, especially in difficult circumstances. Without purpose, we wither, give up hope, and die. He lies because he wants the survivors to hope and avoid despair in the hardest of times.

Some philosophers advocate skepticism since virtually every belief can be questioned based on an argument for the conflicting view. But James shows us that a truly skeptical approach to life can be detri-mental since it requires rejecting potentially rewarding opportunities. And a truly skeptical life is perhaps impossible since so many deci-sions are unavoidably forced. Whether to embrace life and meaning amidst uncertainty is a forced and momentous decision. Blind leaps of faith are dangerous and cynical skepticism concerning everything is unrewarding. The confidence of *certainty* evades many of us, but choices must be made. Avoiding the central choices of life in an attempt to risk nothing, hope for nothing, love nothing, and believe in nothing beyond the indubitable is both impractical and impossible. So say we all.[9]

NOTES

1 Myles Burnyeat, *The Theaetetus of Plato*, trans. M. J. Levett (Indianapolis: Hackett, 1990), 202c.
2 Edmund Gettier, "Is Justified True Belief Knowledge?" *Analysis* 23 (1963): 121–3.
3 See Alvin Goldman, "What Is Justified Belief?" in *Justification and Knowledge*, ed. G. S. Pappas (Dordrecht: D. Reidel, 1976), 1–23.
4 See Alvin Goldman, "Discrimination and Perceptual Knowledge," *Journal of Philosophy* 73 (1976), 771–9.
5 David Hume, "Of Miracles," in *Dialogues Concerning Natural Religion*, ed. Richard H. Popkin (Indianapolis: Hackett, 1998), 110.
6 Alvin Plantinga, *Warranted Christian Belief* (New York: Oxford University Press, 2000), 147.
7 W. K. Clifford, "The Ethics of Belief," in *The Theory of Knowledge*, ed. Louis P. Pojman (Belmont, CA: Wadsworth/Thompson, 2003), 516–17. Further references will be given in the text.
8 William James, "The Will to Believe," in *The Theory of Knowledge*, ed. Louis P. Pojman (Belmont, CA: Wadsworth/Thompson, 2003), 524. Further references will be given in the text.
9 Thanks to Jason Eberl, John Greco, and Rob Arp for their comments on earlier versions of this chapter.

PART V

SAGITTARONS, CAPRICANS, AND GEMENESE: DIFFERENT WORLDS, DIFFERENT PERSPECTIVES

17

Zen and the Art of Cylon Maintenance

James McRae

"I only want you to see the truth of your life. The reason why you suffered and you struggled for so long. That's why God sent me to you" ("Occupation"). Leoben, a Cylon, utters these words shortly after his fifth death at the hands of Kara "Starbuck" Thrace. Though it may be hard to believe at first, the mission Leoben claims to pursue isn't so different from the one taken up by the historical Buddha. Both Buddha and Leoben aim to understand the nature of suffering and seek to eliminate it from the world. In fact, *BSG* explores a number of themes that resonate with key concepts in Zen Buddhism. And, as we shall see, the Buddhist themes suggest that the Cylons are sentient beings who face an existential crisis similar to the one that defines human life. In the end, the solutions to the unsatisfactory existence of both species might be fundamentally intertwined.

"Life is a Testament to Pain": Suffering, Ignorance, and Interdependent Arising

Zen is a Japanese religious and philosophical tradition with roots in Indian Mahāyanā Buddhism. The historical Buddha, Siddhartha Gautama (563–483 BCE), dedicated his life to the study of how to eliminate suffering in the world. His solution to this problem is summarized in his teaching of the Noble Fourfold Truth.[1]

First Noble Truth: Life is characterized by duhkha

The Sanskrit word *duhkha*, which the Buddha uses to describe life, is typically translated as "suffering" or "sorrow," though "unsatisfactoriness" may best capture the full range of its multi-layered meanings. The Japanese translation, *ku*, carries with it the complexity of the Sanskrit term, meaning either suffering—in the sense of *physical* pain—or anxiety—in the sense of *psychological* distress. Death, sickness, poverty, famine, infirmity, racism, and warfare are commonplace and lead to suffering on a large scale. This unsatisfactoriness is even more pronounced in *BSG*. Human civilization has been all but annihilated and the human race is forced to live a nomadic lifestyle, constantly hounded by the Cylons. In "33," for example, the fleet is deprived of sleep for days on end as they make FTL jumps every 33 minutes to avoid their pursuers. Ultimately, they're forced to destroy the *Olympic Carrier* and its 1,345 passengers to save themselves from an apparent nuclear threat.

Second Noble Truth: Duhkha *is a result of our ignorant attachment to false ideals*

Human beings suffer because we attach ourselves to attitudes, doctrines, and prejudices that obscure the way the world really is. This attachment leads to craving, which causes us to act in ways that promote *duhkha*. Leoben explains this concept to Starbuck during his torture:

> I know you. You're damaged. You were born to a woman who believed that suffering was good for the soul, so you suffered. Your life is a testament to pain. Injuries. Accidents. Some inflicted upon others, others inflicted upon yourself. It surrounds you like a bubble. But it's not real . . . It's just something she put in your head. It's something that you wanna believe because it means you're the problem, not the world that you live in. ("Flesh and Bone")

The suffering in our lives is "not real" in the sense that it's self-inflicted through our attachments. Suffering arises because, due to these attachments to false ideals, we're profoundly ignorant of the true nature of reality, which Zen describes as *engi*, or *interdependent arising*. This notion consists of two concepts: no-self and impermanence.[2]

Concerning no-self, Dōgen (1200–1253 CE), founder of the Japanese Sōtō School of Zen, describes the nature of Zen training:

> To study the buddha way is to study the self. To study the self is to forget the self. To forget the self is to be actualized by myriad things. When actualized by myriad things, your body and mind as well as the bodies and minds of others drop away. No trace of realization remains, and this no-trace continues endlessly.[3]

Typically, people experience the world individualistically, as if each person is a unique and detached entity. According to Zen, however, all things in the universe are part of an interrelated web of being, which means that no person is separate from or superior to the rest of reality. In this sense, people can be said to have no-self—*muga*, or *anātman* in Sanskrit—in the sense that no person is an isolated entity. Selfish actions—those that are grounded in the good of the individual at the expense of others—ultimately lead to suffering. Human beings are defined by their relationships with other people and with the world around them. In *BSG*, each person's character is revealed and developed through his relationships. Saul Tigh is characterized by his tumultuous relationship with his wife and his abusive treatment of the crew. Chief Tyrol and Helo are defined by their relationships with the two Sharons. Apollo's character is an extension of his turbulent interactions with his father, his unpredictable relationship with Starbuck, and his sense of self-identity as an officer of the fleet.

The second part of interdependent arising is impermanence—*mujō*, or *anitya* in Sanskrit. Dōgen states, "The thought of enlightenment . . . is the mind which sees into impermanence" (32). All things in the universe are in a constant process of arising, existing, and decaying. Nothing can be taken for granted in life; all things ultimately fall away into oblivion. This isn't meant, however, to be a pessimistic view of reality. Zen aesthetics uses the concept of *mono no aware* to describe the "tragic beauty of impermanent things."[4] In Japan, cherry blossoms appear in the spring for only a few days before they're scattered by the wind. The fact that their beauty is fleeting only intensifies their aesthetic appeal: everything of value in life must be fully appreciated for what it is in each moment, since it might be the last opportunity one has for such an experience. This impermanence is evident in every episode of *BSG*. All twelve colonies have been destroyed, leaving only about fifty thousand humans alive, and President Roslin keeps track of this conspicuously dwindling number. Major characters are routinely killed throughout the series: Billy, Ellen Tigh, and Kat, to name but a few. Roslin accepts the prophesied role of the "leader who suffered a wasting disease and would not live to enter the new land," and her awareness of death strengthens her resolve to find Earth as quickly as possible ("The Hand of God"). The consciousness of constantly impending death sharpens the characters' awareness of the value of life and the particular relationships they have with others.

Third Noble Truth: If we eliminate our ignorant attachment to false ideals, we can eliminate duhkha

Much of the suffering we endure in the world is self-inflicted. Dōgen states that "in attachment flowers fall, and in aversion weeds spread" (69). Our attachment to false ideals leads to injury and suffering, as does our neglect of our responsibilities. Because we view ourselves ego-istically, as if we were separate from and superior to the rest of reality, we inflict suffering upon others, whom we treat as nothing more than raw material for our own satisfaction. The Cylons think of themselves as superior to humans in every way. Human women, for example, are used as tools in the Cylon breeding program ("The Farm"). Humans aren't much better, having originally created the Cylons to do their bidding and thus treating them as nothing more than "walking chrome toasters." After the attack on the Colonies, captured Cylons are sometimes beaten, raped, or executed ("Flesh and Bone"; "Pegasus"). There are exceptions to these attitudes, as evidenced by the Cylon-human relationships between the Sharons and both Helo and Tyrol, and between Baltar and Caprica Six (and later with D'Anna/Three). These relationships lead, on a small scale, to some "humanitarian" efforts on the part of both Cylons and humans to minimize the suffering inflicted upon the other race. Other examples of self-inflicted suffering include Tigh's alcoholism and vitriolic personality, Starbuck's chronic insubordination and inability to maintain interpersonal relationships, and Baltar's perpetual dishonesty and selfishness.

Fourth Noble Truth: Unsatisfactoriness can be eliminated through the cultivation of wisdom, compassion, and meditative practices

Dōgen states that "The great way of all buddhas, thoroughly practiced, is emancipation and realization" (84). Traditionally referred to as the Noble Eightfold Path, a person can eliminate suffering in the world if he cultivates himself so that he removes his attachments to false ideals and understands the true nature of reality as interdependent arising. When he does this, he reaches *satori*, the state of enlightenment. Before we can discuss the possibility of enlightenment in *BSG*, we must first examine Zen Buddhism's understanding of rebirth, divinity, and personhood.

"All of This Has Happened Before . . .": Karma and Rebirth

For Buddhism, the unsatisfactoriness of life is augmented by the fact that all non-enlightened, sentient beings are reincarnated after death. Morally inappropriate acts build up *karma—gō—*which is like a metaphysical record of moral worth. There's no such thing as "good karma"; all karma is "bad karma" in that it binds a person to the cycle of death and rebirth.[5] When people die, their karma carries on to another life and can influence the nature of their rebirths: vicious human beings with significant karma might return as non-human animals, while virtuous beings who have eliminated most of their karma through moral actions might return in a social position that'll make it easier for them to attain enlightenment in that lifetime. This cycle of death and rebirth is known as the wheel of *samsāra—rinne—*and the only way to exit this process is through the complete elimination of karma.

As Leoben tells Starbuck:

> To know the face of God is to know madness. I see the universe. I see the patterns. I see the foreshadowing that precedes every moment of every day . . . What is the most basic article of faith? This is not all that we are. The difference between you and me is, I know what that means and you don't. I know that I'm more than this body, more than this consciousness. ("Flesh and Bone")

Roslin adds to the explanation, "If you believe in the gods, then you believe in the cycle of time, that we are all playing our parts in a story that is told again and again and again throughout eternity" ("Kobol's Last Gleaming, Part 1"). Human beings have lived their lives countless times before and will revisit these same roles again and again. Roslin speaks of herself as "fulfilling the role of the leader" that's mentioned in the Book of Pythia ("Fragged").

The concept of cyclical time and recurring roles is echoed by Number Six:

> *Baltar*: I thought Kobol was supposed to be a paradise or something. Some place where gods lived with the humans in harmony, or . . .
> *Six*: For a time, perhaps. Then your true nature asserted itself. Your brutality. Your depravity. Your barbarism.
> *Baltar*: So the scriptures are all a lie. It's all just a lie, just a cover-up for all this savagery.
> *Six*: Exactly. All of this has happened before, Gaius, and all of it will happen again.
> ("Valley of Darkness")

In Buddhism, the karma that causes our rebirth also predisposes us to commit unethical acts due to the vicious habits acquired in our previous lives.[6] Human beings, due to our selfish attachment to false ideals, have perpetuated a cycle of violence throughout history. A person's karmic predisposition towards certain habits, however, doesn't fatalistically predetermine her course of action. She can choose to change these habits and, through the cultivation of wisdom, compassion, and meditation, eventually eliminate karma. This notion is echoed in Elosha's reassurance to Roslin: "Laura, this is your path, the one the gods picked for you, the one you picked for yourself" ("The Farm"). Though the gods influence the fate of human beings, it would seem that people still must choose the roles that they'll play in life.[7] It's important to note that while this notion of temporal repetition parallels the Buddhist idea of rebirth, there's no mention in *BSG* thus far of a definitive way *out* of this cycle.

Cylon existence also consists of a repeated cycle of birth, death, and resurrection. Cylons who die in the proximity of a resurrection ship have their memories immediately downloaded into another body:

> *Baltar*: The Cylons call this their Resurrection ship. At the moment, we are too far away from the Cylon home world for the normal downloading process to work. Which is why they built this ship. It contains the entire apparatus necessary for Cylon resurrection. Now, this ship has been traveling with the fleet, trailing *Galactica* for the last several months.
>
> *Starbuck*: So it's a safety net. A place where they fall back to when they die.
>
> *Cain*: And if they lose their safety net . . .
>
> *Starbuck*: Then any Cylon who dies out here . . .
>
> *Cain*: Would be dead. As in, really dead. And I dare say they won't like that.
>
> *Starbuck*: No, sir. They might even stop chasing us. Why risk getting killed if you can't just wake up all nice and cozy in a brand-new body?
>
> ("Resurrection Ship, Part 1")

As with karma, the overall moral character of a downloaded Cylon is preserved: Boomer, at first, remains compassionate and loyal to humans, as does Caprica Six ("Downloaded"); Leoben maintains his pursuit of Starbuck despite being killed by her numerous times ("Occupation"); and Scar is "filled with more bitter memories" each time he undergoes the "painful and traumatic experience" of being shot down by a Viper ("Scar"). Unlike Buddhism, it doesn't seem that there's hope for a Cylon to improve her position in life with each rebirth; she simply gets a fresh, identical body. D'Anna and Baltar's quest, however, to unlock the mysteries of the "final five" Cylons suggests that in-between death and downloading, certain metaphysical truths can be obtained that will expand her awareness in the next incarnation ("Hero").

"God Has a Plan for You, Gaius": Religion, God, and *Kenōsis*

Any discussion of religion within the context of *BSG* must take into account the variety of religious traditions depicted in the series. Yet, how is it possible for there to be Zen themes in *BSG* when Buddhism seems to reject the transcendent God or gods to whom humans and Cylons regularly appeal?

Nishida Kitarō (1870–1945), founder of the Kyoto School,[8] is renowned for his Zen-based philosophy of religion that describes God as Absolute Nothingness. For Nishida, the being to whom we appeal when we invoke the notion of God is not a transcendent, personal creator, but the absolute, undifferentiated ground of all existence. A person's true self is found through *kenōsis*, a notion drawn from Christian theology (Philippians 2:5–8) that closely parallels the Buddhist idea of emptiness—*ku*, or *śūnyatā*. *Kenōsis* is a process through which a person empties his individualistic self into his relationships with other people and with the Absolute. Even God takes part in this process of *kenōsis*:

> A God who is simply self-sufficient is not the true God. In one sense, God must empty Himself through *kenōsis*. A God that is both thoroughly transcendent and thoroughly immanent, both thoroughly immanent and thoroughly transcendent, is a truly dialectical God. If it is said that God created the world from love, then God's absolute love must be essential to the absolute self-negation of God and is not *opus ad extra*.[9]

Even God takes part in this process of self-emptying, which means that the Absolute is omnipresent and intensely personal. Leoben echoes this notion: "We're all God, Starbuck. All of us. I see the love that binds all living things together" ("Flesh and Bone"). By emptying themselves into their relationships with God and with each other, humans and Cylons draw closer to the Absolute. This is particularly evident in human-Cylon relationships. Sharon tells Helo that "what we had between us was important . . . Because it brings us closer to God" ("Kobol's Last Gleaming, Part 2").

The Cylons' understanding of God is remarkably similar to Nishida's Absolute. Six describes God to Baltar as pure love:

> If you would give yourself over to God's will, you'd find peace in his love like I have . . . It's important you form a personal relationship with God. Only you can give yourself over to his eternal love. ("Six Degrees of Separation")

If a person empties himself into his relationship with God, this process of self-negation will allow him to embrace the love that is God's

212

very nature. There's only one true, universal God, and though it's polytheistic, the Colonists' religion is directed towards the same Absolute. Leoben tells Starbuck, "Our faiths are similar, but I look to one God, not to many" ("Flesh and Bone"), and Six says to Baltar: "He's not my God. He is God" ("Six Degrees of Separation").[10]

In the Zen tradition, a pupil's study is guided by a *roshi*, an enlightened master of the Buddhist Way. A method of training that's commonplace in the Rinzai tradition of Zen is the use of *kōans*, which are puzzling questions or anecdotes upon which a student is expected to meditate. *Kōans* force the student to doubt the dualistic, false ideals that she has customarily used to interpret the world, and thereby push her closer to enlightenment by bringing about the death of her old, egoistic self.[11] Rinzai master Hakuin states:

> If you are not a hero who has truly seen into his own nature, don't think it is something that can be known easily. If you wish accordance with the true, pure non-ego, you must be prepared to let go your hold when hanging from a sheer precipice, to die and return again to life.[12]

A good roshi uses *kōans* to force students to question themselves, which pushes them to a deeper awareness of the false ideals that lead to their suffering. This ultimately leads to the death of the old self and rebirth as a new, enlightened being.[13]

In *BSG*, Leoben acts as a type of roshi who causes those with whom he interacts to question themselves and their sense of purpose. Trapped with Commander Adama inside Ragnar Station, pretending to be human, he questions human habits of violence that have led to suffering:

> *Leoben*: Suspicion and distrust . . . That's military life, right?
> *Adama*: You're a gun-dealer-philosopher, I take it, right?
> *Leoben*: I'm an observer of human nature. When you get right down to it, humanity is not a pretty race. I mean, we're only one step away from beating each other with clubs like savages fighting over scraps of meat. Maybe the Cylons are God's retribution for our many sins.
> ("Miniseries")

Leoben's speech mirrors the teachings of Buddhism: the selfish attachments of humankind have led to immense suffering in the world. Human beings must realize that their current state of suffering is largely a result of their own actions. Leoben later causes Starbuck to question the personhood of the Cylons and the purpose of human existence. Leoben is not, of course, a moral exemplar; Cylons are guilty of perpetuating at least as much suffering as humans. But, as Six points out to Baltar on this score, "Yes, well, we're your children. You taught us well" ("Valley of Darkness"). The apparent hypocrisy of the Cylons' actions isn't enough to invalidate the moral claims that they make: selfishness and ignorance lead to suffering.

"How Could Anyone Fall in Love with a Toaster?" Cylons as Persons?

On Ragnar, Leoben tries to convince Adama that the Cylons have evolved from mere machines into persons, as evidenced by the fact that "they've developed a culture, a society, an entire way of life."[14] Certainly, the Cylons appear to be human in many respects, but is it possible for Buddhism to consider them persons in the *moral* sense? Buddhism places moral worth on all beings that have sentience, the capacity to feel pain. Some creatures have the ability not only to *feel* pain, but to be cognitively aware of that pain as well, which heightens their capacity for suffering. Cylons clearly have the ability to feel pain and to suffer psychologically, as evidenced by Starbuck's torture of Leoben:

> *Starbuck*: Kind of bad programming, isn't it? I mean, why bother with hunger?
> *Leoben*: Part of being human.
> *Starbuck*: You're not human. How's your lunch?
> *Leoben*: You know how it is. When you're starving, anything tastes good.
> [The guard strikes him]
> *Starbuck*: Did that hurt?
> *Leoben*: Yeah, that hurt.
> *Starbuck*: Machines shouldn't feel pain, shouldn't bleed, shouldn't sweat.
> *Leoben*: Sweat. That's funny. That's good.
> *Starbuck*: See, a smart Cylon would turn off the old pain software about now. But I don't think you're so smart.
> *Leoben*: Maybe I'll turn it off and you won't even know.
> [The guard strikes him again]

Starbuck: Here's your dilemma. Turn off the pain, you feel better, but that makes you a machine, not a person. You see, human beings can't turn off their pain. Human beings have to suffer, and cry, and scream, and endure, because they have no choice.
("Flesh and Bone")

Leoben suggests he can turn off his pain receptors, yet he refuses to do so because it's the capacity to feel hunger and pain that, in his mind, makes him human. But the capacity for suffering alone isn't enough to make the Cylons persons. Buddhists would assert that a rabbit has moral significance and shouldn't be injured, but that doesn't mean it's capable of reaching *satori*.

Suffering is more than the simple capacity to feel pain; it involves the cognitive ability to be aware of the significance of pain and loss in the present, past, and future. Cylons seem to have this ability as well, since Leoben can fear his impending death away from a resurrection ship, and Caprica Six and Sharon can feel remorse—and endure a crisis of character—as a result of their contributions to the destruction of the human race ("Flesh and Bone"; "Downloaded"). Cylons are almost identical to human beings in the functional sense: they're at least our equals cognitively and physically. Because Cylons are volitional beings, they're capable of earning and removing karma, which means that, like humans, they should be capable of reaching *satori*. Thus, in the Buddhist understanding of the term, Cylons ought to be considered persons.

If the Cylons are persons, and if the fate of humans and Cylons is intertwined as Leoben and Six suggest, then the two species ought to seek a peaceful resolution to their conflict. The suffering endured in the war between humans and Cylons comes as a result of both species' attachment to selfish notions of superiority that defy the interdependent nature of reality. Buddhism teaches that awareness of interdependent arising ultimately results in a profound sense of compassion for all sentient beings. If humans and Cylons can learn to be both wise and compassionate, perhaps they can achieve reconciliation. As Dōgen states:

There is a simple way to become a buddha: When you refrain from unwholesome actions, are not attached to birth or death, and are compassionate toward all sentient beings, respectful to seniors and kind to juniors, not excluding or desiring anything, with no designing thoughts or worries, you will be called a buddha. Do not seek anything else (75).

The Noble Eightfold Path of Buddhism consists of three categories of cultivation: *wisdom* (right views and intentions), *ethics* (right speech, actions, and livelihood), and *meditation* (right effort, mindfulness, and concentration). Wisdom comes through the realization of inter-dependent arising, which in turn leads to a profound compassion for all things, since everything is part of a dynamic, interrelated whole. Yet both wisdom and compassion can be gained only through med-itation, the calming of the body and mind that opens a person's perceptions to the truth of interdependent arising. There's no indica-tion that anyone in *BSG* practices seated meditation (right concentra-tion); though some exhibit traces of mindfulness and right effort by honestly acknowledging their own flaws and striving to amend them. Perhaps if meditation were a more common practice, suffering could be eliminated from the *BSG* universe. But how entertaining a show would that be?

NOTES

1 This summary of the Noble Fourfold Truth is drawn from the Buddha's first sermon, translated with commentary by John M. Koller and Patricia Koller in *A Sourcebook in Asian Philosophy* (New York: Mac-millan, 1991), 195–6.

2 In Sanskrit, this term *engi* is *pratitya-samutpāda*, and can be altern-atively translated as "dependent origination" or "dependent co-arising." This concept describes the world as a deeply interrelated process that's in a state of constant flux. The "interdependent" aspect of the world is manifested in the Buddhist doctrine of no-self, while "arising" is evident in the impermanence of all things.

3 Dōgen, *Moon in a Dewdrop: Writings of Zen Master Dōgen*, ed. Kasuaki Tanahashi (New York: North Point Press, 1985), 70. Further references will be given in the text.

4 William Theodore De Bary, "The Vocabulary of Japanese Aesthetics, I, II, III," in *Japanese Aesthetics and Culture: A Reader*, ed. Nancy G. Hume (Albany: State University of New York Press, 1995), 44. Dōgen himself writes a poem celebrating the impermanent beauty of cherry blossoms (14).

5   Good actions, rather than providing "good karma," extinguish the karma a person has accumulated through morally inappropriate actions. This is why the term *nirvana*, which literally means "snuffing out," is used to describe the state of enlightenment that comes when the flames of karma have been doused.

6   See Nishitani Keiji's discussion of karma, rebirth, and time in *Religion and Nothingness*, trans. Jan Van Bragt (Berkeley: University of California Press 1982), 238–50.

7   For discussion of fatalism in the context of *BSG*, see David Kyle Johnson's chapter in this volume.

8   The Kyoto School is based on an East-West philosophical synthesis. It draws on Zen in comparison to Western thought, mostly existentialism.

9   *Nishida Kitarō, Zenshū*, vol. 11, translated by Steve Odin in *The Social Self in Zen and American Pragmatism* (Albany: State University of New York Press, 1996), 106. See also Masao Abe, "Kenotic God and Dynamic Sunyata," in *The Emptying God: A Buddhist-Jewish-Christian Conversation*, ed. John B. Cobb, Jr. and Christopher Ives (Eugene, OR: Wipf & Stock, 2005).

10 Note that the Number Six who appears in the flesh on *Galactica* to test Baltar's faith calls herself "Miss Godfrey."

11 For a thorough explanation of the use of *kōans* in Zen practice, see D. T. Suzuki, *An Introduction to Zen Buddhism* (New York: Grove Press, 1964), 99–117; or T. P. Kasulis, *Zen Action, Zen Person* (Honolulu: University of Hawaii Press, 1981), 104–24.

12 Hakuin, *The Zen Master Hakuin: Selected Writings*, trans. Philip B. Yampolsky (New York: Columbia University Press, 1971), 135.

13 For further discussion of the Buddhist concept of death and rebirth in another sci-fi context, see Walter Robinson, "Death and Rebirth of a Vulcan Mind" in *Star Trek and Philosophy*, ed. Jason T. Eberl and Kevin S. Decker (Peru, IL: Open Court Press, 2008).

14 For further discussion of Cylon personhood, see Robert Arp and Tracie Mahaffey's chapter in this volume.

18

"Let It Be Earth": The Pragmatic Virtue of Hope

Elizabeth F. Cooke

Pragmatism is a philosophy of hope in an uncertain future, hope that we can become something of our own making and our own design. Historically, this worldview emerges in the writings of nineteenth and twentieth-century American thinkers Charles S. Peirce, William James, and John Dewey. But pragmatists believe their worldview captures the universal human condition, cutting across all cultures and all times. So it shouldn't surprise us to find pragmatism within the world of *Battlestar Galactica* right from the beginning. After the Cylon attack, Commander Adama addresses his crew at a funeral for their shipmates who've fallen:

> Are they the lucky ones? That's what you're thinking, isn't it? We're a long way from home. We've jumped way beyond the Red Line into uncharted space. Limited supplies. Limited fuel. No allies. And now no hope! ("Miniseries")

Much more than the Cylons, the loss of hope is the true enemy of humanity. Adama knows his people need hope so badly that he's willing to lie to them. Referring to the myth of the Thirteenth Tribe that had settled on a planet called Earth, Adama reveals that he alone knows the planet's secret location. It's a "noble lie," and President Roslin calls him on it. But Adama doesn't flinch. The people need something to believe in. Our souls are future-oriented, and without hope in becoming something greater, humanity is truly lost. This theme underlies the entire *BSG* series: hope in the promised land, hope in political utopia, hope in the truth of the scriptures, hope

218

against hope in the face of battle, hope for a reconciliation with the Cylons—hope even, on the part of some, in a future race of Cylon-human hybrids—but always hope in each other and for a better tomorrow. Hope holds humanity together, and without it the war is already lost.

Peirce and Adama: Hopeful Pragmatism

Prior to pragmatism, Western philosophy tended to emphasize *doubt*. Because many of our beliefs have been mistaken, skeptical philosophers argued that we should suspend our beliefs until we can secure absolutely certain beliefs, which would count as true knowledge. But pragmatists recognize that absolute certainty is impossible to achieve. Furthermore, we can't suspend beliefs awaiting absolute certainty, since we constantly find ourselves in a world that demands acting upon our beliefs. Yet pragmatists argue that even without certainty, and knowing that many of our beliefs are probably in error, we're able to discover new things about the world by coming together as a community of inquirers and *acting*—forming hypotheses, testing through experiments, and fallibly working toward our cognitive goals.

Charles S. Peirce (1839–1914) first emphasizes the importance of hope within scientific inquiry. Peirce believes hope is an important cognitive value aiding the discovery of new ideas, because without hope, scientists wouldn't engage in experiments in the first place—hope is a sentiment *demanded by logic*.[1] Scientists must hope that their questions will be answered. This hope, however, is justified only because we can do nothing of value without it. Peirce uses the term "abduction" to refer to the formation of hypotheses. Science, he explains, depends on guessing, which in turn depends on the hope that we can come to know the world:

> I now proceed to consider what principles should guide us in abduction, or the process of choosing a hypothesis. Underlying all such principles there is a fundamental and primary abduction, a hypothesis which we must embrace at the outset, however destitute of evidentiary support it may be. That hypothesis is that the facts in hand admit of rationalization, and of rationalization by us. That we must hope they do, for the same reason that a general who has to capture a position, or see his country ruined, must go on the hypothesis that there is some

219

way in which he can and shall capture it. We must be animated by that hope concerning the problem we have in hand, whether we extend it to a general postulate covering all facts, or not. Now, that the matter of no new truth can come from induction or from deduction, we have seen. It can only come from abduction; and abduction is, after all, nothing but guessing. We are therefore bound to hope that, although the possible explanations of our facts may be strictly innumerable, yet our mind will be able in some finite number of guesses, to guess the sole true explanation of them. *That* we are bound to assume, independently of any evidence that it is true. Animated by that hope, we are to proceed to the construction of a hypothesis.[2]

Hope isn't an expectation and isn't quite like other beliefs, since it doesn't rest on evidence. Hope requires *risk*. Yet, despite its lack of warrant, Peirce doesn't consider hope irrational. Rather, it's a most natural and useful faculty (112). Indeed, scientists must *cultivate* hope in order to achieve their goals.

Adama understands this need for hope in achieving goals. But there's a difference between Peirce's view of hope as warrantless and Adama's outright lie. It's one thing to believe without knowing. But Adama appeals to the Sacred Scrolls that describe the lost Thirteenth Colony of Earth, and convinces his crew that he knows where Earth is and can help them find this new home. Yet he doesn't believe this myth—he doesn't share in this hope:

Adama: You're right. There's no Earth. It's all a legend.
Roslin: Then why?
Adama: Because it's not enough to just live. You have to have something to live for. Let it be Earth.
Roslin: They'll never forgive you.
Adama: Maybe. But in the meantime, I've given all of us a fighting chance to survive. And isn't that what you said was the most important thing—survival of the human race?
("Miniseries")

Adama lies because he believes it's in humanity's interests. This is the idea of the "noble lie," which goes back to Plato's *Republic*, in which Plato argues that a city would function best if all the citizens were made to believe a lie about their history. They should be told that they were all born of the earth, as brothers and sisters, but made of different quality "metals," which belong in different social classes. The bronze craft people would be at the bottom, silver guardians in the middle, and golden philosopher kings at the top.[3] This lie is meant to instill a unity, while, at the same time, justify a political hierarchy.

Similarly, Adama believes lying is essential to keep the people unified, even while they're differentiated according to various social roles within the fleet. But Adama's lie is different from Plato's in that he gives them a future rather than a past. By giving them this myth of Earth, he gives them a common goal, a common future. He knows the cognitive and emotional importance of his people thinking their efforts are aimed at something beyond their present survival. Adama sees what Peirce sees: the importance of pressing toward a future goal. And Adama values hope's ability to motivate. The truth of the hope is unimportant.[4]

Adama isn't without hope himself, but his hope seems to rest in other people, even when they've lost hope in themselves. He brings Saul Tigh back from his drunken despair; he has hope in his son's leadership ability; and he regularly rests all his hope on Starbuck's uncanny capacity to do the impossible. But aside from his "noble lie" concerning Earth, Adama doesn't try to instill his personal hopes in the minds of the rest of the fleet, in stark contrast to Roslin.

James and Roslin: Religious Hope

Roslin leads from a very personal hope in the Colonial scriptures, and thus appears to many as fulfilling the Pythian prophecies foretold 3,600 years prior. To others, Roslin's faith seems, at best foolish, and at worst dangerous—her religious convictions are delusions brought on by her cancer and use of chamalla extract. Roslin's hope may be merely self-deception. Yet, while Roslin's brand of hope may not be Adama's, it's still in line with the pragmatist tradition of hope found in the writings of William James (1842–1910).

James argues that religious beliefs may be reasonably based on nothing but personal hope.[5] Affective dimensions, according to James, are at work in all sorts of beliefs. And while these are to be avoided when possible—particularly in science and medicine—sometimes they're unavoidable. Some matters simply don't admit of scientific investigation or empirical support due to the nature of the issue, and yet sometimes we're in a position where we *must* choose and hence, James argues, it's our passions that must decide:

Elizabeth F. Cooke

> Our passional nature not only lawfully may, but must, decide an option between propositions, whenever it is a genuine option that cannot by its nature be decided on intellectual grounds; for to say, under such circumstances, "Do not decide, but leave the question open," is itself a passional decision,—just like deciding yes or no,—and is attended with the same risk of losing the truth. (11)

James is responding to William Clifford's (1845–1879) demand that we must have evidence for every one of our beliefs.[6] Belief in God, for example, isn't permissible, since no evidence can establish God's existence. But James argues that even Clifford's position is a result of a choice based on sentiment. An agnostic chooses to reject belief for fear of being wrong; whereas a believer may choose out of hope for a personal God. James opts for the latter because, otherwise, he risks never having a personal relationship with God if, in fact, God exists. James thus rejects the agnostic's rule for truth seeking: "A rule of thinking which would absolutely prevent me from acknowledging certain kinds of truth if those kinds of truth were really there, would be an irrational rule" (26). James realizes there's no final argument for one sentiment over another, since such sentiments are beyond rational and empirical support. But as long as they're beyond rational argument, James may successfully defend his—and Roslin's—right to choose to believe based on hope. And skeptics should be tolerant of those who choose to believe.[7]

Roslin understands James's point and doesn't flinch when she's challenged for relying on her own religious beliefs as motivating her hope in finding Earth when the Colonials discover New Caprica:

> The issue here, the real question, is not allowing the scriptures to dictate the policy of this government. The question is, do the scriptures contain real-world relevance? Do they contain the information necessary to guide us to a safer home than some completely unknown planet that we've just now discovered? Obviously, my answer to that question is yes. I have always and will continue to feel the scriptures hold real-world relevance. ("Lay Down Your Burdens, Part 1")

Roslin isn't choosing religion over other methods. The scriptures aren't at odds with science, morality, and democracy. Rather, religious doctrine points beyond them and unifies them as an ultimate end of hope in the survival of all those represented by the number she keeps posted in her office. Billy explains the number's significance to Baltar:

"That number means everything to her. It represents hope. It's our future" ("Epiphanies").[8]

Apollo and Tyrol: Social Hope

In contrast to Roslin, Apollo believes humanity's best hope is *polit-ical*. He initially supports Tom Zarek—prisoner and former freedom fighter/terrorist—in his call for free elections when Roslin finishes out President Adar's term ("Bastille Day"). He also defends Baltar against the charge of conspiring with the Cylons, because he believes in the process that ensures justice ("Crossroads"). And when his father wants to assassinate Admiral Cain, Apollo questions Adama's moral judgment ("Resurrection Ship, Part 2"). Apollo even turns his gun on a superior officer for the sake of these moral and political ideals ("Kobol's Last Gleaming, Part 2").

Similarly, Chief Tyrol goes up against Roslin when he supports a worker's strike ("Dirty Hands"). Both Apollo and Tyrol see the military as having a purpose only if the political goals are worthy, as Apollo explains to Adama and Roslin:

> I swore an oath to defend the articles. The articles say there's an election in seven months. Now if you're telling me, we're throwing out the law, then I'm not a captain, you're not a commander, and you are not the president. ("Bastille Day")

Apollo and Tyrol don't work toward otherworldly hopes, but rather toward hopes in a politically immediate future we can fulfill. Their hope is also in line with the pragmatist tradition, resembling the more political versions of pragmatic hope as found in the writings of John Dewey (1859–1952) and neopragmatist Richard Rorty (1931–2007). Dewey replaces the philosophical search for certainty with an emphasis on imagination and self-creation, and as members of a community rather than as individuals. Following Dewey, Rorty wants to replace knowledge as a goal for philosophy with hope—a *social* hope:

> To say that one should replace knowledge by hope is to say much the same thing [as Dewey]: that one should stop worrying about whether what one believes is well grounded and start worrying about whether one has been imaginative enough to think up interesting alternatives to one's present beliefs.[9]

Rorty argues for a political pragmatism that avoids appeals to transcendent ideals, but yet is explicitly *utopian*. He doesn't necessarily expect to achieve utopia, but believes such hopes are essential for achieving political goals.[10] Rorty contends, "If we fail in national hope, we shall no longer even try to change our ways" (254). Hope motivates us to make efforts we wouldn't otherwise make—like coming together as a species to expand democracy. For Apollo and Tyrol, purpose comes from within, rather than above and beyond or from the distant future. We must become our own moral compass and achieve moral goals by our own actions, rather than hope for divine intervention, luck, or destiny.

Hope vs. Fear

As important as hope is, however, it can also be dangerous. Hope, or the need for hope, can work against our survival. We see this when Baltar's presidential campaign succeeds on the promise of settlement on the recently discovered New Caprica. The hope for Earth is replaced with more immediate fulfillment. Roslin has her doubts:

> *Roslin*: This is a rest stop, a place to load up on food and water. We're not settling here, obviously . . .
>
> *Tory*: Suddenly, Baltar is holding out hope of breathing real air, growing real food, sleeping in a bed instead of a bunk, living in a house instead of a ship.
>
> *Roslin*: It's a fantasy . . . What, are we now assuming that Cylon technology is not sufficient to find this planet? We just found it.
>
> *Tory*: Madame President, in my opinion, people vote their hopes, not their fears. Baltar is offering them what they want to hear, and you're offering them a bitter reality.
>
> *Roslin*: I'm offering them the truth.
>
> *Tory*: They don't want to hear the truth. They're tired, exhausted. The idea of stopping, laying down their burdens and starting a new life right now is what is resonating with the voters.
>
> ("Lay Down Your Burdens, Part 1")

Indeed, Tory is correct, and the voters give in to this dangerous hope at their peril.

In addition to being dangerous, hope can also sometimes resemble madness. When Tyrol becomes frustrated with the scarcity of ships and spare parts, he appears to go off the deep end and begins to build another ship from scratch ("Flight of the Phoenix"). Everyone thinks he's lost it, but he's simply acting out of hope. And as he begins to make progress, others join him because they want to believe they can do something positive. Tyrol and the others know their future is uncertain, but they refuse to face it passively and eventually finish the ship. It's appropriately christened *Laura* after Roslin, who never loses hope for humanity's future or her own in the face of her cancer. She commends the project as "an act of faith." Sometimes hope can be of value not for the goal it achieves, but because it transforms the way we view our present situation. It reminds us that we can transform our situation—our future isn't completely written for us.

But if Tyrol had failed, then he would have been judged insane, not to mention what it would have done to the crew's morale. There's a danger with such ambitious, seemingly mad, hope. True ambition and human progress depend on success, but always risk failure that may destroy the individual or the collective. Within the history of scientific discovery, we see such mad hope play an integral role, and once again the pragmatists are there to analyze it. Italian pragmatist Umberto Eco studies the methods of Renaissance genius Leonardo da Vinci and argues for the importance of the great thinker's almost naïve assumptions for scientific discovery—for example, that a human being could build wings and fly. Yet, had physics not borne out da Vinci's vision, Eco knows that history would have treated him as more of a madman than a visionary: "To define [da Vinci] as a utopian genius means exactly that the community recognizes that he was in some way right but in some other way madly wrong."[11]

Great minds know that their successes and failures, and history in general, will bear out their madness or genius. Their mad hope will be met with praise or mockery by the community long after they're gone. And yet they risk all anyway. The great men and women of *BSG*—Adama, Roslin, Tyrol, and so on—stand together with historical giants like da Vinci. All great leaders are *visionaries*, willing to take great risks, often against all evidence and common sense, in order to achieve great results.

But what happens when an individual completely lacks hope? Baltar has no hope in political ideals, religious fulfillment, or even humanity's survival, because he doesn't value anything more than himself. He lacks commitment to anything that he isn't willing to trade the moment he feels threatened, which is why he's "not on any-one's side"—neither the Colonials nor the Cylons. Baltar is motivated out of *fear*, rather than hope, and he thus lacks a moral center.

Of course, Baltar isn't all bad. He tries, when he can, to be good or understand that there might be something more to the world than himself. When Baltar's inner Six tries to convince him of God's plan for him, Baltar tries to believe. But he can't consistently maintain this hope because of fear and self-doubt. He doubts that Six is anything more than part of his delirium as a result of his guilt for aiding in humanity's massacre, or part of a Cylon chip implanted in his brain ("Home, Part 2"). His worry about the lack of justification for the belief that God has a plan for him keeps him from getting onboard completely with Six's vision for him.

Yet, because he can believe in nothing but himself, Baltar is easily used by the Cylons—either by his inner Six or the other Cylons, to whom he offers no resistance when they take over New Caprica. Either way, Baltar is rarely in control of his own destiny. He's always a slave to the situation or to his compulsion—be it fear, ego, or Six. He isn't free because he isn't attached to anything beyond his own survival. Perhaps this is why Adama lied to the survivors in the begin-ning—he didn't want them to live solely out of fear like Baltar does. Living from fear is a kind of madness, which is why Baltar so often appears to hover on the edge of insanity. In fact, Baltar is, in a way, the polar opposite of Tyrol's mad hope. One who has extreme hope borders on madness, but so does one who has none at all.

"A Flawed Creation"

In stark contrast to Baltar, the Cylons are never without hope. Though they have lost virtually all hope in their creators, they have unbounded hope in their God of *love*. The Cylons' view of the future is what they believe to be God's plan for them—procreation out of love:

> *Anders*: Supposedly, they can't reproduce, you know, biologically, so they've been trying every which way to produce offspring.
> *Starbuck*: Why?
> *Sharon*: Procreation, that's one of God's commandments. "Be fruit-ful." We can't fulfill it. We've tried . . .

Helo: They have this theory. Maybe the one thing they were missing
  was love. So Sharon and I, we're set up—
Starbuck: To fall in love?
("The Farm")

Caprica Six is convinced of her ability to love Baltar and to be loved
by him. She's also convinced that she's a genuine individual. She
makes the turn when she, Boomer, and a Three/D'Anna are bombed
and trapped under rubble. Six is severely injured, and D'Anna offers
to kill her to spare the pain and allow her to be downloaded into a
new body. But Six betrays a very human emotion when she chooses
to endure her pain, rather than "give up on life" ("Downloaded").
She believes her present life is what's important and has hope for who
she is *now*.

But while some Cylons envy the human ability to love, most have
given up hope in the human race. When Adama asks Sharon why the
Cylons hate humans so much, she responds,

It's what you said at the ceremony . . . You said that humanity was
a flawed creation. And that people still kill one another for petty jealousy and greed. You said that humanity never asked itself why it
deserved to survive. Maybe you don't. ("Resurrection Ship, Part 2")

The Cylons don't think humans are morally worthy of survival because they're petty, selfish, and murderous. Humans constantly squan-
der opportunities and forget themselves. Sharon explains this point to
Adama as he struggles in deciding whether to assassinate Cain to save
the fleet. Deciding at the last minute against the assassination, Adama
says, "It's not enough to survive. One has to be worthy of surviving"
("Resurrection Ship, Part 2").

Sharon serves as Adama's conscience. After four months of Cylon
occupation, Adama despairs over the humans he left behind on New
Caprica and Sharon is again his moral compass:

Sharon: Do you feel guilty about leaving the people behind on New
  Caprica?
Adama: I don't do guilt.
Sharon: You know, a year ago, when you put me in this cell, I was at
  a crossroads. I sat in here for weeks just consumed with rage at all
  the things that had happened to me. And at some point I realized
  it was all just guilt. I was angry at myself for the choices I had

made, betraying my people, losing the baby. So, I had a choice. I could either move forward or stay in the past. But the only way to move forward was to forgive myself. You know I don't think we can survive, I don't think the fleet, or *Galactica*, or the people on New Caprica, can survive unless the man at the top finds a way to forgive himself.

("Occupation")

While Adama believes survival depends on hope, Sharon argues survival actually depends on forgiving ourselves. Even if the past doesn't justify our belief that we're worthy of survival, we must hope that we can become worthy tomorrow. The future is open and we must always assume we're free to act and make a change. Our destiny is always, in the most important ways, in our own hands.[12]

NOTES

1   Charles S. Peirce, *The Essential Peirce*, vol. 1, ed. C. Kloesel and N. Houser (Bloomington: Indiana University Press, 1992), 81–2. Further references will be given in the text.

2   Peirce, *The Essential Peirce*, vol. 2, ed. the Peirce Edition Project (Bloomington: Indiana University Press, 1998), 106–7.

3   Plato, *Republic*, trans. G. M. A. Grube, revd. C. D. C. Reeve, in *Complete Works*, ed. John M. Cooper (Indianapolis: Hackett, 1997), 414b–d.

4   For a discussion of the epistemological implications of Adama's lie, see Eric Silverman's chapter in this volume.

5   William James, *The Will to Believe and Other Essays in Popular Philosophy* (New York: Dover, 1956), 1–31. Further references will be given in the text.

6   William Clifford, *The Ethics of Belief and Other Essays* (New York: Prometheus Books, 1999).

7   For additional discussion of James's religious epistemology, see Eric Silverman's chapter in this volume.

8   There is, of course, a similarity between *faith* and hope insofar as both go beyond evidence or argument. But here we're considering Roslin's faith as a kind of hope, because she lets it guide her overall outlook for the future. There's some debate about whether faith is a gift, an act of the will, or a commitment. And this same question might be raised about hope. Why are some more hopeful than others? The relationship between faith and hope, however, is beyond the scope of this chapter.

For further discussion of the rationality of religious faith, see Jason Eberl and Jennifer Vines' chapter in this volume.

9   Richard Rorty, *Philosophy and Social Hope* (New York: Penguin, 1999), 33–4. Further references will be given in the text.

10 Rorty, *Consequences of Pragmatism* (Minneapolis: University of Minnesota Press, 1996), 208.

11 Umberto Eco, Richard Rorty, Jonathan Culler, and Christine Brooke-Rose, *Interpretation and Overinterpretation*, ed. Stefan Collini (Cambridge: Cambridge University Press, 1994), 145.

12 I'm very grateful to Jason Eberl, Bill Irwin, and J. J. Abrams for reading and commenting on an early draft of this chapter.

19

Is Starbuck a Woman?

Sarah Conly

While *Battlestar Galactica* frequently portrays women as strong and powerful, and sometimes even as ruthless, Starbuck is the character to whom the traditional restrictions of femininity have meant the least. In the original series, Starbuck was played by a man, and the character's re-creation as a woman is one of the more interesting—and initially controversial—choices the re-creators of *BSG* have made. Has Starbuck successfully made the transition? Or has Starbuck, in her complete liberation from gender roles, simply become a man in a female body?

What Is a Woman?

The philosopher Simone de Beauvoir (1908–1986) famously argues that a woman is not born, but *made*.[1] While many feminists of the modern era had argued for increased political rights for women, de Beauvoir focuses on the philosophical question of what exactly a woman is, and how she is different from a man. For de Beauvoir, writing shortly after World War II, which awakened many people's interests in the nature of freedom and equality, there are three significant things we need to understand in order to grasp fully the difference between men and women. And it's only once we've understood them that we can improve women's position in the world.

The first is that the difference between men and women isn't really a question about what the body is like. The physical question of who is male and who is female is settled relatively simply by reference to

230

reproductive capacity. When we think of what it is to be a woman, though, we mean more than that: we have a host of character traits, values, standards of appearance, mannerisms, and activities which we associate with being a woman, and which are really what we care about when we say, "She is a woman." Being a woman is more than having a certain kind of body.

Second is de Beauvoir's contention that these non-physical elements of being a woman are *artificial*. It is society, not nature, which demarcates women as being different from men in character, emotion, and mind. In this way women are not born, but made. A baby is born a female, but it's society which establishes the standards of what the girl, and later the woman, should be like, and which tries to impose these standards on her as she grows up. For de Beauvoir, there's no such thing as a feminine *nature*—no natural woman's character, no natural woman's role. All of that is artificial; she asserts, "Men have presumed to create a female domain" (65).

Third, this creation—the social understanding of what it is to be a woman—*injures* women: they're created to fulfill a role in which no being can be comfortable. The social understanding of what a woman is forces women to be what they can't be, and wouldn't want to be if they could. Women need to be liberated from these constraints to become what they're capable of—to become *themselves*.

This raises a puzzle. It seems odd to say that we've created something and set up standards for what it is to be that thing, and that these standards cut against the very nature of that thing in a way it can't accommodate. It's as if we refined tylium ore precisely to produce fuel, and it did that, and then someone complained that we were really unfair to constrain tylium to producing fuel when it should be used to produce explosives. We could respond that it *can't* be a travesty for tylium ore to make it produce fuel—that's what its nature is, and we can be completely sure of what its nature is precisely because it's artificially refined to be fuel. Thus, if we've created women as a certain sort of thing, how can it be a travesty for women's nature when they end up being precisely that sort of thing?

The answer is twofold. First, women aren't just women, they're human beings. For de Beauvoir, the true nature of every human being is to be free to make decisions and define itself, to *choose* what it wants to be. So, if we take a free human being and try to mold it into a set form from which it's told it can't deviate, it can never comfortably do that. Society, dominated by men, has come to see women not just as a particular kind of thing, but a kind defined by its difference from men. Rather than emphasizing common humanity, we exaggerate the differences between men and women. Worse, men are seen as the "normal," basic sex, and women as a deviation. Woman, in de Beauvoir's language, is defined as "Other," as something distinctive in being different from men. Not only do men see women as defined by their deviant nature; but women also come to see men as normal and themselves as abnormal, and believe that this abnormality makes them what they are.

Thus, in order to define themselves, women always have an eye on someone else, to see what he's like, and to see themselves as, and indeed to *make* themselves, different. To construct oneself exclusively in opposition to something else is as servile as defining oneself by imitation—instead of choosing what to be, a woman models her life on being different from men, who become her focus. Woman is "being towards man," rather than an independent nature: she "sees herself and makes her choices not in accordance with her true nature in itself, but as man defines her" (138). It can't be fulfilling to a woman's truly free nature to deny this freedom to herself and make herself live as the inverted mirror of someone else.

Second, when we mold women into this perverted form, we constrain their activities to a particular sort which, for de Beauvoir, is especially unfree. Women are, traditionally, held to domestic positions: having and caring for children, cooking, and maintaining the house. These activities emphasize the physical nature of humans, and while there is such a nature—de Beauvoir never denies that we're biological creatures—this isn't an interesting side, because our physical nature is to some extent given and thus at odds with what makes us truly special: our freedom to choose. So women are told they have a determinate nature and a special sphere of activity, and that nature and sphere are particularly linked to the maintenance of the body. Men, on the contrary, are taught that they can choose what to do, including whether or not they want to live. Their role is one of freedom, and is admired. The *warrior*, throughout history a male, proves

> that life is not the supreme value for man but on the contrary that it should be made to serve ends more important than itself. The worst

curse that was laid upon woman was that she should be excluded from these warlike forays. For it is not in giving life but in risking life that man is raised above the animal; that is why superiority has been accorded in history not to the sex that brings forth, but to that which kills. (64)

Women, in the constrained domestic sphere, are taught to be *passive*, to accept what others do rather than act themselves. This passivity is pervasive. Women, for de Beauvoir, are generally physically passive, constraining their movements to the delicate and petite; sexually, they're the recipient of others' advances, doing no more to engage in sexual satisfaction than trying to attract men's attention by exaggerating their delicacy and weakness, and finally receiving the active male into their bodies; and they seek men's admiration for their self-esteem, rather than directly pursuing lives they themselves could consider valuable.

All this is a perversion of human nature, but it's not always unpleasant. De Beauvoir thinks that while it's our nature to be free, we're often frightened by our freedom and enjoy, at least at times, telling ourselves that we aren't free, that there's nothing we can do but comply with standards others have created for us, even where those standards are at odds with our underlying nature. Both men and women are in danger of hiding their own freedom from themselves; but women in particular, given the social structure, are in danger of loving their chains, so that they may be complicit in destroying their underlying freedom. This complicity shouldn't, however, be mistaken for real satisfaction; and even when women cling to their subordinate and secondary roles, they're creating lives that can't yield real contentment: "Woman, too, feels the urge to surpass, her project is not mere repetition but transcendence towards a different future" (64). Women need to recognize the construction of womanhood for what it is: both artificial and destructive. Men also need to realize this, for de Beauvoir doesn't think women can achieve freedom without the cooperation of the other sex. For men to see women differently, they need to see themselves differently; for the exaggeration of difference which shapes women has an effect, though less extreme, on men. We need a general change in society, in its structures of education, job opportunities, and expectations of the two sexes.

"I Am a Viper Pilot"

On all these counts, it looks as if Starbuck is a smashing success story and a signpost for what women today may strive to become. No one could say that Starbuck lives for men. Socially, of course, Starbuck admires particular men (Adama), has very close friends who are men (Apollo and Helo), and has male lovers for whom she cares deeply (Anders and Apollo). But no one would say that Starbuck defines herself by exaggerating her differences from men, or that she lives for their approbation. Indeed, one of the moments of clearest pride for Starbuck is when Admiral Cain, a woman, tells Starbuck she's proud of her ("Resurrection Ship, Part 2"). Starbuck typically has other things on her mind than her love life, and we never see her willing to give up her own goals and principles to please a man—or anyone else. She's *active*, in just the ways de Beauvoir admires. On the small scale, she's physically unconstrained, whether she's boxing, playing pyramid, pushing someone up against a wall, or simply walking. She smokes cigars, she sweats, and her hair is practical and short— except, significantly, during the time she opts for the life of a Colonist on New Caprica. The diffidence and exaggerated delicacy that de Beauvoir believes unfortunately characterizes women in her own time is gone.

It is not that Starbuck can't play the part of the traditional woman when she wants. After Apollo chides her for neglecting her clothes and "hygiene," she shows up at a party decked out in an evening dress with all the feminine accoutrements—just hours after having engaged in a barroom brawl and interrogating a prisoner with threats of immediate execution ("Colonial Day"). She dances and flirts, and it's no accident that she ends up in bed with Gaius Baltar, a man not at all in the style she usually admires. Starbuck recognizes that there is a traditional feminine role, and that she can play it, reflecting the views of contemporary philosopher Judith Butler, who has inherited and extended de Beauvoir's analysis of woman. For Butler, the feminine and masculine roles are *performances*, artificial roles we enact, with no basis in nature.[2] For Butler, it's by the "performative" actions of dressing, talking, and thinking according to gender that we create gender. For contemporary men and women, these roles are socially enforced, and in turn create a gendered reality. For Starbuck, though,

234

this is a choice, an act to be consciously adopted. The next morning, like an inverted Cinderella, she turns back into her liberated self, which we, prisoners of a different culture, can't do.

Starbuck also lives the warrior life that de Beauvoir admires for its willingness to risk life in the service of a greater cause. It's this warrior life that the Cylons both admire and want to destroy by channeling Starbuck away from it and back to the domesticity de Beauvoir thinks is without value. But the Cylons' attempts to domesticate Starbuck utterly fail. Simon, masquerading as a human doctor, tries to convince Starbuck that in these times of reduced human population a woman of childbearing age can do more good by producing children. Her answer is uncompromising: "I am a Viper pilot" ("The Farm"). While Simon tries to convince her that this rejection of motherhood is a function of her own abused past, there's no reason to think that Starbuck's choice is solely a neurotic one based in fear: she *is* a fighter.

The later, extended Cylon attempt to domesticate Starbuck has a more ambiguous result. During the occupation of New Caprica, Leoben imprisons her with him in an atmosphere of artificial domesticity, a sort of suburban love nest constructed within the detention center. Rather than trying to conquer her through violence, his goal is to get her to love him; and to that end he's unendingly, if irritatingly, gentle. With unlimited opportunities to beat, rape, or kill her, he never even raises his voice until the very end. Starbuck responds by murdering him over and over again, even though she knows he'll simply download into a new body ("Exodus, Part 1").

Leoben then tries a more indirect weapon by introducing a child into their ersatz home, a toddler—Kacey—he tells Starbuck is biologically hers. While this is a lie, it provides telling insight into Starbuck's character, because she comes to care for Kacey in a maternal way. When *Galactica* returns to save the colonists on New Caprica, Starbuck refuses to leave without her. She finds Kacey with Leoben, who insists that Starbuck tell him that she loves him and that she kiss him. In order to save Kacey, Starbuck does so, convincingly enough to distract Leoben so that she can murder him one more time ("Exodus, Part 2"). This shows Starbuck to be absolutely unyielding in her resistance towards the position of feminine partner; yet she's softened in regards to Kacey and accepts, at least momentarily, the indignity of playing the role of a compliant female. From de Beauvoir's perspective,

Starbuck's rejection of traditional feminine activity isn't, as Simon claims, because she's too traumatized to allow affection for a child. Rather, she has a great capacity for affection, but she won't sacrifice her integrity. Starbuck, of course, has her own demons: her mother's physical and emotional abuse has wounded her ("Maelstrom"); and she admits that while others fight to get back what they've lost, she fights because it's all she knows ("Valley of Darkness"). Despite these psychological obstacles, we see during the occupation of New Caprica that it's not an inability to love that keeps her from motherhood, but a commitment to living a different kind of life that she's made for herself.

This isn't a choice she can make without society's help. De Beauvoir stresses that women can't change unless society changes and men change their attitude towards women. Fortunately, this has happened in the world in which Starbuck lives. Colonial society is less *gendered* than our own: Starbuck is one of many female pilots, the Colonial President is a woman, and the only surviving battlestar besides *Galactica* is commanded by a woman who's Adama's superior officer. It's clear that the Colonials have developed the educational opportunities and general social support that de Beauvoir sees as necessary for the liberation of women. While both President Roslin and Admiral Cain have had their naysayers, they're not attacked for simply being women in men's roles. The Colonials have many problems, but gender doesn't seem to be one of them. In that respect, *BSG* affords us, like all great science fiction, a compelling vision of a very different world.

But Aren't Men and Women Different?

Starbuck exemplifies the changes in our conceptualization of women that de Beauvoir believes necessary—and probably sufficient—for women to reach equality with men, and provides a vivid example of what such equality might be like. The problem, for some critics, is that this vision of equality rests largely on a premise of *sameness* between men and women. Many women contend that, to be treated equally, they shouldn't have to be just like men. Women have their own culture and ways of doing things, and to require complete assimilation to the male seems a high price to pay for respect. Starbuck is so extremely ungendered that perhaps, in all but body, she's simply become a man.

But why is this so bad? If we accept de Beauvoir's idea that our construction of the idea of woman has been artificial and destructive, why not get rid of it and allow that females are basically the same as males? Recent movements in feminism have discarded the essentially negative feminist project, where all we seek is to free women from obstacles that prevent equality, in favor of a more positive celebration of a distinctive female nature. Harvard psychologist Carol Gilligan, after interviewing boys and girls, men and women, contends that women have a distinctive ethical outlook that is uniquely insightful.[3] While Gilligan doesn't argue that the feminine outlook is superior to the masculine, she argues that it's both distinct and valuable as an alternative way of solving moral problems. Others have gone further to argue that the female ethical outlook is better than the male and is the key to moral progress.[4]

While Gilligan doesn't speculate as to whether the difference between men's and women's outlooks is based in biology or social conditioning, many of the specific female virtues she discovers are ones we can imagine arising from, and lending themselves to, care of the family. Whereas men tend to see morality as a system of demands one can make of others, women see it as organized around attempts to help others and satisfy their needs. Whereas men see other people as threats from whom they must protect themselves, women see others as sources of support with whom they want to bond. Whereas men tend to prioritize duties hierarchically, so that, say, the duty to save a life always outweighs the duty not to steal, women see moral dilemmas more contextually, so that a particular value—like honesty—might predominate in one situation but not in another. These feminine virtues are clearly useful in the home, where we see other family members not as threats, but as those we want to help and who will help us in turn; where mothers have to be flexible in making decisions about the allocation of resources or chores; and where we're generally optimistic that a satisfactory solution can be reached without anyone ending up with the short end of the stick. For Gilligan, these virtues and methods can be useful outside the home, and may be taken as a whole new outlook on our relationships with other people. Rather than seeing conflicts of interests as inevitable and irresolvable, we'd see them as based on misunderstandings which can be worked out with the cultivation of good will and understanding.

Starbuck doesn't exemplify these virtues. A Gilligan-esque woman might have softened towards Leoben, and tried to make him understand her position. She wouldn't have felt that mutual understanding was a lost cause, or that the conflict was entirely irresolvable and could end only in death. She probably would have hesitated before murdering him six times. On Gilligan's terms, Starbuck definitely does what a guy would do.

But we need to consider whether Gilligan's distinction is legitimate. While she introduces this distinction as between men and women, the difference may not be so absolute. Gilligan concedes that, especially with more experience, men take on more of the traditionally female perspective and women take on more of the male approach—especially when it comes to sticking up for themselves. It may be that *BSG* presents a post-Gilligan worldview: both women and men have matured, and both have aspects of the other. Commander Adama exhibits central aspects of the *ethic of care* Gilligan attributes to women. Nothing is oversimplified: he recognizes the many and various conflicts he needs to address; he tries to meet the conflicting needs of his own soldiers and the civilians; and he's endlessly flexible in balancing values in each and every context. Adama arrests Roslin when he thinks she's a danger to their survival ("Kobol's Last Gleaming, Part 2"), but he doesn't demonize her. He's able to differentiate his condemnation of her plans from condemnation of her character, and continues to treat her respectfully. Adama often stresses the importance of the military chain of command and obedience to superior officers; yet, when Cain condemns Helo and Tyrol to death, he trains *Galactica*'s guns on the *Pegasus* without hesitation. Sometimes loyalty must triumph over discipline. Roslin, while demonstrating more of the mannerisms found in traditional maternal care, can be ruthless in advocating violence against those she sees as a danger: she airlocks Leoben without remorse ("Flesh and Bone"), advocates the assassination of Cain ("Resurrection Ship, Part 1"), plots to commit genocide against the Cylons ("A Measure of Salvation"), and wants no forgiveness for Baltar's betrayal of humanity during the occupation of New Caprica ("Taking a Break from All Your Worries"). *BSG* portrays a malleability of male and female character that is quite in line with de

Beauvoir's belief that there's no given nature for men or women, other than the ability to choose.

Crossroads

BSG is, of course, fiction, so we can't say it reveals what men or women are really capable of. But what it presents reveals our conceptual abilities, and makes us wonder what we can become. *BSG* is profound in its revelation of psychological complexity—no character, not even Caprica Six or Baltar, is seen as all bad. Characters who blend feminine and masculine aspects make sense. If Starbuck has become like a man, it's in part because men on *BSG* are different. They've become more like women: more attached, more varied in their values, and more respectful of women than in de Beauvoir's time or our own. Gilligan's argument that there are distinctive ways of looking at moral questions isn't so much refuted by *BSG* as left behind as history. There are different ways of approaching moral problems, but they don't have to be linked to sex and aren't mutually exclusive. *BSG* represents an evolution in moral thinking, as well as a great and positive social change. It's an *androgynous* society—one where social roles aren't limited by sex, and where opportunities are open such that de Beauvoir's wish for "every human life to be pure transparent freedom" is realized.[5] Starbuck isn't a perfect person, but she's nonetheless a model of what women can be: equal to men in their courage, their achievement, and their flaws.[6]

NOTES

1 Simone de Beauvoir, *The Second Sex*, trans. H. M. Parshley (New York: Knopf, 1952), 267. Further references will be given in the text.
2 Judith Butler, *Gender Trouble: Feminism and the Subversion of Identity* (New York: Routledge, 1990); and *Bodies that Matter: On the Discursive Limits of Sex* (New York: Routledge, 1993).
3 Carol Gilligan, *In a Different Voice* (Cambridge, MA: Harvard University Press, 1983).
4 See Nel Noddings, *Caring: A Feminine Approach to Ethics and Moral Education* (Berkeley: University of California Press, 1984); and Sara

Ruddick, *Maternal Thinking: Towards a Politics of Peace* (Boston: Beacon Press, 1989).
5 Simone de Beauvoir, *The Blood of Others*, trans. Roger Senhouse and Yvonne Moyse (New York: Knopf, 1948), 128.
6 I want to thank Owen Conly and Luke Cummiskey for their help on this chapter.

20

Gaius Baltar and the Transhuman Temptation

David Koepsell

The desire to surpass one's natural state is the original sin. According to Earth religion and mythology, humanity fell when, in the Garden of Eden, we dared to eat the fruit of the Tree of Knowledge in order to become like God. Lucifer didn't know his place either: jealous of God's love for humanity, he rebelled and earned eternal damnation by his pride, his hubris. Prometheus was punished for improving the lot of us lowly humans by bringing us fire against the will of the gods. Icarus suffered for flying too close to the sun, because it challenged the gods' rightful place. The divine seem to be a jealous bunch, who don't appreciate humans encroaching on their turf. So the lesson appears to be this: Don't let your reach exceed your grasp, petty humans. But, as the poet Robert Browning asks, "What's a heaven for?"

Humans have a long history of seeking things we ought not to have, like knowledge or immortality. Dr. Faust and Dorian Grey are prime examples of the folly of human betterment, at least beyond a certain point, and Dr. Frankenstein, of course, for daring to create life—a pastime only for divine tinkerers. Dr. Gaius Baltar joins this long list of those who sin by their arrogant quest to become more than human. Like Faust, Frankenstein, Lucifer, and Adam and Eve, Baltar yearns and strives to walk where mortals fear to tread.[1]

The desire to surpass our innate human limitations survives today beyond fiction, in a movement which is growing in numbers, if not necessarily in public acceptance. *Transhumanism* embraces the philosophy of Faust, Lucifer, and Baltar by seeking to legitimize the quest to overcome our humanity. Transhumanists invest in technologies that would be right at home on a Cylon baseship. Bionics, stem cells,

computer-enhancements of the human mind, uploading of consciousness into computers, are all being explored as means to achieve limit-
less knowledge or extend the human lifespan, perhaps even to the
point of immortality. These desires and plans meet with a skeptical
public, conditioned to view modern transhumanists as the moral
equivalent of Lucifer. Even the most secular among us may blanche
at the thought of cheating nature, devising means to re-engineer
ourselves, remaking ourselves in the image of the divine, or even
transcending ourselves altogether by creating a whole new species.
Baltar, a complicated and evolving character, represents humanity in
its hubris and cowardice. Much as Lucifer in Milton's *Paradise Lost*,
Baltar is both anti-hero and everyman, both loathsome and sympathetic as a depiction of the "transhuman" temptation that we all suffer
from time to time.

The Fall of Baltar

Baltar's frailty is central to the main conceit of *BSG*: the apocalyptic
destruction of humanity by its own creation, the Cylons. Baltar's
narcissism leads to the Colonies' destruction. Enticed by the affections
of Caprica Six, whom he presumes to be merely a corporate spy,
Baltar gives her access to the Colonial defense mainframe. This initial
treachery also results from Baltar's hubris. Having been contracted to
write a Command Navigation Program that's critical to coordinating
the Colonial fleet, he finds himself unable to design some of the more
complex algorithms. So, instead of admitting his shortcomings, he
enlists Six's help. By outsourcing critical defense work to a Cylon—
albeit while not knowing she's a Cylon—Baltar enables the near
destruction of humanity.

At first, Baltar merely intends to give away trade secrets for sex and
his own career advancement, and suffers from not being able to
admit his own intellectual limitations. But he compounds his treachery with cowardice, seeking refuge and accepting the help of the very
enemy he's enabled. Baltar's fall mimics a number of anti-heroes who
share his aspiration to ascend to something for which they mistakenly
believe they're worthy. Like Lucifer, Prometheus, or Adam and Eve,
Baltar's reach exceeds his grasp, and pride leads to the downfall, not
just of one person, but all of humanity. It's a sin for which Baltar

enters his own brand of hell, tormented by the ghost of his betrayer, the "serpent" whispering in his ear, who continues to manipulate him with flattery and affection.

The fallen Baltar joins the human survivors and serves at once as possible savior, and likely scapegoat if ever the truth becomes known. But with the rest of humanity, Baltar will seek to transcend his mortality, climb back from the depths of his private hell, and ascend to his rightful place among the gods. We'll trace Baltar's path from hubris to shame, and then up the steep slope again to fulfill his perceived "messianic" role. What drives this impulse? Why does it pervade our mythology? And why do some real-life groups today aspire to Baltar's goal of overcoming humanness, transcending mortality, and becoming divine?

The Transhuman Temptation . . . Really!

The desire to transcend our humanity runs deep in fiction, from ancient demigods—such as Hercules—to modern superheroes—such as the X-Men. These aren't demonic, fallen characters, but heroes, saviors of mortals who often have mortal origins. Even the fallen characters—Lucifer, Prometheus, Faust, and Frankenstein—are sympathetic in most tales. Should we add Baltar to that list? To answer this, we need to explore transhumanism more deeply.

What drives modern transhumanists who seek ways to augment themselves, using technology, to surpass what they see as unfair limitations produced by chance and evolution? They seek, among other things, to redefine their natural lifespans, arguing that the notion of a *natural* lifespan is now moot given modern medical technologies. There's theoretically no definite limit to human life, and stem cell technology, nanotechnology, genetic augmentations, or other innovations on the near horizon will enable us to cheat death.

Transhumanists seek to surpass their mortality through various *augmentations*. New technologies could literally give us superhuman powers, or merge us with our machines in useful (or terrifying) ways. Imagine being able to plug into the Internet without a computer; using bionic eyes to see in infrared, complete with zoom; running comfortably at 15 or 20 miles per hour; or jumping a fence 12 feet high "in a single bound." Consider a computer-enhanced brain, capable of recalling every memory, or carrying *Encyclopedia Britannica* right behind our eyelids. These enhancements all hover now within the range of technical possibility, and only scratch the surface of dreams that people are now expressing, and searching for ways to realize, to remake themselves in the divine image.

The modern transhumanist movement seeks essentially to legitimize behavior punished in fiction and mythology for thousands of years. The desire to become something more than human would no longer be ridiculed or feared as the stuff of humanity's fall from grace, but rather embraced as human destiny. There are credible philosophical arguments justifying this position, such as the incontrovertible fact that there's nothing "natural" about humanity's current state. We've augmented and altered ourselves considerably since the dawn of civilization through the development of agriculture, intercontinental transportation, clothing, weaponry, and any other device or method we employ to cheat nature. Without these innovations, fueled by a growing brain, humanity would have been wiped out by stronger, faster, hungrier predators; we also wouldn't inhabit cold environments, deserts, or anything but tropical zones abundant with food.

Modern transhumanist thought emerges from the fictional anti-heroes and heroes we've discussed, but also owes its roots to the age of the Enlightenment in Europe. René Descartes and Giovanni Pico della Mirandola each considered a benefit of science to be the ability for humans to better ourselves, to ease or eliminate our frailties, and even extend lifespans.[2] Philosopher Marquis de Condorcet (1743–1794) wrote:

> Would it be absurd now to suppose that the improvement of the human race should be regarded as capable of unlimited progress? That a time will come when death would result only from extraordinary accidents or the more and more gradual wearing out of vitality, and that, finally, the duration of the average interval between birth and wearing out has itself no specific limit whatsoever?[3]

Philosophers, utopians, and their dystopian critics speculated, wished for, and warned against a range of human improvements as science and technology began to make their possibility imminent. The term "transhumanist" didn't emerge until the twentieth century, coined by the biologist Julian Huxley, brother of Aldous Huxley, whose dystopian novel *Brave New World* ironically serves as a utopian vision to the small but growing transhumanist community. Julian Huxley defined transhumanism as involving "man remaining man, but transcending himself, by realizing new possibilities of and for his human nature."[4]

In the last three decades of the twentieth century, transhumanism began to coalesce into a *movement*, under the influence of several philosophers and public intellectuals, including Marvin Minsky, Ray Kurzweil, Hans Moravec, and a fellow who began calling himself FM-2030 at the New School in New York City. In his course "New Concepts of the Human," FM-2030 used the term "transhuman" to denote any "transitory human" who's in the process of directing her own evolution past human by adopting technology to enhance perceived shortcomings of evolution thus far. FM-2030's book, *Up Wingers: A Futurist Manifesto*, features a call-to-arms for transhumanist rights and activism.[5] In 1980, the first international transhumanist conference took place at UCLA. And in the 1980s technology seemed to be catching up with the hype—specifically, computer technology. In fact, much of the renewed energy in the transhumanist movement finds its roots in the "cyberculture" that emerged in the 1980s and matured in the 1990s.

Given a voice in magazines like *Omni*, *Mondo 2000*, and eventually *Wired*, and given intellectual support by Eric Drexler's *Engines of Creation* and later Kurzweil's *The Singularity Is Near*, transhumanists focused not on the dystopian cultural icons of technology's tendency to alienate and dehumanize individuals, but rather on the promise that technology holds for bettering us and continuing where evolution left off: to make us healthier, heartier, smarter, and better looking.[6] Drexler and Kurweil envision *Star Trek*-like futures, where scarcity is eliminated and human desires are met by nearly magical machines. In 1998, the World Transhumanist Association was formed by Nick Bostrom and David Pearce to advance the causes and concerns of transhumanists in the realms of science and public policy.[7]

Emerging out of the increased visibility of transhumanists is a growing and more vocal stream of warnings and ethical opponents. Jeremy Rifkin began sounding the alarm over genetic engineering in the 1980s, centered around environmental concerns and issues of "human dignity."[8] Other critics and cautionaries include Bill Joy, founder of Sun Microsystems, who warns of dangers posed by artificial intelligence, robots, and nanotechnology.[9] Among the dangers he envisions is the emergence of "gray goo," where nanobots run amok and basically eat the world.[10] Francis Fukuyama warns of the dangers of genetic engineering and biotechnology in undermining our humanness and individuality.[11] Bill McKibben raises similar warnings in the context of concerns for the environment and a sort of "back-to-the-earth" ethos.[12]

Philosophical opponents of transhumanism offer a spectrum of objections. Among them are those implicitly expressed in warnings both biblical and science-fictional. Bioethicist Leon Kass argues against human enhancement technologies from the age-old position that it's akin to "playing God."[13] This objection echoes the moral of myths and literature from the Bible to Faust. It underlies the themes of *BSG* as well in the conflict between the "old" religion of the Colonials and the heresy of the Cylons.

Other philosophical objections to transhumanism include arguments regarding the feasibility of transhuman technologies. Gregory Stock argues that despite the advances in biotechnology on the horizon, many of the cyborgian predictions of human and machine integration are far-fetched, and we will remain essentially biological and human.[14] Other technologists and futurists point to the often hyped accounts of the future from the past, with expectations of flying atomic cars, and note that the actual rate of change has been much less radical than once predicted. They argue that human enhancement technologies have been similarly hyped.[15]

Others argue that manipulating human limitations would deprive us of the "meaning" of human life, which is defined in part by our limits. McKibben makes this argument, and also contends that enhancement technologies will result in an unjust divide among rich and poor, privileged enhanced humans and the un-enhanced masses.[16] Philosopher Jürgen Habermas also suggests that a "human species ethic" will be undermined by genetic alterations.[17]

In many ways, the fears and uneasiness expressed by opponents of transhumanism are the motivating emotions behind the entire backstory of *BSG*, and echoed by the human heroes of the series. Burned by its creation, humanity has adopted a sort of neo-Luddism,[18] embracing certain technologies, but fearing others. In the "Miniseries," we see the Cylon Doral explaining this to a group touring *Galactica* while posing as a public relations agent during its decommissioning:

> You'll see things here that look odd or even antiquated . . . Antiquated to modern eyes. Phones with cords, awkward manual valves, computers that barely deserve the name. It was all designed to operate against an enemy who could infiltrate and disrupt even the most basic computer systems. *Galactica* is a reminder of a time when we were so frightened by our enemies that we literally looked backward for protection.

When Secretary of Education Roslin asks Commander Adama about installing a networked computer system to "simply make it faster and easier for the teachers to be able to teach," Adama shuts her down with extreme prejudice: "Many good men and women lost their lives aboard this ship because someone wanted to make a faster computer to make life easier." Baltar represents the opposite view, as he contends in an interview just before the Cylon attack: "The ban on research and development into artificial intelligence is, as we all know, a holdover from the Cylon Wars. Quite frankly, I find this to be an outmoded concept. It serves no useful purpose except to impede our efforts . . . [cut to hot Cylon-human sex]." Let's examine further Baltar's motivations, weaknesses, and especially his sympathy for humanity's would-be destroyers that characterize him as either hero or victim of the transhuman temptation.

The First and Last Temptations of Baltar

Baltar is the quintessential man of science—just like Faust or Frankenstein, and we know what happens to them. Tempted by the perfection of their creations, and rebelling against the imperfections of humanity, they stand ready to betray us. Yet Baltar's a survivor, he narcissistically believes in *himself*, so he ingratiates himself to Roslin and Adama and practices measured use of his scientific knowledge to safeguard humanity. But he does nothing without the whispered advice of the demonic/angelic Six. It's clear that Baltar holds the Cylons in some degree of respect; he seeks their approval. It isn't merely fear that motivates him occasionally to throw his lot in with the Cylons, even while fearing constantly that someone will learn of his betrayal. He even assists the Cylons, motivated perhaps as much by his love for Six as for himself. He lies to Boomer, for example, about being a Cylon, which endangers the whole fleet and results in

Adama's near-assassination. Over time his own hubris, combined with Six's prodding, leads him to believe he's special, chosen above the rest of humanity, for some divine purpose. "The Hand of God" ends with Baltar exclaiming, while striking a Christ-like cruciform pose, that he's "an instrument of God." Baltar's fascination with the Cylons leads him to his destiny of protecting the first Cylon-human hybrid, Hera, who represents at the same time both transhumanism and transcylonism.[19]

Baltar commits the ultimate betrayal after being elected President and allowing most of humanity to settle on New Caprica—all according to Six's advice and planning. Baltar has established himself in a place of esteem that he believes he truly deserves. At the moment of his achievement, however, the version of Six Baltar had rescued from *Pegasus* (Gina) detonates a nuclear warhead that he'd given her, which enables the Cylons to invade New Caprica a year later ("Lay Down Your Burdens, Part 2"). As the puppet President of the occupied New Caprica colonists, Baltar authorizes atrocities with the stroke of his pen ("Precipice"). And when New Caprica is liberated, he must flee with the Cylons, where he succumbs even more to the conceit that he's truly now where he belongs. Six tries to convince Baltar that he may be one of the "final five" Cylons and that he's the "chosen one" who'll see "the face of God." After being taken prisoner by the Colonials and awaiting trial for treason, Baltar is convinced by Six to kill himself to determine whether he's a Cylon. He dreams of waking up in a resurrection pod:

> *Baltar*: I'm alive? I'm alive. [laughing] Thank God, I'm alive!
> *Six*: I always told you to have faith.
> *Baltar*: Then no one was betrayed. I was never one of them. I am one of you.
> *Six*: Is that what you think, Gaius?
> *Baltar*: I knew it. I knew it. I always knew I was different, special, maybe a little gifted.
> ("Taking a Break from All Your Worries")

Baltar represents the mad-genius model of evil, led by his belief only in himself and his brilliant mind to be better than everyone else. And he believes his "specialness" absolves his guilt; he tells Number Three that if he's a Cylon, then he can "stop being a traitor to one set of people, and be a hero to another" ("The Passage"). Later, when he's given psychotropic drugs during interrogation, he tells Roslin and Adama:

> *Baltar*: She . . . Caprica Six. She chose me. Chose me over all men. Chosen to be seduced. Taken by the hand. Guided between the light and the dark. But is she an angel or is she a demon? Is she imaginary or is she real? . . . the final five . . . I thought I might be one of them. I told them I wanted to be one of them.
> *Roslin*: A Cylon, why?
> *Baltar*: All my sins forgiven. A new beginning.
> *Roslin*: Are you a Cylon, Dr. Baltar?
> *Baltar*: No . . . [and in his hallucination, he allows himself to die]
> ("Taking a Break from All Your Worries")

Now, having been cast down and giving in to his own sacrifice, Baltar will rise again at the conclusion of his trial. No longer the Luciferian anti-hero, but rather nearly Christ-like, Baltar is spared his sacrifice when he's acquitted and a small group of followers—who just happen to all be young, attractive women—whisk him away ("Crossroads, Part 2"). Perhaps they're the core of *BSG*'s new transhumanist movement, accepting Baltar's role as their "chosen one."

"There Must Be Some Way Out of Here"

While much of *BSG* seems to be steeped in a form of Luddism, it's clear at the end of three seasons that things aren't quite what they seem. Technology, after all, abounds and saves the "ragtag fleet" time and again. Technology keeps humanity alive, enclosed in artificial spaceships, as they seek their new Eden: Earth. Pursued by their own creations, they follow the guide left by their creators: the Sacred Scrolls. Humanity's downfall came from reaching too far, to imbue its creation with the spark of life, and to enslave it, leading to a rebellion.[20] This was God's first error too, as first Lucifer rebels, then humanity. The tyranny, in transhumanism, is nature, not the divine. Like the Cylons, we're trapped in an endless cycle of birth and death, and we've sought all along to extend that cycle or break it, to slip our mortal coil. Baltar is no different, except perhaps by having the natural intelligence and extreme self-love to possibly succeed. He's special, and appears to have been chosen by that which humankind created, enslaved, fought, and all but lost to.

The cycle of sin and redemption plays out in the character of Baltar. His salvation from this cycle is to become the "chosen one," to be different, to aspire to something greater than humanity. While *BSG* begins with the flavor of Rifkin, McKibben, and other anti-transhumanists, Season Three ends with a sort of redemption for the Cylons—especially as we learn that their ranks include some of our beloved heroes—and the possibility that the best path for the salvation of humanity may lie with the reconciliation of creator and created, the final transcendence of human to transhuman. The four who are revealed to be Cylons in "Crossroads, Part 2" appear comfortable with their humanity, even when it becomes apparent that they're not human. Baltar may yet be the fifth Cylon, but I wouldn't put money on it. Rather, he's the link, the spark of genius in humanity that could begin to grasp the soul of the new machine. That soul, it would seem, is rather like his—and ours, if we'd only admit it.

Do we not all aspire to be something more, whether by faith or technology, when we seek immortality in this life or the next? Baltar personifies this transhumanist ethic, first as accidental villain and then as potential savior. As a metaphor for our times, *BSG* offers both warning and hope, that somehow within the possibilities of our own technologies lie the seeds of both destruction and salvation. We, too, travel like the Colonials, in a largely technological shell, apart from nature, and as something new. Perhaps, like Baltar, we can learn to embrace this, to become something greater, to dare to yearn for more. We've already reshaped our world in the image of our dreams, built our technology well beyond our individual abilities to control it. We're all transhumanists now.[21]

NOTES

1   See John M. Steadman, "The Idea of Satan as the Hero of 'Paradise Lost'," *Proceedings of the American Philosophical Society* 120 (1976), 253–94.
2   Nick Bostrom, "A History of Transhumanist Thought" (2005): www.nickbostrom.com.

3   Marie Jean Antoine Nicolas Caritat, Marquis de Condorcet, *Sketch for a Historical Picture of the Progress of the Human Mind* (Westport, CT: Greenwood Press, 1979).

4   Julian Huxley, "Transhumanism," in *New Bottles for New Wine* (London: Chatto & Windus, 1957), 13–17.

5   FM-2030, *UpWingers: A Futurist Manifesto* (New York: John Day, 1973).

6   K. Eric Drexler, *Engines of Creation: The Coming Era of Nanotechnology* (New York: Anchor Books, 1986); Ray Kurzweil, *The Singularity Is Near: When Humans Transcend Biology* (New York: Penguin, 2005).

7   James J. Hughes, "Report on the 2005 Interests and Beliefs Survey of the Members of the World Transhumanist Association," World Transhumanist Association (2005): www.transhumanism.org.

8   Jeremy Rifkin, *Biosphere Politics: A New Consciousness for a New Century* (New York: Crown, 1991).

9   Bill Joy, "Why the Future Doesn't Need Us," *Wired Magazine*, April 2000: www.wired.com/wired/archive/8.04/joy_pr.html.

10 Nanotechnology is a field of science working on the miniaturization of complex machines. Such machines could, for instance, unblock arteries from inside our bodies, or construct huge complex structures one molecule at a time. Neal Stephenson's novel *The Diamond Age* envisions a future where huge airships constructed molecularly out of diamond transport us without pollution. "Gray goo" happens when, as Joy predicts, these nanobots go to war with one another, or run amok and digest everything they come into contact with.

11 Francis Fukuyama, *Our Posthuman Future: Consequences of the Biotechnology Revolution* (New York: Farrar, Straus and Giroux, 2002).

12 Bill McKibben, *Enough: Staying Human in an Engineered Age* (New York: Henry Holt, 2003).

13 Leon Kass, *Beyond Therapy: Biotechnology and the Pursuit of Happiness* (Darby, PA: Diane Publishing, 2003).

14 Gregory Stock, *Redesigning Humans: Our Inevitable Genetic Future* (New York: Houghton Mifflin, 2002), 4.

15 Bob Seidensticker, *Future Hype: The Myths of Technology Change* (San Francisco: Berrett-Koehler, 2006).

16 Bill McKibben, *Enough: Staying Human in an Engineered Age* (New York: Times Books, 2003).

17 Jürgen Habermas, *The Future of Human Nature* (Cambridge: Polity Press, 2003).

18 "Luddism" is the distrust of machines and technology in general. Named after a fictional character "Ned Ludd," whom workers used to rally other workers to smash new machines at the dawn of the modern

industrial age in the United Kingdom. The original Luddites opposed the elimination of jobs by technology; modern Luddites may oppose technology for any number of reasons, including concern for the environment, fear of alienation, and so on.

19 While Baltar doesn't literally care for Hera, he intervenes on several occasions to protect her existence. For example, in "Epiphanies" he discovers that Hera's blood contains a cure for Roslin's cancer and thereby prevents her from being aborted under Roslin's orders; and in "Exodus, Part 2," he finds her in the arms of her dead adoptive mother after the Colonials flee New Caprica.

20 For discussion of the Cylon rebellion against their creators from a Nietzschean perspective, see Robert Sharp's chapter in this volume.

21 For further discussion of transhumanism in the context of *BSG*, see Jerold J. Abrams' chapter in this volume.

There Are Only Twenty-Two Cylon Contributors

Jerold J. Abrams is Associate Professor of Philosophy at Creighton University. His publications appear in *The Philosophy of Film Noir* (2006), *The Philosophy of Neo-Noir* (2007), and *The Philosophy of Martin Scorsese* (2007), and he's the editor of *The Philosophy of Stanley Kubrick* (2007). Abrams is currently a sleeper Cylon hiding among the cows and cornfields of Nebraska where absolutely no one will ever find him.

Robert Arp is the editor of *South Park and Philosophy* (Blackwell, 2007) and has contributed to numerous pop culture volumes. He's currently doing postdoctoral research at the National Center for Biomedical Ontology through SUNY Buffalo, where it frakkin' snows way too much!

Erik D. Baldwin received his MA in Philosophy from California State University, Long Beach and is expecting to earn his PhD from Purdue University in 2008. He has published in the areas of philosophy of religion, epistemology, and ethics. He's the proud owner of vintage "original series" *Battlestar Galactica* bed sheets, the same ones he had as a kid.

Jason P. Blahuta has taught at Carleton University, the University of Ottawa, and Saint Paul University, and is currently Assistant Professor of Philosophy at Lakehead University. He has published essays on political theory in the journals *Dialogue: Canadian Philosophical Review* and *Iyyun: The Jerusalem Philosophical Quarterly*. His research interests include Machiavelli, Asian philosophy, Schopenhauer,

253

and applied ethics. He *really* wants to throw Helo out of an airlock and broadcast it on Colonial pay-per-view.

Sarah Conly teaches Philosophy at Bowdoin College. She has a BA from Princeton and a PhD from Cornell, and has enjoyed recent research fellowships from the National Endowment for the Humanities and Harvard University. In the summer she walks by the water and writes, and in the winter she watches *Battlestar* and writes.

Elizabeth F. Cooke is Associate Professor of Philosophy at Creighton University, where she researches in the philosophy of science, applied ethics, and American pragmatism. She's the author of *Peirce's Pragmatic Theory of Inquiry: Fallibilism and Indeterminacy* (2006). Currently, she's cooling her heels in Admiral Adama's brig for assaulting a superior scholar.

George A. Dunn teaches Philosophy at Indiana University-Purdue University Indianapolis, where he regularly co-teaches a course on "Philosophy Thru Pop Culture" with his colleague Jason Eberl. He has also been a visiting lecturer at Purdue University and the University of Indianapolis. Recently, at a Bob Dylan concert, he discovered he was a Cylon.

Jason T. Eberl is Assistant Professor of Philosophy at Indiana University-Purdue University Indianapolis where he directs a graduate program in bioethics. He also teaches medieval philosophy and metaphysics. He's the co-editor (with Kevin Decker) of *Star Wars and Philosophy* (2005) and *Star Trek and Philosophy* (forthcoming). He has contributed to similar books on Stanley Kubrick, Harry Potter, and Metallica. He and his wife, Jennifer, own two cars, affectionately known as the "Bucket" and the "Beast."

Randall M. Jensen is Associate Professor of Philosophy at Northwestern College. His philosophical interests include ethics, ancient Greek philosophy, and philosophy of religion. He has also contributed to *South Park and Philosophy*, *24 and Philosophy*, and *The Office and Philosophy*. Opinions probably vary on whether he's evolved or devolved, but thankfully there's only one of him. And most of the time he's very glad not to have a plan.

David Kyle Johnson is Assistant Professor of Philosophy at King's College. His philosophical specializations include philosophy of religion, logic, and metaphysics. He wrote a chapter in Blackwell's *South Park and Philosophy*, and has forthcoming chapters on *Family Guy*, *The Office*, Quentin Tarantino, Johnny Cash, and *Batman*. He has taught many classes that focus on the relevance of philosophy to pop culture. Kyle recently bought Edward James Olmos's trimmed mustache hair on eBay, but was outbid on Jamie Bamber's "fat suit" by BSGFaNaTiC247.

Amy Kind is Associate Dean of the Faculty and Associate Professor of Philosophy at Claremont McKenna College. Students have told her that she's the highest-ranking *BSG* fan at the college. She works mainly in the philosophy of mind, and her papers have appeared in journals such as *Philosophy and Phenomenological Research*, *Philosophical Studies*, and *Philosophical Quarterly*. Having recently survived a vicious malware attack on her home PC, she agrees with Admiral Adama that computers should never be networked.

David Koepsell has a Law degree and a PhD in Philosophy, and is a Research Assistant Professor at SUNY Buffalo. He has authored numerous articles and books, including *The Ontology of Cyberspace: Law, Philosophy and the Future of Intellectual Property* (2000) and a sci-fi novel, *Reboot World* (2003). David has recently developed a troubling fear of his toaster.

Taneli Kukkonen is Professor in the Study of Antiquity at the University of Jyväskylä, Finland. He has published widely on topics in ancient and Arabic philosophy, principally cosmology. Away from prying eyes he has a home altar, at the center of which sits a small stainless steel toaster.

J. Robert Loftis teaches Medical and Environmental Ethics at Lorain Country Community College. His publications include "Germ Line Enhancement in Humans and Nonhumans" in the *Kennedy Institute of Ethics Journal* and "The Other Value in the GMO Debate" in the volume *Ethics and the Life Sciences*. As of June 25, 2007, he's betting that the final Cylon is Laura Roslin, and the series will end with a mystical union of the human and Cylon races.

James McRae is an Assistant Professor of Asian Philosophy and Religion and the Coordinator for Asian Studies at Westminster College. He earned his PhD at the University of Hawaii at Manoa in 2007, and has published a number of articles and book reviews in the field of

Asian and comparative philosophy. An avid martial artist since 1996, he practices and teaches Jeet Kune Do and Jiu-Jitsu. He spends most of his free time wondering if he might be a Cylon.

Tracie Mahaffey is a PhD candidate in Philosophy at Florida State University. Her research interests include the philosophy of mind and action, ethics, and feminist theory. Although she's sure that she isn't a Cylon, she's deeply suspicious of others and therefore has joined the Church of the Mystic Cylon-Detector.

David Roden is a Research Associate in the Department of Philosophy at the Open University. He has published works on Donald Davidson, Dan Dennett, and Jacques Derrida in journals such as *Ratio* and *Continental Philosophy Review*. He's also co-editor, with Christopher Norris, of the *Sage Derrida* boxed set. He recently installed a freeware Cylon "logic bomb" on his laptop in the hope of receiving his due reward from our new posthuman masters. The machine was drunkenly trashed at a Christmas party, so the apocalypse has been averted—for now.

Robert Sharp is an Instructor at the University of Alabama, where he teaches ethics, existentialism, and logic. He received his PhD from Vanderbilt. His research focuses on value pluralism's political implications and on the nature of online communities. He also contributed to *Family Guy and Philosophy* (Blackwell, 2007). After noticing that their cats consistently exhibit red eyes in photographs, Robert and his wife began developing a device that specifically detects feline Cylons (patent pending).

Eric J. Silverman is a PhD candidate in Philosophy at Saint Louis University. His interests include ethics, medieval philosophy, and epistemology. He has 47,905 philosophical tasks to complete, requiring 11 hours each, totaling 21,956 days or 60.1534 years' worth of work.

Andrew Terjesen is Visiting Assistant Professor of Philosophy at Rhodes College. He previously taught at Washington and Lee University, Austin College, and Duke University. His interests are in the history of ethics and moral psychology, and he has written essays on the philosophical underpinnings of *Family Guy*, *The Office*, and dogs. He only wishes there were many copies of him and that they had a plan, so he might be able to juggle his many interests.

Jennifer A. Vines earned a BA in Philosophy from Florida State University. She's currently Assistant Director of Graduate Financial Aid at Indiana University-Purdue University Indianapolis. Jen's made pretty good on the black market, having hoarded ambrosia before the Cylon attack.

Brian Willems is Assistant Professor of Literature at the University of Split, Croatia and a PhD candidate at the European Graduate School, Saas-Fee, Switzerland. He's currently giving favorable odds as to whether D'Anna Biers will be taken out of cold storage.

The Fleet's Manifest

tyrant 30–2, 34–8
Tyrol, Cally 62, 68, 70, 80, 110, 112, 123, 129, 160
Tyrol, Galen 7, 11, 13, 24, 26, 44, 59, 62, 65, 68, 70, 108–10, 112, 114–16, 119–20, 122, 138, 144, 160, 186–7, 195, 197, 207–8, 223–6, 238
Tyrol, Nicholas 144, 150

uploading *see* downloading
utilitarianism 102–3, 105, 107, 109–10, 115–17, 121

Valerii, Sharon "Boomer" 20, 26, 33, 42, 57, 59–60, 64–5, 67, 69–71, 73, 74n7–8, 74n10, 80, 93, 127–39, 145, 147–8, 186, 193, 195–6, 211, 227, 247
value 15–18, 25, 27, 43, 50, 64, 103–4, 116, 118, 125, 128, 133, 137, 145, 161, 164–6, 208, 219, 221, 225, 231–2, 235, 237–9
veil of ignorance 142–5; *see also* Original Position; Rawls, John

vice 9, 19, 32, 37, 123
da Vinci, Leonardo 225
violence 112, 117, 142, 169, 210, 213, 235, 238
Viper 6–8, 10, 23, 38, 56, 66–7, 101, 109, 117, 165, 185, 211, 235
virtue 7–10, 12, 17–18, 23, 25, 41, 44, 123, 134, 149, 237–8
virus 19, 49, 58, 77, 89, 96

warrior 11, 17, 38, 232, 235
wealth 4, 8–9, 14n4, 21, 25, 37, 134, 145
Wilkins, Burleigh 117–18
Williams, Bernard 67
wisdom 19, 34, 36, 85, 89, 209–10, 216
World Transhumanist Association 245
World War II 40, 48, 230

Xenophanes 170

Zarek, Tom 16, 23–4, 42, 61, 120, 124, 174, 223
Žižek, Slavoj 136